上海紧缺人才培训工程教学系列丛书

英语中级口译资格证书考试

中级口译教程

第二版

An Intermediate Course of
Interpretation

Second Edition

梅德明　编著

外教社

上海外语教育出版社
SHANGHAI FOREIGN LANGUAGE EDUCATION PRESS

图书在版编目(CIP)数据

英语中级口译资格证书考试中级口译教程/梅德明编著.
2 版. —上海：上海外语教育出版社,2003
(上海市紧缺人才培训工程教学系列丛书)
ISBN 7-81080-741-2

I. 英… II. 梅… III. 英语—口译—资格考核—
教材 IV. H315.9

中国版本图书馆 CIP 数据核字(2003)第 000541 号

出版发行：上海外语教育出版社
　　　　　　（上海外国语大学内）　邮编：200083
电　　　话：021-65425300（总机），35051812（发行部）
电子邮箱：bookinfo@sflep.com.cn
网　　　址：http://www.sflep.com.cn　　http://www.sflep.com
责任编辑：梁晓莉

印　　　刷：常熟市华顺印刷有限公司
经　　　销：新华书店上海发行所
开　　　本：880×1230　1/32　印张10.125　字数304千字
版　　　次：2003 年 2 月第 2 版　　2003 年 6 月第 2 次印刷
印　　　数：20 000 册

书　　　号：ISBN 7-81080-741-2 / G · 365
定　　　价：16.70 元
　　　本版图书如有印装质量问题,可向本社调换

"上海市外语口译资格证书考试"
专家组顾问：戴炜栋

"英语中级口译教程丛书修订项目"负责人
齐伟钧　　孙万彪

"上海市英语中级口译资格证书考试"
教材编委会成员

主编：孙万彪
编委：周国强　严诚忠
　　　梅德明　陈汉生

第一版总序

由上海市人民政府教育卫生办公室、市成人教育委员会、中共上海市委组织部、市人事局联合组织编写的"九十年代上海紧缺人才培训工程教学系列丛书"将陆续出版。编写出版这套丛书是实施上海市紧缺人才培训工程的基础工作之一,对推动培养和造就适应上海经济建设和社会发展急需的专业技术人才必将起到积极的作用。

九十年代是振兴上海、开发浦东关键的十年。上海要成为国际经济、金融、贸易中心之一,成为长江流域经济发展的"龙头",很大程度上取决于上海能否有效地提高上海人的整体素质,能否培养和造就出一大批坚持为上海经济建设和社会发展服务,既懂经济、懂法律、懂外语,又善于经营管理,擅长国际竞争,适合社会主义市场经济新秩序的多层次专业技术人才。这已越来越成为广大上海人的共同认识。

目前上海人才的状况不容乐观,与经济建设和社会发展的需求矛盾日趋突出。它集中地表现在:社会主义市场经济的逐步确立,外向型经济的迅速发展,新兴产业的不断崛起,产业产品结构的适时调整,使原来习惯于在计划体制下工作的各类专业技术人才进入了一个生疏的境地,使原来以面向国内市场为主的各类专业技术人才进入一个同时面向国内外市场并参与国际竞争的新天地,金融、旅游、房地产和许多高新技术产业又急切地呼唤一大批新的专业技术人才,加强了本市专业人才总量不足,结构不合理的状况。此外,本市的从业人员和市民的外语水平与计算机的应用能力普遍不高。这种情况如不能迅速改变,必将会影响上海的经济走向世界,必将影响上海在国际经济、金融、贸易中的地位,和在长江流域乃至全国经济发展中的作用。紧缺人才培训问题已引起上海市委、市政府的高度重视。

"机不可失，时不再来。"我们要大力加强紧缺人才的培训工作和外语、计算机的推广普及工作。鉴于此，及时出版本丛书是当前形势之急需，其意义是深远的。诚然，要全面组织实施九十年代上海紧缺人才培训工程还有待于各有关方面的共同努力。

　　在"九十年代上海紧缺人才培训工程教学系列丛书"开始出版之际，感触颇多，简述代序。

上海市副市长　谢丽娟

第一版序

处于世纪之交的中国,改革开放正不断深化和发展,作为国际大都市的上海与世界各国在经济、文化、教育以及其他领域内的交流与合作日趋密切和频繁。来上海投资、经商、讲学、旅游和参加会议的海外人士也接踵而至。外语是中外交流的桥梁。英语作为国际通用语,其重要性更是显而易见的。精通英语,并能熟练进行英汉互译是保持交际渠道畅通的必不可少的条件,作为"上海紧缺人才培训工程"项目之一的"上海市英语中级口译资格证书"的培训和考试,与"上海市英语高级口译资格证书"相衔接。这两个项目是由上海市委组织部、市人事局、市教育委员会和市成人教育委员会联合主办,并委托上海高校浦东继续教育中心具体负责,旨在为上海经济和文化发展培养更多中级和高级层次的英语口译工作者,以适应上海地区进一步改革开放的需要。

一个合格的口译工作者应在听、说、读、写、译五个方面都达到较高的水平。以孙万彪为主编的英语口译资格证书教材编委会根据《上海市英语中级口译资格证书考试大纲》的要求精心设计编写了中级《翻译教程》、《听力教程》、《口语教程》、《口译教程》和《阅读教程》,分别供笔译、听力、口语、口译和阅读五门课程教学使用。这五门教材在供反复试用的基础上,吸收了使用本教材的教师的部分建议,由编者数易其稿,并经主编通读和编委会集体讨论后最后定稿。这套教材编写目的明确、编排新颖、选材丰富,以实践为重点兼顾必要的理论阐述,是一套科学性、实用性、针对性都非常强的教材。学生经过培训学完这套教材后,就可以在全面提高五项基本技能的基础上,使自己的英语综合能力达到一个新的水准,以适应内容包括这五项技能的笔译和口译,顺利通过"上海市英语中级口译资格证书"考试。

我个人阅读这套教材后,深感这是一套很好的教材,不仅对有志参加培训和考试以获得"上海市英语中级口语资格证书"的读者十分有用,而且对其他英语学习者提高英语综合能力和口译水平也很有裨益,值得推荐给广大英语爱好者。教材的出版将使"上海市英语中级口译资格证书"项目日臻完善,在世纪之交为上海紧缺人才的培训作出贡献。

上海外国语大学校长

戴炜栋

再版前言

"上海市英语中级口译资格证书"培训和考试是"上海紧缺人才培训工程"的项目之一,由上海市委组织部、市人事局、市教育委员会和市成人教育委员会联合主办,并委托上海高校浦东继续教育中心负责具体实施。通过该项目市统考者,可获得这四个部门统一颁发的"上海市英语中级口译岗位资格证书"。

为满足培训需要,该项目专家组成立了英语口译资格证书教材编委会,负责教材的策划、设计和撰稿,委托五位编者分头编写《中级翻译教程》、《中级口译教程》、《中级听力教程》、《中级口语教程》和《中级阅读教程》,经主编通读修改后定稿。这五本配套教材是根据"上海市英语中级口译资格证书考试大纲"的要求及其细则编写的。分别适用于笔译、口译、听力、口语和阅读五门课程的教学,使学生在经过培训之后,能适应内容包括这五个项目的笔试和口试。未参加培训者,只要在英语水平上达到参加培训的相应的要求,也可以通过自学这套教材来应试。

这套教材的适用对象,是大学英语"四级"水平以上的大专院校学生、英语专业二年级学生以及具有同等英语水平的其他人员。以此为起点,教材编委会确定了统一的编写原则、范围和要求。这套教材的总体构想是,学生在接受240学时(以每周15学时,共16周计)系统培训并通过市统一考试之后,"英语中级口译资格证书"获得者应能较好地承担生活接待、导游和一般性会议的口译任务。

我们以为,要胜任口译工作,译员必须在听、说、读、写、译五个方面全面发展,五种能力缺一不可。只有这五项基本技能都达到较高的水准,才能成为合格的口译工作者。这就是为什么口译培训要涵盖这五个项目,要分别使用五本不同的《教程》来培训学生的英语综合能力。作为一套完整的教材,这五本《教程》是相辅相成的,既有统一的要求,又有各自的重点。在教学进度上,各《教程》均规定每周(次)完成一个单元(或一课内容),五项训练齐头并进。在教材内容上,所选编的语言材料有一定的横向联系,往往围绕若干相同或类似的主题或题目展开,以便于学生在这些话题范围内掌握更多的相关词汇、表达方法和应用技巧,进而增强驾驭英语的能力。在教学方法上,每本《教程》都强调实践的重要性,要求在培训过程中始终贯彻以"操练"为主,充分调动学生的主观能动性,让学生在反复实践中不断提高英语水平和各项技能。

当然,这五项技能各有其不同的培训方法和学习规律,体现在各本《教程》中,又各有其特色。五本《教程》的具体编写体例及不同的教学要求,在各自的"编者的话"和"使用说明"中都分别作了阐述,这里不再一一赘述。

这套教材的初稿完成于1996年8月,随即以胶印本形式交付全市各英语口译培训点试用。1998年2月,经修订的五本《教程》由上海外语教育出版社出版发行。在过去的四年多时间里,参加培训和使用这套教材的学生及购买这套教材的自学者人数逐年递增。据统计,参加英语中级口译资格证书考试的人数,从1997年开考时的400余人猛增到2002年9月第十二次考试时的14000多人。从项目的发展趋势看,使用这套教程的人会越来越多,其中不乏以全面提高自身英语水平和翻译能力为目的而学习这套教程的各界人士。根据这一情况,教材编委会决定对现行《教程》进行全面修订,使之能更快地跟上时代步伐,与时俱进,适应21世纪经济高速发展对人们整体素质(其中包括外语能力)上的要求。为此,在上海高校浦东继续教育中心的领导下,专门成立了"英语中级口译教程丛书修订项目",确定了项目负责人,协助开展《教程》的修订工作。全体编委在广泛征求和听取使用《教程》的教师和学生的意见的基础上,经认真讨论,确定了框架和体例基本不变,内容作大幅度调整的修订原则。

从现已修订完成的书稿来看,每一本《教程》都更换了三分之一以上、甚至超过一半的材料,新增的内容与国际和国内形势、我国改革开放的深化及世界经济的发展更贴近,因而也更为实用。在教材编写方面,除了修正第一版中的谬误和疏漏外,各本《教程》的质量也有较大提高。总体而言,第二版在实用性、科学性和可操作性上均有长足的进步。

我们认为,在知识经济和信息技术高速发展的新千年,教材只有不断更新,才能保持其存在价值,为广大使用者所接受。此次修订,是我们向更高目标迈进的又一步。我们自信,这套教材会越编越好。当然,限于我们的学识,现在的第二版可能还有不尽如人意之处,甚至存在各种差错。在此,我们恳请专家、学者、使用本《教程》的教师和学生及广大读者提出宝贵意见,以便编者及时修正。

在第二版付梓之际,我们谨向上海高校浦东继续教育中心表示感谢,在中心领导的关心和支持下,这套教材的修订工作才得以圆满完成。同时,我们还向上海外国语大学校长戴炜栋教授表示深切的谢意,感谢他为这套《教程》作序。戴校长一直很关心"英语中、高级口译"项目,从一开始就对专家组的工作给予热情的指导,有力地推动了本项目的发展。我们还要感谢专家组的其他成员,他们为教材修订提出过不少建设性意见。我们也不会忘记上海外语教育出版社社长庄智象教授及《教程》的各位责任编辑,他们为这套教材的出版和修订花费了大量的时间和精力,在此我们向他们表示由衷的感谢。我们深信,在上海市有关部门的领导、关心和支持下,这个项目一定会日臻完善,为上海紧缺人才的培训作出一份贡献。

主编 孙万彪

2002 年秋

编者的话

《中级口译教程》属"上海市英语口译资格证书"应试培训教材之一,以拟参加"上海市英语中级口译资格证书考试"的学生为主要对象,同时也适用于高校英语口译课教学。对因种种原因无法参加口译培训而又有志参加口译考试者,本教程也可用作应考生自学教材。

作为一本用以培养英语中级口译人员的教材,《中级口译教程》要求学生在培训前应已具有相当程度的英语水平,即学生在听、说、读、写诸方面必须具有较好的基本功,尤其是直接影响口译成败的口头表达能力和耳听会意能力,必须达到可以同英语为本族语人士进行一般性交谈的水平。当然,这些能力也可以在整个培训期间通过其他科目的学习和训练,不断提高和完善。必须指出,一个人的口译能力不仅涉及其对两种语言之间言语符号的转换技能,而且还关系到其对各项交际技能综合运用的能力。

《中级口译教程》根据口译工作的特点和范围取材与编写,体现了口译工作的基本要求以及当代中国改革开放的时代特征。《中级口译教程》分为三部分。第一部分为"口译概论",对口译的性质、特点、标准、过程、类型、难点以及译员的素质作简要阐述。第二部分为"培训教程",共含 14 个单元,涉及"会话口译"、"访谈口译"、"礼仪性口译"、"介绍性口译"、"说服性口译"、"学术性口译"、"商务性口译"和"科普性口译"等,前两个单元含三篇课文,其余各单元均含四篇课文。课文内容涉及外事接待、商务会谈、礼仪演讲、会议发言、宣传介绍、参观访问、人物访谈、学术研讨、科普报告、饮食文化、经济改革、经贸合作等。第三部分为"口译测试",介绍英语中级口译测试部分的要求、题型和形式,并提供六套中级口译测试模拟卷,用以检测英语中级口译教学的效果,同时也为意欲参加"上海市英语中级口译资格证书考试"的学生提供应考训练的机会。

　　编者根据自己从事口译教学工作的体会认识到,口译是一门实践性很强的课程,只有通过精讲勤练方能有所收效。编者认为,口译是一项高技能的语言交际活动,因此口译教学既要重视语言能力的培养,也要根据课文内容和口译形式训练口译技能。

　　《中级口译教程》第一版自 1998 年出版以来,受到全国各地教育机构和广大师生的普遍欢迎,四年内重印达 13 次。编者在对第一版部分内容进行更新和充实的基础上,现推出第二版。对于时代性很强的口译教材,《中级口译教程》第二版仍需不断充实完善。对本教材可能出现的纰缪或疏漏之处,祈望专家学者、外语界的同行以及本教程使用者不吝指正。

梅德明

上海外国语大学英语学院

2002 年秋

使用说明

  《中级口译教程》按照《上海市英语中级口译资格证书考试大纲》而编写,用以培养和提高具有中级以上英语水平、有志从事专职或兼职英语口译工作之人士的口译能力,使学习者在短期内达到参加"上海市英语中级口译资格证书考试"或从事一般口译工作所需具备的英汉／汉英口译水平。

  《中级口译教程》作为一本主要用以课堂教学的教材,按一学期至少16周、每周至少3课时的培训期要求而编排教学内容。换言之,本教程所需课堂教学的课时不宜少于48个课时。

  《中级口译教程》以"口译概论"为教学先导,以"培训教程"为教学核心,以"口译测试"为教学检测。

  "口译概论"概要地讨论了口译的性质、特点、标准、过程、类型,难点,以及译员必须具备的素质。"口译概论"旨在帮助学生从理论的角度来认识口译这门学科,解答"什么是口译"、"如何进行合乎规范的口译"、"合格的译员应具备何种条件"等问题。"口译概论"这部分的重要性还在于它向学生传递了这样一种信息,即一个人的口译能力不完全等同于其语言水平加翻译技巧,而是现代社会跨语言交际活动中译员的双语能力、翻译技巧和人的素质之综合体现。"口译简述"所讨论的这些问题应成为口译教学第一周的主要内容。

  "培训教程"构成口译教学的主要内容,共有14单元。除了第1单元和第2单元各含3篇课文之外,其余各单元均由4篇课文组成。除了篇章课文外,每单元还含有一些精选的单句,供复习之用。本教程的教学安排为每周学习1个单元,课堂教时不少于3课时。以下教学建议仅供参考:

每单元的教学可始于"词汇预习"部分,作为一项"热身"活动。然后播放课文录音两至三遍,与此同时可组织学生将录音内容从来源语翻译成目标语。通常,播音与翻译宜以句子为单位进行,即学生耳听一句,而后口译一句。若因条件受限(或无课文录音带,或无放音设备),或为活跃课堂教学气氛,也可采取(或部分采取)教师一边朗读(或讲述)课文内容、学生一边口译的方法。课文操练之后,教师应对课文内容作必要的讲解,同时对学生的口译情况并结合参考译文给予必要的讲评,讲评的重点应该放在口译的准确性和流畅性这两方面。为了巩固所学课文的基本内容,教师应安排时间让学生在课堂上操练"句子精练"部分的内容。至于第2、3、4篇课文的教学步骤,教师亦可采用上述方法。每单元教学的后期,教师应安排一定的时间,组织学生结成"英汉"或"汉英"口译对子,上讲台就课文的主要内容进行口译实践。

　　作为《上海市英语中级口译资格证书考试》的推荐应试教材,《中级口译教程》依据《上海市英语中级口译资格证书考试大纲》要求,在教程的最后部分简要地介绍了英语中级口译资格证书考试中口译测试部分的要求、题型和形式,并提供六套口译测试模拟试卷供师生检测教学成果,教师可在最后一周专门组织学生,或以小组形式,或以个别形式,参加模拟口译面试,并作适当的讲解。

　　虽然许多口译技巧的掌握可通过学习、操练和讲评本教程中的课文与练习而达到,虽然口译技巧与笔译技巧有许多相通之处,然而一些反映口译特殊性的技能则需要通过适时的强化训练以及不间断地实践,方能成为译员驾轻就熟的本领。有鉴于此,教师应该结合课文内容以及学生在口译操练中遇到的一些问题或难题,如词序、数字、成语、笔记、表达、怯场等问题,作必要的讲解和讨论,点拨迷津,指导实践。

　　以上使用说明,反映了编者对本教程的一些编写意图,其中也融入了编者自己的口译教学经验。所提建议,仅供本教程使用者参考。编者欢迎各位同行勇于探索,独创口译教学的佳径。

目　录
CONTENTS

第一部分　口译概论
PART ONE　An Overview of Interpretation

口译与译员简述　**Interpretation and the Interpreter** ……………(3)

一、口译的今昔　The Past and Present of Interpretation ……(3)

二、口译的定义　The Definition of Interpretation ………(5)

三、口译的特点　The Characteristics of Interpretation ………(7)

四、口译的标准　The Criteria of Interpretation …………(9)

五、口译的过程　The Process of Interpretation …………(11)

六、口译的类型　The Classification of Interpretation ……(13)

七、口译的难点　Difficulties in Interpretation ……………(15)

八、译员的素质　Interpreter Qualification Requirements …(27)

第二部分　培训教程
PART TWO　A Training Course

第 1 单元　会话口译

UNIT 1　**Interpreting Conversations** ……………………………(31)

1—1　欢迎光临　Welcome ………………………………(31)

1—2　投资意向　A Wish to Invest .... （33）

1—3　合资企业　Establishing a Joint Venture .... （35）

　　　句子精练　Sentences in Focus .... （38）

　　　参考译文　Reference Version .... （39）

第 2 单元　访谈口译

UNIT 2　Interpreting Interviews .... （46）

2—1　行在美国　Travel in America .... （46）

2—2　艾滋哀之　The AIDS Epidemic .... （49）

2—3　经营之道　Business Management .... （52）

　　　句子精练　Sentences in Focus .... （55）

　　　参考译文　Reference Version .... （57）

第 3 单元　礼仪性口译(英译汉)

UNIT 3　Interpreting Ceremonial Speeches

　　　　　English-Chinese Interpretation .... （64）

3—1　故地重游　Revisiting the Old Haunt .... （64）

3—2　愉悦之旅　A Pleasant Trip .... （66）

3—3　欧亚合作　Euro-Asian Cooperation .... （68）

3—4　新的长征　A New Long March .... （70）

　　　句子精练　Sentences in Focus .... （72）

　　　参考译文　Reference Version .... （74）

第 4 单元　礼仪性口译(汉译英)

UNIT 4　Interpreting Ceremonial Speeches

　　　　　Chinese-English Interpretation .... （81）

4—1　新春联欢　Celebrating the Spring Festival .... （81）

4—2　圣诞晚会　At the Christmas Party .... （82）

4—3　开幕祝词　An Opening Speech .... (83)

4—4　展望未来　Looking Ahead .... (85)

　　句子精练　Sentences in Focus .... (86)

　　参考译文　Reference Version .... (88)

第 5 单元　介绍性口译(英译汉)

UNIT 5　Interpreting Informative Speeches

　　　　　English-Chinese Interpretation .... (95)

5—1　股票市场　The Stock Market .... (95)

5—2　浪漫香槟　The Romantic Champagne .... (97)

5—3　游客之居　A Place to Stay .... (100)

5—4　教堂之游　A Tour around the Cathedral .... (101)

　　句子精练　Sentences in Focus .... (103)

　　参考译文　Reference Version .... (104)

第 6 单元　介绍性口译(汉译英)

UNIT 6　Interpreting Informative Speeches

　　　　　Chinese-English Interpretation .... (110)

6—1　传统节日　Traditional Holidays .... (110)

6—2　集团公司　An Ambitious Conglomerate .... (111)

6—3　出版王者　A Super-Publisher .... (113)

6—4　丝绸之路　The Silk Road .... (114)

　　句子精练　Sentences in Focus .... (116)

　　参考译文　Reference Version .... (117)

第 7 单元　说服性口译(英译汉)

UNIT 7　Interpreting Persuasive Speeches

　　　　　English-Chinese Interpretation .... (125)

7—1　应试之灾　The Examination-oriented Education ...... (125)

7—2　广而"误"之　The Effects of Misleading Advertising

　　　　　　　　　　　　　　　　　　……………………… (127)

7—3　共创未来　The Future Is Ours to Build ………… (130)

7—4　继往开来　The New Beginning of an Old Story …… (132)

　　　　句子精练　Sentences in Focus ………………… (135)

　　　　参考译文　Reference Version ………………… (137)

第8单元　说服性口译（汉译英）
UNIT 8　**Interpreting Persuasive Speeches**

　　　　Chinese-English Interpretation ………………… (144)

8—1　第二文化　Acquiring a Second Culture ………… (144)

8—2　环境保护　Environmental Protection …………… (145)

8—3　迎接挑战　Meeting the Challenge ……………… (147)

8—4　习武健身　Practicing Martial Art for Your Health

　　　　　　　　　　　　　　　　　　……………………… (148)

　　　　句子精练　Sentences in Focus ………………… (150)

　　　　参考译文　Reference Version ………………… (151)

第9单元　学术性口译（英译汉）
UNIT 9　**Interpreting Academic Speeches**

　　　　English-Chinese Interpretation ………………… (159)

9—1　语言系统　The Linguistic System ……………… (159)

9—2　人机之争　Two Kinds of Brain ………………… (161)

9—3　生物革命　The Biological Revolution ………… (163)

9—4　信息时代　The Information Age ………………… (167)

　　　　句子精练　Sentences in Focus ………………… (169)

　　　　参考译文　Reference Version ………………… (171)

第 10 单元　学术性口译(汉译英)
UNIT 10　Interpreting Academic Speeches
　　　　Chinese-English Interpretation .... (178)

10—1　文化冲突　On Cultural Clashes .... (178)

10—2　语用能力　Communicative Competence .... (180)

10—3　中国书法　Chinese Calligraphy .... (181)

10—4　社区服务　Community Service .... (183)

　　　　句子精练　Sentences in Focus .... (184)

　　　　参考译文　Reference Version .... (185)

第 11 单元　商务性口译(英译汉)
UNIT 11　Interpreting Business Speeches
　　　　English-Chinese Interpretation .... (194)

11—1　企业文化　Entrepreneurial Culture .... (194)

11—2　认识债券　Getting to Know Bonds .... (196)

11—3　硅谷之贵　The Unique Silicon Valley .... (199)

11—4　专利法规　On Patent Laws .... (202)

　　　　句子精练　Sentences in Focus .... (204)

　　　　参考译文　Reference Version .... (206)

第 12 单元　商务性口译(汉译英)
UNIT 12　Interpreting Business Speeches
　　　　Chinese-English Interpretation .... (213)

12—1　金融扩展　The Growing Financial Industry ...... (213)

12—2　亚洲合作　Asian Cooperation .... (215)

12—3　外资企业　Foreign-capital Enterprises .... (217)

12—4　经济关系　Economic Links .... (218)

　　　　句子精练　Sentences in Focus .... (220)

　　　　参考译文　Reference Version .... (222)

第 13 单元　科普性口译(英译汉)

UNIT 13　Interpreting Popular Science Speeches

　　　　　English-Chinese Interpretation ....（234）

　13－1　睡眠与梦　Sleep and Dream ....（234）

　13－2　音响今昔　The Sound Reproduction Industry ......（236）

　13－3　遗传信息　Genetic Information ....（238）

　13－4　左脑之优　Left Hemispheric Dominance ....（240）

　　　　　句子精练　Sentences in Focus ....（242）

　　　　　参考译文　Reference Version ....（244）

第 14 单元　科普性口译(汉译英)

UNIT 14　Interpreting Popular Science Speeches

　　　　　Chinese-English Interpretation ....（250）

　14－1　汉语概要　The ABC of Chinese ....（250）

　14－2　热量传递　Energy Transfer ....（252）

　14－3　蚊虫之祸　The Power of the Petty Mosquito ...（253）

　14－4　用筷技艺　The Magic Chopsticks ....（255）

　　　　　句子精练　Sentences in Focus ....（257）

　　　　　参考译文　Reference Version ....（258）

第三部分　口译测试

PART THREE　Interpretation Test in Brief

口译测试概要与实践

Interpretation Test：Essentials and Practice ....（269）

英语中级口译模拟测试

Model Tests for the Intermediate Interpretation Test ....（271）

　　Model Test One ....（271）

Model Test Two .... (274)

Model Test Three .... (277)

Model Test Four .... (280)

Model Test Five .... (283)

Model Test Six .... (285)

Reference Version .... (288)

第一部分　口译概论

PART ONE
An Overview of Interpretation

口译与译员简述
Interpretation and the Interpreter

一、口译的今昔
The Past and Present of Interpretation

一种语言文字的意义经由另一种语言文字表达出来叫做翻译。翻译有两种主要形式,即口译和笔译。口译可以是两种不同的民族共同语之间的翻译,也可以是标准语同方言之间或一种方言同另一种方言之间的翻译。本书所讲的口译属第一类翻译,即汉语同英语之间的翻译。

口译的历史源远流长,可追溯到人类社会的早期。在漫长的人类原始社会,原始部落群体的经济和文化活动属一种各自为政的区域性活动。随着历史的发展,这种自我封闭的社会形态显然阻碍了人类经济和文化活动的进一步发展,于是各部落群体便产生了跨越疆域、向外发展的愿望,产生了同操不同语言的民族进行贸易和文化交流的需要。语言不通显然成了影响这种跨民族交流的最大障碍,而口译作为中介语言媒介可以使人们与外界进行经济和文化交往的愿望得以成为现实。于是,构筑人类跨文化、跨民族的交际活动的桥梁——双语种或多语种口译便应运而生。

在人类社会的发展史上,口译活动成了推动人类社会的车轮滚动的润滑剂。人类的口译活动忠实地记录了千百年来世界各族人民之间的政治、经济、军事、文化、科技、卫生和教育的交往活动。古代社会东西方文明成果的交流,佛教、基督教、儒教和伊斯兰教的向外传播,文成公主婚嫁西域,马可·波罗东游华夏,哥伦布发现新大陆,郑和下西洋,鉴真东渡扶桑;近代社会西方世界与中国之间在政治、军事、经济、文化诸方面交往的风风雨雨;现代社会两次世界大战的爆发,"联合国"的建立,"世贸组织"的形成;当代社会中国全方位的对外开放,经济持续高速发展;今日信息时代"地球村"的发展,欧元区的创建,亚太经合组织的成立,欧亚峰会的召开……,人类历史上的各大事记无不烙有口译的印记。显然,在人类的跨文化、跨民族的交往中,口译无疑起着一种催化剂的作用。

口译作为一种专门职业,在我国已有两千多年的历史。古时,从事口译职业的人被称之为"译"、"寄"、"象"、"狄鞮"、"通事"或"通译"。《礼计·王制》中记载:"五方之民,言语不通,嗜欲不同。达其志,通其欲,东方曰寄,南方曰象,西方曰狄鞮,北方曰译。"《癸幸杂识后集·译者》作了这样的解释:"译,陈也;陈说内外之言皆立此传语之人以通其志,今北方谓之通事。"《后汉·和帝纪》提到了当时对译者的需求:"都护西指,则通译四万。"

数百年来西方各国虽然也有专司口译之职的人员,但是大部分的译员属临时的兼职人员。口译作为一种在国际上被认定为正式专门职业是 20 世纪初的产物。第一次世界大战结束后的 1919 年,"巴黎和会"的组织者招募了一大批专职译员,他们以正式译员的身份为"巴黎和会"作"接续翻译"(或被称为"连续翻译")。"巴黎和会"结束后,这批译员中的不少杰出人士陆续成了欧洲许多翻译学院和翻译机构的创始人。从此,口译的职业性得到了认可,口译基本方法和技能的训练开始受到重视。第二次世界大战结束后,纽伦堡战犯审判的口译工作采用了原、译语近乎同步的方法。以"同声传译"为标志的新的口译形式的出现使人们对高级口译的职业独特性刮目相看。随着联合国的创立,随着各类全球性和地区性组织的出现,国际间交往日趋频繁,世界的多边和双边舞台上演出了一幕幕生动的现代剧,口译人员在这些剧目中扮演了独特的角色。职业国际会议译员的地位越来越高,联合国成立了专门的翻译机构,高级译员组织"国际会议译员协会"在日内瓦隆重宣告成立。与此同时,口译作为一门学科对其原则和方法的研究也进入了高等学府。半个世纪以来,高级口译人才一直受到各类国际机构、各国政府、各种跨文化机构和组织的青睐。专业口译已成为备受尊敬的高尚职业,尤其是高级国际会议译员,他们既是聪慧的语言工作者,同时也是博学的国际外交家。

新中国成立以来,我国在国际舞台上日趋活跃。我国在世界政治、经济、贸易、文化、体育等领域里发挥着越来越重要的作用,这使优秀口译人员成了国家紧缺人才。20 世纪 70 年代初,中国重返联合国,自此我国的国际地位快速上升。进入以改革开放为标志的 80 年代后,我国的经济开始腾飞,对外开放的国门也因而越开越大。在东西方许多国家和地区经济陷于衰退的 90 年代,我国的经济列车仍以其强劲的活力,沿着通向世界经济发达国家之列的轨道继续高速运行。一个义无反顾的选择了社会主义市场经济并已取得巨大成功的中国,成了许多海外投资者和观光客的首选目标。一个以稳健的步伐走强国之路的全面开放的中国,对外交流的接触点越来越多,接触面越来越大。各类口译人才的需求与日俱增,高级译员的供需矛盾越来越突出。

今天,历史的车轮已把我们带入了一个新的世纪。这是我国全面振兴的世纪,再造盛唐辉煌的世纪,是中华文化同世界各族文化广泛交流、共同繁荣的世纪,这也是口译职业的黄金时代。这些年来,我国同世界各国开展了全方位、多层次的交流,让我们更好地了解世界,也让世界更好地了解我们。涉外口译工作者作为中外交往的一支必不可缺的中介力量,肩负着历史的重任。今日的中国比以往任何时期更需要一大批合格的专职或兼职译员来共同构筑和加固对外交往的桥梁。今日的翻译界比以往任何时期更需要对口译理论和方法进行研究。"上海市英语口译资格证书考试"应运而生,全国各高校的英语本科专业纷纷开设口译实践课,"口译研究与实践"作为一门理论与实践相结合的课程已被越来越多的高校列入英语硕士研究生班的教学大纲。一些高校还举办了全国或国际口译学术研讨会。这是时代的需要,国家的需要,市场的需要。同时,也丰富了语言学与应用语言学理论(如心理语言学研究、话语研究、双语研究和翻译研究)。

二、口译的定义
The Definition of Interpretation

口译是一种通过口头表达形式,将所听到(间或读到)的信息准确而又快速地由一种语言转换成另一种语言,进而达到传递与交流信息之目的的交际行为,是人类在跨文化、跨民族交往活动中所依赖的一种基本的语言交际工具。

人类的口译活动不是一种机械地将信息的来源语符号转换为目标语符号的"翻语"活动,而是一种积极地、始终以交流信息意义为宗旨的、具有一定创造性的"译语"活动。因此,口译不是孤立地以词义和句子意义为转换单位的单一性语言活动,而是兼顾交际内容所涉及的词语意义、话语上下文意义、言外寓意、语体含义、体语含义、民族文化含义等信息的综合性语言活动。从这个意义上说,口译不仅仅是语言活动,而且还是文化活动、心理活动和社交活动。

从事上述口译工作的人叫做译员。在相当长的时期里以口译为职业的人叫做职业译员。除了职业译员外,还有一些人叫做兼职译员和自由人译员。自由人译员以承接口译任务为基本职业,他们可能有固定的服务对象,但不从属于任何一个正式的翻译机构。偶尔做些简单应急之类口译工作的人不是通常意义上的译员。

译员必须是掌握两种语言(或两种以上语言)的语言知识和语言能力的双语人。但是,一个能说两种语言的双语人却非自然而然是一名称职的译员。这就是说,译员的前提是双语人,而双语人不等同于译员。这好比说,一个本族语为英语的人并非自然而然是一名英语教师,能够称职地向母语为非英语的人士教授英语。又譬如说,发音器官无障碍的人都会唱歌,但一个发音器官正常的人不一定是一个歌手。口译所需的双语知识和双语能力仅仅是口译的语言基础。口译依赖双语符号系统的有效转换以传递信息,保持交际双方信息渠道的畅通。暂且不论两种语言符号系统之间存在着种种非对等性,即便一个能流利讲两种语言的人具备一定的双语转换知识和技巧,但语言符号的有效转换不仅涉及一个人的语言知识,而且还涉及这个人的语言解意能力、反应记忆能力、信息组合能力、语言表达能力以及文化背景知识。具有双语能力的人可以通过系统学习、强化训练和勇于实践,进而较好地掌握口译知识和技能,成为一名合格的职业译员。

三、口译的特点
The Characteristics of Interpretation

口译是一项很特殊的语言交际活动。说其特殊是因为口头翻译工作有一些突出的特点。

首先,口译是一种具有不可预测性的即席双语传言活动。口译人员需要在准备有限的情况下,即刻进入双语语码切换状态,进行现时现场的口译操作。有些口译场合,如记者招待会和商务谈判,口译话题千变万化,往往难以预测的。译员或许可以通过事先确定的交谈主题来预测交谈各方的话题。但是,译员的任何估计都不可能是充分的,而且主观预测也是靠不住的,甚至是危险的。此外,交际各方都希望能连贯表达自己的思想,并能迅速传递给对方。但是由于在语言不同的交际双方之间介入了一个传言人,这在一定程度上影响了信息表达的连贯性和接收的快捷性。正因如此,交际双方都希望作为交际中介的译员不要过多地占用他们的交谈时间,尽可能地做到捷达高效。这就要求译员具有高超的即席应变能力和流利的现时表达能力。

现场气氛压力是口译工作的另一特点。口译场面有时非常严肃庄重,如国际会议和外交谈判。正式场合的严肃气氛会给经验不足的译员造成不良的心理压力,紧张的情绪会影响译员的自信,怯场的心态会使译员口误频生。瞬息万变的现场气氛的会使译员反应迟钝,从而影响口译水平的正常发挥。一般说来,译员的翻译行为不可有意掩饰或调和现场气氛。如实反映口译现场的气氛和主题是口译的基本职业规范。交际现场气氛无论是热烈的,还是沉闷的,无论是严肃的,还是随和的,都不应该因译员不恰当的过滤而受到损失。译员的口译精神不可超脱现场气氛,更不应该凌驾于现场气氛之上。译员的口译神态应该是一面如实反映场景气氛的镜子。

口译的另一特征是个体性操作,译责重大。译员属单打一的个体工作者,其劳动具有很强的独立操作性。通常,译员在整个口译过程中基本上是孤立无援的。译员必须随时独立处理可能碰到的任何问题。有些问题属语言类,与译员的双语知识有关;有些属文化传统类,与译员的民族知识有关;有些属自然科学类,与译员的学科知识有关;更多的属社会科学类,与译员的社会、文化、国情、时事等方面的基本知识有关。译员无法回避面临的任何一个问题,无路可退,只有正视每一道难题,及时处理每一道难题。在口译过程中,译员不可能查询工具书或有关参考资料,也不能频频打断说话者,要求对方重复自己所讲的内容,解释其中的难点。作为个体劳动者,译员要对自己的口译负责,不可胡编乱造,信口雌黄,自我得意;不可"自圆其说",瞎猜乱凑,以期歪打正着;不可"你说你的,我译我的",两条铁轨,永不相交。译员应该认识到,"译(一)语即出,驷马难追"。自己的译语,字字句句,重如千金,随意不得。有些场合口译出错,还可期望在以后起草书面协议时予以纠正。然而许多口译,如国际会议口译,没有后道工序的补救机会。对于口译,所谓的"译责自负"原则没有多大意义。译员自知"译责"重大,只是在重要口译场合铸成大错,恐怕自己想"负"此责,也"负"不了。

口译是一种综合运用视、听、说、写、读等知识和技能的语言操作活动。"视"是指译员须具有观察捕捉说话者的脸部表情、手势体姿、情绪变化等非语言因素的能力。"听"是指译员能够耳听会意各种带地方口音以及不同语速的话语的能力。"说"是指译员能用母语和外语进行流利而达意地表达的能力。"写"是指译员在口译过程中能进行快速笔记的能力。"读"是指译员在视译时能进行快速阅读和理解的能力。口译属一种立体式、交叉型的信息传播方式。多层次的信息来源和传播渠道,既给口译工作带来了一定的困难,如说话者浓重的地方口音和过快的语速给译员带来的耳听会意的困难,同时又为口译工作创造了颇为有利的条件,如说话者抑扬顿挫的语音语调,生动直观的体语表现,现场各种与口译内容有关的景物,如旅游景点和博物馆的实景实物,所有这一切都是辅助口译的有利条件。

交流的信息内容包罗万象,是口译的又一特点。职业译员的口译范围没有界限,内容可以上至天文,下及地理,无所不涉,无所不包。毋庸置疑,口译是一门专业性很强的职业,口译要求译员有扎实的语言知识功底、流利的双语表达能力和娴熟的转译技能。口译要求译员成为一名语言专家和交际能手,这非一日之功。然而,这些仅仅构成译员的语言基本功。由于口译的服务对象是各界人士,他们来自各个阶层、各行各业,有着不同的教育背景和文化背景,在交际过程中他们会有意或无意地将自己所熟悉的专业知识表达出来,这是译员无法回避的现实。

当然，无人能够精通百家，博晓万事，无人能说自己天文地理、古今中外，无所不知，无所不晓。但是，口译内容繁杂无限却是不争的事实。坐在翻译席上的译员，自然而然地被视为既是一名精通语言的专家，同时又是一名通晓百事的杂家。

四、口译的标准
The Criteria of Interpretation

衡量口译优劣有两条基本标准：一是准确，二是流利。

自从严复提出了"信"、"达"、"雅"翻译三标准之后，翻译界尽管对"信、达、雅"的解释各有不同，但是大部分学者对这些标准所持态度是肯定的。翻译能做到"信、达、雅"固然不错，问题在于翻译不是照相业的复制行当，难以做到"信、达、雅"三全。基于不同文化的各族语言在翻译过程中难保原汁原味、原形原貌，因而"信、达、雅"只能是相对的。有时"信"虽然达标，而"达"和"雅"却有所不达，有所不雅。于是便出现了"信、达、雅"三标准之主从关系的争论。时至今日，争论仍在延续，焦点无非集中在是翻译究竟应以"直译"还是"意译"为本。

其实，"信"、"达"、"雅"作为衡量笔译作品质量之优劣的三条标准，是一个互为依存、缺一不可的整体，片面强调"直译"或"意译"的孰主孰辅是无意义。一篇上乘的笔头译文从内容到形式都应忠实反映原文的内容是形式，都应被译文的目标读者所感知和理解。译文的内容、精神和风格不可顾此失彼，应该基本做到"信"、"达"、"雅"。任何刻意的直译或意译行为，单方面地求"信"、"达"、"雅"中的某条标准，严格说来都不是真正意义上的翻译，而是"改译"或"编译"。

至于口译的标准，套用笔译的"信、达、雅"三原则是不恰当的。口译不同于笔译，口译的"现时"、"现场"、"限时"的特点决定了口译的标准有别于笔译的标准。衡量口译质量的基本标准应该是"准确"和"流利"。

首先，口译必须"准确"。不准确的口译可能是"胡译"，可能是"篡译"，也可能是"误译"，是不能容忍的。准确是口译的灵魂，是口译的生命线。准确要求译员将来源语这一方的信息完整无误地传达给目标语那一方。具体说来,口译的准确涉及口译时的主题准确、精神准确、论点准确、风格准确、词语准确、数字准确、表达准确、语速准确以及口吻准确等方面。归根结底,准确的译语应该同时保持原语的意义和风格。准确的口译不仅是双语交际成功的保障,而且也是译员职业道德和专业水平的集中体现。准确的口译不仅体现了译员对交际活动的尊重和负责,而且也体现了译员对交际双方的尊重和负责。必须指出,我们所讲的准确性并非是那种机械刻板的"模压式"口译或"盖章式"口译。例如,对原语者明显的口吃,不可妄加模仿。如法炮制说话人的语疾不是忠实翻译,而是人身侮辱。对交际一方过快或过慢的语速、明显的口误或浓重的口音,译员也不可模压炮制,鹦鹉学舌般地如数传递给另一方。

"流利"是译员必须遵循的另一大标准。译员在确保"准确"口译的前提下,应该迅速流畅地将一方的信息传译给另一方。如果说"准确"也是笔译的基本要求,那么"流利"则充分体现了口译的特点。口译的现场性、现时性、即席性、限时性、交互性等因素要求口译过程宜短不宜长,节奏宜紧不宜松。口译是交际的工具,工具的价值在于效用和效率。工具首先得有效用,否则就不成其为工具,但有效用而无效率(或低效率)的工具绝不是好工具。那么,如何来衡量口译的流利程度呢?口译的流利程度包括译员对来源语信息的感知速度和解析速度,及其用目标语进行编码和表达的速度。通常,口译时译员对母语信息的感知速度和解析速度快于对外语信息的感知速度和解析速度,同时用母语编码和表达的速度也快于用外语编码和表达的速度。在口译场合,译员对信息的感知和解析受到"现时"、"限刻"的制约,无法"自由自在"的调节速度,所以必须同步加工。而在编码和表达阶段,译员可以按自我控制速度,所以,目标语为母语的口译所需要的时间相对少于目标语为外语的口译所需要的时间。当然,口译的类型、内容、场合、对象、风格等因素都会对口译的速度产生影响,用同一把尺子来衡量不同类别的口译是不合理。一般说来,我们可以依据译员所用的口译时间是否同发言者的讲话时间大体相等来衡量某场口译是否属于流利。以两倍于来源语发言者的讲话时间进行口译显然不能被视为流利。

五、口译的过程
The Process of Interpretation

口译的基本过程是输入、解译、输出：

| 输　　入 | → | 解　　译 | → | 输　　出 |

从口译过程的形式上看，口译将信息的来源语形式转换为目标语形式，即由"源语"转码为"译语"：

| 源语输入 | → | 语码转换 | → | 译语输出 |

从口译过程的内容上看，口译从信息的感知开始，经过加工处理，再将信息表达出来：

| 信息感知 | → | 信息处理 | → | 信息表达 |

口译过程的这三个阶段可具体分解为信息的接收、解码、记录、编码和表达这五个阶段：

| 接收 | → | 解码 | → | 记录 | → | 编码 | → | 表达 |

译员对信息的接收有两种渠道：一种为"听入"，一种为"视入"。听入是口译中最基本、最常见的信息接收形式，是口译的重要环节。语言信息的听入质量与译员的听觉能力有关。视入是视译时的信息接收形式，这种形式在口译中较少见，有时用作听译的辅助手段。当译员听入母语所表达的信息时，除了不熟悉地方口音、怪僻语、俚语、古语、专业词语或发生"耳误"情况外，听入一般不会发生困难。当译员听入非本族语所表达的信息时，接收信息将可能构成一道难关，译员对外语信息可能会少听入或者无听入，甚至会误听。接收有被动接收和主动接收两种，被动接收表现为孤立地听入单词和句子，译员的注意力过分集中在信息的语言形式上。主动接收是指译员在听入时十分注意信息发出者的神态和语调，注重信息的意义（包括信息的语境意义和修辞意义）。译员在接收时应该采取主动听入的方法。解码是指译员对接收到的来源语的信息码进行解意，获取语言和非语言形式所包含的各种信息。来源语信息码是多方面、多层次的，有语言码，如语音、句法、词汇等信息，也有非语言码，如文化传统、专业知识、信息背景、表达风格、神态表

情等信息,也有介于两者之间的,如双关语、话中话、语体意义等信息。由于来源语信息码丰富复杂,既呈线形排序状,又呈层次交叠状,所以译员对原码的解译处理不可能循序渐进、逐一解码。对语言信息的立体式加工处理是人脑的物种属性,译员在解译语言信号的同时会综合辨别和解析各种微妙的非语言信号以及它们同语言信号之间可能发生的关系。这就是智能翻译机无法取代人工口译的主要原因之一。有必要指出,译员的感知和解码能力与其储存在长时记忆中的知识和经验有着密切的关系,尤其是译员的解码能力,随着知识面的扩大和经验的丰富而增强。

记录,或者叫做暂存,是指将感知到的语码信息暂时储存下来。当以某一种语码形式出现的信息被感知后,在转换成另一种语码前,须暂时储存下来。口译的信息记录采用两种形式,一种以"脑记"为主,一种以"笔记"为主。口译记录可以使感知到的信息尽可能完整地保存下来,经过转码处理后再完整地传送出去。记录不善往往导致来源语的信息部分甚至全部丢失。由于口译内容转瞬即逝,良好的记录显得十分重要,它反映了口译职业的独特要求。记录,尤其是"脑记"形式,往往与解码同步发生。越是简短的信息越便于大脑记录,越是容易解码的信息越容易记录。短时记忆能力强的译员常以"脑记"代替"笔记",但对于大段大段的信息,重"脑记"而轻"笔记"是危险的,是靠不住的。无论采用"脑记"还是"笔记",译员所记录的内容主要是信息的概念、主题、论点、情节、要点、逻辑关系、数量关系等。对于单位信息量较大的口译,译员宜采用网状式的整体记忆法,避免点状式的局部记忆法。孤立的记录不仅低效率,而且没有意义。有意义的记录是以有意义的理解为前提,没有理解的记录会导致误译或漏译。

编码是指将来源语的信息解码后,赋予目标语的表达形式。编码涉及信息语言的结构调整和词语选配,译员必须排除来源语体系的干扰,将原码所表达的意义或主旨按目标语的习惯表达形式重新遣词造句,重新组合排序。经过编码加工后的信息不仅要在语言形式上符合目标语的表达规范,而且还应该在内容上保持信息的完整性,在风格上尽可能保持信息的"原汁原味"。口译的编码技巧与笔译的编码技巧相仿,所不同的是,口译要求快速流利,所以无法像笔译那样有时间斟酌字眼,处理疑难杂症,追求目标语的"雅致"。

表达是指译员将以目标语编码后的信息通过口头表达的方式传译出来。表达是口译过程的最后一道环节，是全过程成败的验收站，也是口译成果的最终表现形式。口译表达的成功标志是准确和流利，只有准确流利的表达才能在交际双方中间构筑一座顺达的信息桥梁。口译表达虽无需译员具备伶牙俐齿、口若悬河、能言善辩的演说才能，但口齿清楚、吐字干脆、音调准确、择词得当、语句通顺、表达流畅却是一名职业译员必备的条件。

六、口译的类型
The Classification of Interpretation

口译类型的划分有三种不同的方法，即"形式分类法"、"方向分类法"和"任务分类法"三种。

口译按其操作形式可以分为以下五种：

交替口译(alternating interpretation)　交替口译是指译员同时以两种语言为操不同语言的交际双方进行轮回交替式口译。这种穿梭于双语之间的口译是最常见的一种口译形式。交替口译的场合很广，可以是一般的非事务性的交谈，可以是正式的政府首脑会谈，也可以是记者招待会。这种交谈式的传译要求译员不停地转换语码，在交谈双方或多方之间频繁穿梭，来回传递语段简短的信息。

接续口译(consecutive interpretation)　接续口译是一种为演讲者以句子或段落为单位传递信息的单向口译方式。接续口译用于多种场合，如演讲、祝词、授课、高级会议、新闻发布会等。演讲者因种种原因需要完整地表达信息，所以他们往往作连贯发言。这种情况需要译员以一段接一段的方式，在讲话者的自然停顿间隙，将信息一组接一组地传译给听众。

同声传译(simultaneous interpretation)　同声传译，又称同步口译，是译员在不打断讲话者演讲的情况下，不停顿地将其讲话内容传译给听众的一种口译方式。因为译员的口译与讲话者的发言几乎同步进行，所以这种口译也被称之为同步口译。同声传译的最大优点在于效率高，可保证讲话者作连贯发言，不影响或中断讲话者的思路，有利于听众对发言全文的通篇理解。同声传译被认为是最有效率的口译形式,是国际会议最基本的口译手段。同声传译有时也用于学术报告、授课讲座等场合。

耳语口译(whispering interpretation) 耳语口译顾名思义是一种将一方的讲话内容用耳语的方式轻轻地传译给另一方的口译手段。耳语口译与同声传译一样,属于不停顿的连贯性口译活动。所不同的是,同声传译的听众往往是群体,如国际会议的与会者等,而耳语口译的听众则是个人,其对象往往是接见外宾、参加会晤的国家元首或高级政府官员。

视阅口译(sight interpretation) 视阅口译(通常叫做"视译")是以阅读的方式接收来源语信息,以口头方式传出信息的口译方式。视译的内容通常是一篇事先准备好的讲稿或文件。除非情况紧急,或出于暂时保密的缘故,译员一般可以在临场前几分钟(甚至更长的一段时间)得到讲稿或文件,因而译员可以将所需口译的文稿快速浏览,做一些必要的文字准备。与同声传译和耳语口译一样,视阅口译同属不间断的连贯式口译活动。

口译按其传译方向,可呈单向口译和双向口译两种:

单向口译 (one-way interpretation) 单向口译是指口译的来源语和目标语固定不变的口译,译员通常只需将某一种语言口译成另一种语言即可。

双向口译 (two-way interpretation) 双向口译是指两种不同的语言交替成为口译来源语和目标语的口译。这两种语言既是来源语,又是目标语,译员在感知、解码、编码、表达时必须熟练而又快捷地转换语言。

在前面所讲的五种口译形式中,交替口译自然属于双向口译的范畴;接续口译因场合不同可以表现为单向口译,也可以是双向口译;同声传译、耳语口译和视阅口译这三种形式通常表现为单向传译。

口译按其操作内容可以分成导游口译、礼仪口译、宣传口译、会议口译、会谈口译等类型:

导游口译(guide interpretation) 导游口译的工作范围包括接待、陪同、参观、游览、购物等活动。

礼仪口译(ceremony interpretation) 礼仪口译的工作范围包括礼

宾迎送、开幕式、闭幕式、招待会、合同签字等活动。

宣传口译（information interpretation）　宣传口译的工作范围包括国情介绍、政策宣传、机构介绍、广告宣传、促销展销、授课讲座、文化交流等活动。

会议口译（conference interpretation）　会议口译的工作范围包括国际会议、记者招待会、商务会议、学术研讨会等活动。

谈判口译（negotiation interpretation）　会谈口译的工作范围包括国事会谈、双边会谈、外交谈判、商务谈判等活动。

上述分类旨在说明口译活动的几种不同类型，而在口译的实际工作中，界线分明的口译类别划分往往是不可能的，也是不必要的，因为许多场合的口译不是单一性的，而是混合性的。所以，一名优秀的译员应该是兼容性强的通用性译员，是一名能胜任各种类型口译工作的多面手。

七、口译的难点
Difficulties in Interpretation

1. 称谓的口译

在外事接待活动中，译员首先面临的一道难题是称谓的翻译。称谓代表了一个人的职位、职衔或学衔，体现了一个人的资历和地位。称谓的误译不仅是对有关人员的不尊重，而且也会产生种种不良的后果。称谓的准确翻译其关键在于译员对有关人员的身份及其称谓的表达是否有一个正确的理解，尤其是对称谓词语指义的认识。一个称谓词很可能表示多种身份，例如，英语的头衔词 president，译成汉语时可视具体情况分别译作共和国的总统、国家主席、大学的校长、学院的院长、学会或协会的会长或主席、公司的总裁或董事长等等。同样，当介绍中国各类机构或组织的首长时，不可千篇一律地将他们的头衔译作 head，而应该使用相应的、规范的称谓语。

一般说来，首席长官的汉语称谓常以"总……"表示，而表示首席长官的英语称谓语则常带有 chief、general、head、managing 这类词，因此当翻译冠以"总"字的头衔时，需遵循英语头衔的表达习惯，例如：

总工程师　chief engineer

总经理　general manager; managing director

总教练　head coach

总干事　secretary-general

有些部门或机构的首长或主管的英译,可以一些通用的头衔词表示,例如下列机构的负责人可以用 director、head 或 chief 来表示,例如:

局长　director of the bureau, head of the bureau, bureau chief

汉语中表示副职的头衔一般都冠以"副"字,英译时需视词语的固定搭配或表达习惯等情况,可选择 vice、associate、assistant、deputy 等词。相对而言,vice 使用面较广,例如:

副总统　vice president

副省长　vice governor

副市长　vice mayor

学术头衔的"副"职称往往用不同的词表达,最为常用的英语词是associate,例如:

副教授　associate professor

副研究员　associate research fellow

副主任医师　associate senior doctor

以 director 表示的职位的副职常以 deputy director 表示。此外,secretary、mayor、dean 等头衔的副职也可冠以 deputy,例如:

副秘书长　deputy secretary-general

副院长　deputy dean

学术头衔系列除了含"正"、"副"级别的高级职称和中级职称外,还有初级职称如"助理","助理"常用 assistant 来表示,例如:

助理工程师　assistant engineer

助理农艺师　assistant agronomist

还有一些行业职称头衔,其高级职称不用"正"或"副"表示,而直接用"高级"或"资深"来表示,我们可以用 senior 来称呼,例如:

高级编辑　senior editor

高级工程师　senior engineer

资深翻译　senior translator

有一些行业的职称或职务系列中,最高级别的职位冠以"首席"一词,英语常用 chief 来表示,例如:

首席执行官　　chief executive officer(CEO)

首席法官　　　chief judge

首席记者　　　chief correspondent

有些头衔会含诸如"代理"、"常务"、"执行"、"名誉"这类称谓语,例如:

代理市长　acting mayor

常务理事　managing director

执行主席　executive chairman / chair(或 presiding chairman)

名誉校长　honorary president

有些职称或职务带有"主任"、"主治"、"特级"、"特派"、"特约"等头衔,英译不尽相同,例如:

主任秘书　chief secretary

主治医师　attending / chief doctor; physician; consultant

特级教师　special-grade senior teacher

特派记者　accredited correspondent

特约编辑　contributing editor

许多职称、职务的头衔称谓其英语表达法难以归类,需要日积月累,逐步登录在自己的称谓语料库中。

2. 谚语的口译

谚语的口译大致可分为三种类型,一种是"形同意合"的口译,第二种是"形似意合"的口译,第三种是"形异意合"的口译。

英语和汉语两种语言中都有许多"形"同"意"合的谚语。例如英语的 A fall into the pit, a gain in your wit 与汉语的"吃一堑,长一智",其形其意可谓"形同意合"。两种语言中存在着形意相合的谚语,这对译员来说,无疑是可喜可慰的。

Facts speak louder than words.　事实胜于雄辩。

Failure is the mother of success.　失败乃成功之母。

Like father, like son.　有其父,必有其子。

Pride goes before a fall.　骄者必败。

The style is the man.　文如其人。

More haste, less speed.　欲速则不达。

Man proposes, God disposes.　谋事在人,成事在天。

The tongue cuts the throat.　祸从口出。／言多必失。

英汉语言中有许多谚语虽然"形"有所不同,但表意却有惊人的相似之处,例如英语中有 Love me, love my dog 一语,汉语里也有"爱屋及乌"之说。通常对反应较快的译员来说,这类谚语的转译也比较容易应付。例如:

Speak of the devil (and he will appear).　说到曹操,曹操到。

A new broom sweeps clean.　新官上任三把火。

Teach fish to swim.　班门弄斧。

Have a card up one's sleeve.　胸有成竹。

Put the cart before the horse.　本末倒置。

Gifts blind the eyes.　拿了手短,吃了嘴软。

The same knife cuts bread and fingers.　水能载舟,亦能覆舟。

A sparrow cannot understand the ambition of a swan.　燕雀安知鸿鹄之志。

译员遇到第三类谚语时,常常会因"形"生"意",造成误译。例如英语谚语 A horse stumbles that has four legs,若将其直译成"有四条腿的马会失蹄",这自然会给听者的理解带来困难,甚至会产生一种莫名其妙的感觉。对于这类谚语的翻译,应采取"形相远而意相近"的译法,即以完全不同的词语将甲方语句的寓意准确地传达给乙方。如果我们将上例 A horse stumbles that has four legs 译成"人非圣贤,孰能无过"或"金无足赤,人无完人",不失之为成功的处理方法。汉译后,其形虽变,然其意依存。例如:

Late fruit keeps well.　大器晚成。

A hedge between keeps friendship green.　君子之交淡如水。

Rest breeds rust.　生命在于运动。

Many kiss the baby for the nurse's sake.　醉翁之意不在酒。

Everybody's business is nobody's business.　三个和尚无水吃。

The moon is not seen when the sun shines.　小巫见大巫。

The pot calls the kettle black.　五十步笑百步。

Misfortune might be a blessing in disguise.　祸兮福所倚,福兮祸
　　　所伏。

　　当然,掌握了以上三种谚语的翻译方法并不等于找到了一把可以
翻译所有谚语的万能钥匙。有些谚语的翻译需要译员"转形解意",而
有些谚语的翻译宜"以不变应万变",以保其"原汁原味"。例如 One
swallow does not make a summer,译作"一燕不成夏"即可。

　　除了谚语之外,成语、习语、歇后语、诗句等语句的临场翻译也是译
员颇感棘手的问题。以上所述的有关谚语的口译方法有"举一反三"之
意。一般说来,译员在充分理解有关词语所含寓意的情况下,可采用意
译或半意译的方法,只需将词语的意思传译过去即可。至于歇后语的
口译,例如"小葱拌豆腐———清二楚"、"猪八戒照镜子——里外不是
人"、"张飞穿针眼——大眼瞪小眼"、"和尚打伞——无法无天"等歇后
语,一般不必将歇后语的前后两部分无一遗漏地都译成英语,以免给英
语听众带来困惑。口译时,原则上只需翻译歇后语所表达的主要意思,
即歇后语中后半句的内容。

3. 引语的口译

　　经常为政府首脑、高级官员、文化人士、社会名流做口译的译员都
有相同的体会,即这些人员在接待或访问时常常在演讲中引用一些名
家名言、经典诗句,以表达自己的感情、观点和立场,或赞颂对方国家的
文化传统。

　　例如,1999 年 10 月 22 日江泽民主席在英国剑桥大学发表演讲时
说到:"中华民族历来尊重人的尊严和价值。还在遥远的古代,我们的
先人就已提出'民为贵'的思想,认为'天生万物,唯人为贵'(Man is
the most valuable among all the things that heaven fosters.),一切社
会的发展和进步,都取决于人的发展和进步,取决于人的尊严的维护和
价值的发挥。"江主席在结束讲话时引用了孔子的一句话:"中国两千五
百五十年前诞生的杰出教育家、思想家孔子说过:'逝者如斯夫! 不舍
昼夜。'(The passage of time is just like the flow of water, which goes
on day and night.)时光流逝不可逆转。"

　　朱镕基总理在 1999 年春访美时,在一次记者招待会上回答某个记
者提出的有关"人权"问题时也引用了"民为贵,社稷次之,君为轻"

（The people are the most important element in a state; next are the gods of land and grain; least is the ruler himself. ）这句古话,以表明中国政府十分重视人权问题。

又如,美国前总统里根 1984 年 4 月访华时在欢迎宴席上引用了《易经》中的一句话,他说道:And as a saying from The Book of Changes goes, "If two people are of the same mind, their sharpness can cut through metal.（二人同心,可以断金。）"

再如,美国克林顿总统 1998 年 6 月下旬访华时在人民大会堂的国宴上致辞时引用了孟子的一句话,他说道:In so many different ways, we are upholding the teachings of Mencius, who said:"A good citizen in one community will befriend the other citizens of the community; a good citizen of the world will befriend the other citizens of the world."(一乡之善士斯友一乡之善士,天下之善士斯友天下之善士。）。

在这种场合,一个称职的译员必须准确、流利地将这些引语译成目标语。这就要求译员掌握一定数量的名家名言、经典诗句,尤其是中国古代思想家流传下来一些名言佳句。对于不少译员来说,这是一道难以逾越但又必须逾越的难关。有着五千年文明史的中国,历经沧海巨变,文化底蕴深厚,儒道墨法争鸣,阴阳纵横齐放,哲人智者如云,传世绝句如林,信手拈来,为我所用。因此,译员平时需要加强学习,做一个有心人,注意收集古今名人的经典名言,以不断充实自己的语料库。

4. 数字的口译

数字的翻译是口译中的一大难关,即使是老翻译,当遇到数字时,尤其是遇到五位数以上的数字时,亦不敢有半点松懈。这不仅仅是因为数字难译,更重要的是在商贸谈判或外交活动中,数字误译所造成的后果是不堪设想的。如果说遇到难译的词语时,译员还可以通过解译的方法绕道走,而数字的口译却无道可绕。

数字之所以难译,其中一个主要原因在于英汉对于四位数以上的数字的表达上,这两种语言有不同的段位概念和分段方法。英语学习者都知道,英语数字的表达以每三位数为一段位,这与汉语以每四位数为一段位的表达方法完全不同:

英语数字分段法

第一段位：one　　　　　　ten　　　　　　　　hundred
第二段位：thousand　　　　ten thousand　　　　hundred thousand
第三段位：million　　　　　ten million　　　　　hundred million
第四段位：billion　　　　　ten billion　　　　　hundred billion
第五段位：trillion

汉语数字分段法

第一段位：个　　　十　　　　　百　　　　　千
第二段位：万　　　十万　　　　百万　　　　千万
第三段位：亿　　　十亿　　　　百亿　　　　千亿
第四段位：兆（万亿）

如果我们将英汉数字对照排列，我们可以清楚地体会到英汉数字分段上的差异给译员带来的困难：

阿拉伯数字	英语	汉语
1	one	一
10	ten	十
100	one hundred	一百
1,000	one thousand	一千
10,000	ten thousand	一万
100,000	one hundred thousand	十万
1,000,000	one million	一百万
10,000,000	ten million	一千万
100,000,000	one hundred million	一亿
1,000,000,000	one billion	十亿
10,000,000,000	ten billion	一百亿
100,000,000,000	one hundred billion	一千亿
1,000,000,000,000	one trillion	一兆（万亿）

英汉数字的不同分段方法使同一组阿拉伯数字具有不同的读法规则，现以一组 13 位数字为单位的阿拉伯数字 1234567891234 为例，在用英语和汉语表达时，前者按下标分段记号（，）为单位朗读，而后者则按上标分段记号（'）为单位朗读：

英语朗读法

1,234,567,891,234

one trillion

two hundred and thirty-four billion

five hundred and sixty-seven million

eight hundred and ninety-one thousand

two hundred and thirty-four

汉语朗读法

1'2345'6789'1234

一兆／万亿

二千三百四十五亿

六千七百八十九万

一千二百三十四

几乎所有英汉口译人员都对英汉两种语言在数字上的不同表达习惯感到头痛。因此在口译教学中,集中一段时间专门训练数字口译是必不可少的一个教学环节。提高数字口译的准确性和速度可以采取三种方法。第一,在日常生活中,经常不断地进行英汉数字互译练习,其中包括操练转译孤立的数字和出现在语境中的数字。第二,在正式口译工作中,尽可能将语句中的数字记录下来,然后用原文复述一遍,确证无误后方可传译给另一方。第三,做笔记时,可先以下标或上标的分段记号写下英语或汉语的原始语数字,然后标上目标语的段位记号,再将数字传译给另一方。

以下各句介绍了世界上五个英语国家的人口与国土面积,可试译成汉语:

The United States has a population of 269,857,000, with a total area of 9,372,610 square kilometers, or 3,618,765 square miles.

Canada, a country with a population of only 28,529,000, has a total area slightly larger than that of the United States, that is, an area of 9,946,140 square kilometers, or 3,851,788 square miles.

The United Kingdom, whose population amounts to 59,283,000, has a total land area of 244,820 square kilometers, or 94,525 square miles.

Australia, with its landmass of 7,686,850 square kilometers, or

2,967,893 square miles, has a population of 18,742,000.

New Zealand has the smallest population of only 3,605,000, with a territory of 268,680 square kilometers, or 103,723 square miles.

以下是选自英国杂志《银行家》某期有关世界前 1,000 家银行中 7 家中国银行的实力状况（数字以千美元为单位）。请给这些数字加分隔符（下标或上标），然后用英语和汉语分别说出这些数字。

世界 1000 家银行中我国 7 家银行实力排名表

Bank Name	Primary Capital	Total Assets	Profits
Industrial & Commercial Bank	22213000	391213000	417000
Bank of China	14712000	299007000	425000
Construction Bank of China	5988000	203116000	1215000
Agricultural Bank of China	4802000	190095000	95000
Bank of Communications	2816000	58454000	322000
Merchants Bank	974000	16679000	242000
Xiamen International Bank	163000	1208000	22000

以下是 2002 年 10 月 22 日上海股市的成交情况。请给这些数字加上分隔符（下标或上标），然后用英语和汉语分别说出这些数字。

沪市成交综述

	成交金额	增 减	成交量(手数)	增 减
A 股	554909.96	260319.05	7191568	3380274
B 股	9480.59	5386.62	171386	98150
合计	564390.55	265705.67	7362954	3478424

5. 口译的笔记

口译成功与否在很大程度上取决于译员在口译表达前对感知的信息进行记录的情况。记录分为"脑记"和"笔记"两种。

人脑的记忆由短时记忆和长时记忆两部分组成。短时记忆是一种操作性暂时记忆，长时记忆属一种储存类的永久记忆。记忆是人脑的自然属性，是一个心智正常人的天赋能力。但是，不是所有人都具有相同的记忆能力。

短时记忆不仅因人而异，而且容量十分有限。影响一个人短时记忆能力的因素很多,其中最主要的因素是记忆内容的意义性。通常,一个人的短时记忆最多只能容下一组由六个意义毫不相干的单词组成的词群,或一组无意义的七位数的数字。当感知的信息有意义时,人的短时记忆可容纳由二十多个单词组成的句子,或者一组十位数的数字。即便如此,这种记忆能力仍然十分有限,不足以应付长段信息的口译。对于口译工作者来说,完全依赖脑的记忆能力是危险的。因此做口译时,尤其是做接续性的口译,记笔记便显得十分重要。常言道,好记性不如赖笔头(The worst pen is better than the best memory.),讲的就是这个道理。

口译笔记应记要点,切忌记"全"。口译笔记是记忆的延伸或补充,不应也不必取代记忆。在口译工作中,我们无需也不可能采取听写的方法,整句整段地记录源语信息。记过多的笔记会影响对源语信息整体的理解。口译笔记的内容主要是概念、命题、名称、数字、组织机构和逻辑关系(如大小、先后、正反、上下、升降、因果关系等),笔记单位以表达意群的词语和符号为主。

口译笔记求快求精,但不可潦草。感知到的信息转瞬即逝,而笔记的速度往往赶不上表达的速度。译员要培养快速笔记的能力,书写时笔划要干脆利落,不可拖泥带水。同时,行书不宜潦草,速记代号不宜过多,以防"笔记欺主"的尴尬局面。译员可以选用或编造一些自用的简明速记符号,但需熟练掌握后方可在正式口译的场合中使用。

口译笔记可以使用来源语,也可使用目标语,也可以双语兼用。以信息的来源语作为笔记的基本记录语言通常比较安全,可以减少信息的丢失。至于以何种文字、何种符号记录为佳,这完全取决于译员个人的听辨能力、解析能力、笔记习惯、缩写能力、速记经验、翻译能力,以及信息来源语和目标语的书写特点。手段服务于目的,只要有利于口译的准确性和流利性,我们不必拘泥某种文字或符号。有经验的译员往往会混合使用来源语、目标语和其他符号。例如,"联合国大会"可笔录为"UN 大"或"联大"。

译员应该随身携带一本开本稍窄、可上下翻动的记事本。记录时纸上的行幅宜窄,行间稍宽,两边留有空间。每行记录的信息量不宜多,书写字体和符号不宜过小,笔墨不宜过浅,以减少串行、混译、误译、漏译等现象的发生。

口译笔记使用大量常见略语,学习者应该熟悉这些略语,例如:eg (for example), etc (and so on), ie (that is), cf (compare), esp (especially), min (minimum), max (maximum), usu (usually), ref (reference), Co (company), std (standard) 等。

口译学习者是否需要学习速记? 速记是一项特殊的技巧,速记语言是由一套完整符号组成的体系。除非时间和条件许可,我们一般不主张另设速记课,也不鼓励初涉译界的口译新手使用不为自己所熟悉的速记符号。但是,向口译学生介绍一些常用速记符号,使他们在口译实践中逐步掌握一些简单的速记符号还是有益的。以下列举一部分简易速记符号,供参考使用。

信息意义	速记符号
上一个台阶	↱
下一个台阶	↳
交换	⊂⊃
压力,影响	↓
会议,会面	⊙
国家	□
国与国	□ / □
促进,发展	↗
上升,增加	↑
下降,减少	↓
进入	∩
越来越强等	↟↟
越来越弱等	↡↡
双向交流	↑↓
接触,交往	∞
对立,冲突	><
分歧	⊥
波折	<<
非常,十分重要	* *
属于	∈

胜利	V
坚持	≡
奇观	!
有关	@
一方面	・ /
另一方面	/ ・
关系	・ / ・
问题,疑问	?
关键	!
将来	→
过去	↵
错误,否,不,否定	×
正确,对,好,肯定	√
不同意	N
同意	Y
优秀	★
强,好	+
更强,更好	++
弱,差	—
更弱,更差	——
因为	∵
所以	∴
原因	←
导致,结果	→
结论是	⇒
大于	>
小于	<
小于或等于	≤
大于或等于	≥
等于,意味着	=
不等于	≠
约等于	≈

替换为	∽
但是	‖
与……比较而言	//
和，与	&
空洞	○
代表	△

八、译员的素质
Interpreter Qualification Requirements

　　口译是一门专业要求很高的职业。虽然粗通两国语言的人也可以做一些简单的口译工作，但是他们却无法承担正式的口译任务。要成为一名优秀的职业译员，除了一些必要的生理条件和心理条件之外，通常需要经过专门学习和强化培训，培养和提炼职业译员所必须具有的素质。一名专职译员应具备哪些基本条件呢？

　　译员必须具有良好的职业道德和爱国主义的情操。译员的活动属外事活动，译员的一举一动、一言一行都关系到祖国的形象、民族的风貌、机构的利益。译员在口译工作以及与口译工作有关的活动中，应遵守外事纪律和财经纪律，严守国家机密，严格按口译工作的操作程序办事。译员必须忠于职守，对交谈双方负责，严守服务对象的机密。译员要洁身自爱，不谋私利，不自行其是，不做有损国格和人格的事。

　　译员必须有扎实的两种语言或两种以上语言的功底。译员的双语能力不仅指通晓基本语言知识，如语音语调、句法结构、词法语义等知识的掌握，更重要的是指运用语言知识的能力（如听、说、读、写、译）。此外，译员还应该了解各种文体或语体风格和语用功能，掌握一定数量的习语、俚语、术语、谚语、委婉语、略语、诗句等词语的翻译方法。

　　译员必须具备清晰、流畅、达意的表达能力。在做口译时，要做到语速不急不缓，音调不高不低，吐字清晰自然，表达干净利落，择词准确恰当，语句简明易解，译文传神传情。

　　译员必须有一个敏捷、聪颖的头脑，具备良好的心脑记忆能力、逻辑思维能力、辨析解意能力和应变反应能力。

译员必须有广博的知识,对时事要闻、政经知识、人文知识、科技知识、商贸知识、法律知识、史地知识、国际知识、民俗知识、生活常识等等,都要略窥门径。

译员必须具有高尚、忠诚、稳重、谦虚的品格和大方素雅、洁净得体的仪表。译员必须讲究外事礼仪、社交礼节和口译规范。译员在口译工作时,要忠实翻译,做到不插话、不抢译、不随意增减原文内容;要把握角色,不可喧宾夺主、炫耀学识。译员要随时检点自己的服饰和仪容,戒除不拘小节、不修边幅的习惯。总之,一名高级口译应该是一个仪表端庄、举止大方、态度和蔼、风度儒雅、言谈得体的外交家。

以上论述简要介绍了口译的理论和范畴,旨在对"什么是口译"作一番概述。至于"如何进行口译","如何处理口译的难题"、"如何成为一名合格的译员",则需要学习者积极参与口译培训,勇于参与现场实习,一步一个脚印地学习口译的基本知识和技巧,从坚持不懈的口译实践中逐步掌握规范的口译方法。

第二部分　培训教程

PART TWO
A Training Course

第1单元 会话口译

UNIT 1 Interpreting Conversations

1—1 欢迎光临
Welcome

邮电   look over the seas
海外部主任   幽默感
感到骄傲和荣幸   字面意思
gracious invitation   下榻
a distinguished group   国际机票
寄托   school break
外宾专用别墅

课文口译
Text for Interpretation

Interpret the following conversation alternatively into English and Chinese:

A：欢迎来上海，罗伯茨先生。我是上海邮电服务发展公司海外部主任陈天明。

B：Nice to meet you，Director Chen. I'm very excited to visit your company and of course，to tour around Shanghai and the whole country.

A：您专程从英国赶来，我很高兴。我们为您来此参加工作，成为我部门的一员而感到骄傲和荣幸。我真诚地希望您的来访有价值、有意义。

B：It is indeed my pleasure and privilege to have received your gracious invitation and work with a distinguished group of people like Director Chen. I had been looking forward to this visit for years. I had a dream that someday I would visit China and work in the beautiful city of Shanghai for a while. I'm very grateful that you have made my dream come true.

A：您对这次来沪短期工作有如此高的期望，真令人高兴。我们会尽力使您在沪期间过得舒适愉快。考虑到您的方便和舒适，您可以居住在公司的外宾专用别墅。别墅紧挨着海滩，从那里骑自行车15分钟可到我海外部的办公楼。您一定会喜欢的。

B：That's wonderful. Isn't it nice that not only your "Overseas" Department looks "over the sea", but also my residence?

A：罗伯茨先生，我真的很喜欢您的幽默感。您可知道"上海"这两个字在汉语里的字面意思是"海上之埠"？我们为能够安排英国朋友在临海的寓所下榻而感到骄傲。英国不是海上岛国吗？

B：I like what you said, Mr. Chen. We have much in common with Shanghai and its people. I believe my wife will like here, too.

A：我希望您的家人能早日与您在此团聚。我公司会支付包括国际机票在内所需的一切费用。

B：Thank you so much for your concern. My wife teaches at a university and the best time for her and our son to come over is when school breaks in the summer. Two more months. We simply can't wait to see each other here in Shanghai.

A：真遗憾，您还要等那么久。

B：You're very nice, Mr. Chen, really.

A：长途飞行后您一定很累了。今晚有招待晚宴，您需要休息一下。晚上6时我派车来接您。

B：Very good.

A：我得走了，我们晚上再见。

B： Bye now.

1－2 投资意向
A Wish to Invest

share my thoughts with you

洗耳恭听

foreign firm

investment destination

翻了两番

投资热

对外全面开放

沿海城市

内地

有利可图

I'm all ears to

最大程度

发挥有关双方的优势

幅员辽阔

税收

消费者市场

基础设施

诱人的投资政策

资金

管理知识

研究资料

利润

合资／独资企业

enlightening

consultant

Interpret the following conversation alternatively into English and Chinese:

A：您好，罗伯茨先生。

B: Hi, Mr. Chen. I have been thinking about something lately and I'd like to share with you my thoughts.

A: 愿洗耳恭听。如能为您效劳，我将很高兴。

B: In the West everybody is talking about going to the East and making an investment. Apparently a growing number of foreign firms have been pouring into China, and the Pudong area of Shanghai is among the best choices of their investment destinations. Today it is not a matter of whether to go east, but when and how.

A: 您说的完全对。海外人士在上海及其周边地区的投资近年来翻了两番。出现这一高涨不止的投资热有多种缘由。除了中国是世界上经济增长最快的国家之一这个原因外，中国政府和地方政府很重视对外全面开放，不仅开放沿海城市，也开放内地，尽可能吸引外资。另外，许多海外团体与个人投资者认为在中国直接投资比同中国公司做生意更有利可图。

B: I'm not sure if I understand the logic behind this preference. I'm all ears to your explanation.

A: 好的。基本情况是这样的，外国直接在华投资可以在最大程度上发挥有关双方的优势。中国幅员辽阔，自然资源丰富，廉价劳动力充裕，税收低，消费者市场不断增长，基础设施不断改善，当然罗，我们还有稳定的社会政治环境以及诱人的投资政策。所有这些优势难以在其他国家找到。而来自发达国家和地区的外国投资者则有充足的资金，先进的技术和管理知识。同做进出口贸易生意相比，在华直接投资的经济回报则更高。

B: You're right. I have friends who are interested in direct investment in China. Do you have any idea of the best place in which to invest?

A: 就我个人来说，我希望你们在上海的浦东地区投资。这倒不是因为浦东是我的家乡，而是因为浦东的确是投资者的理想场所。如果您或您的朋友有兴趣，我可以向你们提供许多研究资料。我也听说过许多关于在中国内地和其他沿海城市进行投资而获得成功的例子。真的很难说哪一个地方为最佳。也许应该说在某一时期的某一地点做投资相对比较为好。

B： My next question concerns the forms of investment that are allowed in China currently.

A： 投资方式很多，您可以同中方合资办企业，也可以独资办公司。

B： What are the differences?

A： 投资兴办合资企业时，通常外方提供资金、机械、先进技术和管理方法，而中方则提供土地、劳工以及部分用于基础设施建设的资金。至于独资企业嘛，外商提供所有资金，赚取所有利润，同时承担所有风险。您可以选择自己喜欢的方式经营独资公司，当然不可超越中国法律。

B： Your explanations are very enlightening. If we ever decide to invest in Shanghai，we'd like you to be our Chinese consultant. I hope you won't refuse our offer then.

A： 我深感荣幸。希望能早日为您的投资效劳。

1—3　合资企业
Establishing a Joint Venture

词汇预习
Vocabulary Work

cordless / mobile phone	at a moderate rate and a safe scale
投资意向	in the vicinity of
明智的	投资比重
制造公司	利润分配
persuasive	权益关系
express train	营销
potential market	外汇储备
initially	天晴还需防雨天
embark on	convertible currency

the term of our partnership   正合吾意

the board of directors   a rewarding day

Interpret the following conversation alternatively into English and Chinese:

A：罗伯茨先生，很高兴再次见到您。有什么需要我做的吗？

B：Hi, Mr. Chen, it's been ten months since I left China. I would like to discuss with you the possibilities of establishing a joint venture with your company to manufacture cordless phones and mobile phones.

A：好极了。您的投资意向是明智的。我公司也正在寻求外资，合办一家生产无绳电话和移动电话的制造公司，您的提议很好。罗伯茨先生，我还记得一年前曾同您讨论过有关外国在华投资的事情。

B：Yes, you did a good job. The whole idea of my investing in a joint enterprise with your company is the direct result of your wonderful lecture. Your answers were direct and honest. And your explanations were sincere and persuasive. May I get on China's economic express train and share your economic gains?

A：当然可以。欢迎罗伯茨先生加入我们的行列！我们来讨论一下合资企业的事宜吧。您能告诉我您的设想吗？

B：I did a lot of research in the market of telecommunications equipment lately. There's a potential market for cordless and mobile phones in China and the world as a whole. Initially, I would like to embark on this joint venture business at a moderate rate and a safe scale. My suggestion for the amount of total capital investment is in the vicinity of eight million US dollars, a lucky number in China, I suppose.

A：很好。800万岂止是个吉利的数字，我认为这对启动这家合资企业来说，是很合适的。那么您在合资中打算占有多少投资比重呢?

B : My contribution is 50% of the total investment，including the construction funds and the cost of all the imported equipment，and the engineers，technicians and management staff from my home company.

A : 我对您这个 5:5 对半开的合伙投资比例感到满意。这就是说，我们在经营管理和利润分配上也保持一种 5:5 对半开的权益关系。

B : You're absolutely right.

A : 接下来的问题是产品的营销。无绳电话在中国有很大的需求量，但是我们无法保证在国内推销 50% 移动电话。此外，我们需要增加外汇的储备，"天晴还需防雨天"嘛。我建议贵方负责向海外推销 65% 以上的移动电话，您看如何? 我相信您对外汇的需求大于对我人民币的需求。

B : I love *renminbi*. And I have heard that the Chinese *yuan* will become a convertible currency soon. But I accept your proposal and we will be responsible for the international marketing of two-thirds of the mobile phones.

A : 好极了。

B : Two more questions. One concerns the term of our partnership and the other the management's structure of the venture.

A : 至于我们的合作期限，我们可以定为 15 年，只要双方愿意，合同期满后我们还可以续签。您意下如何?

B : That's quite logical. May I suggest that we set up a board of directors for the management of the company and share rights and obligations as equal partners?

A : 正合我的想法。下周我们是否再举行一轮会谈，详细讨论一些技术性问题?

B : That's fine. I like to work with you, as I did before. It's been a very rewarding day.

A : 收获确实很大。罗伯茨先生，祝您周末愉快。

B : You, too.

句子精练
Sentences in Focus

Interpret the following sentences into English or Chinese:

1. 我希望您的太太能早日与您在此团聚,我公司会支付包括国际机票在内所需要的一切费用。

2. 今晚我们为您举行招待晚宴,晚上 5:30 我派车来接您。

3. 中央政府很重视全面对外开放,不仅开放沿海城市,也开放内地,尽可能吸引外资。

4. 由于外国直接在华投资可以在最大程度上发挥有关各方的优势,所以许多海外机构个人投资者认为,他们在中国直接投资比同中国公司做生意更有利可图。

5. 中国幅员辽阔,自然资源丰富,劳动力低廉,税收低,消费者市场潜力大,社会环境稳定,投资政策诱人,经济回报率高。

6. 在华投资的方式很多,你可以同中方合资办企业,也可以独资办公司,选择自己喜欢的方式经营,但不可超越中国法律。

7. 投资兴办合资企业时,通常外方提供资金、机械、先进技术和管理方法,而中方则提供土地、劳工以及部分用于基础设施建设的资金。

8. 我们来讨论一下建立合资企业的事宜吧。您能告诉我您的设想吗? 例如您打算在合资企业中占有多少投资份额?

9. 我们之间的投资份额可以对半开,在经营管理和利润分配上也可对半开。

10. 我们的合作期定为 10 年,只要双方愿意,期满后我们还可以续签合同。

11. 我们的想法不谋而合。

12. 我们是否可在下周再举行一轮会谈,集中讨论一些技术性的问题?

13. It is my great pleasure and privilege to have received your gracious invitation and work with a distinguished group of China's automobile specialists.

14. A growing number of American firms have been pouring into

China's inland provinces, although coastal cities such as Shanghai and Tianjin are still among their first choices of investment with many foreign investors.

15. I would like to discuss with you the possibilities of establishing a joint venture with your company to manufacture progressive-scan DVD home cinema systems of the latest model.

16. I suggest that we should set up a board of directors for the management of the company and share rights and obligations as equal partners.

参考译文
Reference Version

1－1 欢迎光临
Welcome

A: Welcome to Shanghai, Mr. Roberts. I'm Chen Tianming, from Shanghai Post and Telecommunications Service Development Company. I'm director of the company's Overseas Department.

B: 很高兴见到您,陈主任。能访问贵公司我很兴奋,当然罗,我还能看看上海和整个中国,真令人兴奋。

A: I'm very happy that you have come all the way from Britain. We are very proud and honored that you will work with us, and be part of our department. I sincerely hope that your visit will be worthwhile and meaningful.

B: 受到贵公司的友好邀请,来此与陈主任这样杰出的人士一起共事,我深感愉快和荣幸。我曾梦想有朝一日能访问中国,能在美丽的上海工作一段时间。我很高兴您使我的梦想成了真。

A: I'm very glad that you have so high expectations for this business trip in Shanghai. We will make an all-out effort to make your stay comfortable and pleasant. For your convenience and comfort, we accommodate you in one of the company's villas for overseas visitors. It is located by the beach, fifteen minutes' bicycle ride from the office building of the Overseas Department. I'm sure you will like it.

B：好极了。不仅您的"海外"部面向着大海，而且我的寓所也面向着大海，这不很有意思吗？

A：I really like your sense of humor, Mr. Roberts. Do you know that the word "Shanghai" in Chinese literally means "a port on the sea". We're very proud that we can offer our British friends a residence overlooking the sea. Britain is a country of islands on the sea, isn't it?

B：您说得好，陈先生。我们与上海以及上海人有许多共同之处。我太太也一定会喜欢这里。

A：I hope your family will join you soon. Our company will pay for all their expenses including international flights.

B：非常感谢您的关心。我太太是大学教师，她与我们儿子来此的最佳时间是暑期。还要等上两个月。我们真的等不及在上海相会。

A：I'm sorry you have to wait for that long.

B：陈先生，您真是个好人，真的。

A：You must be very tired after a long flight, Mr. Roberts. You'll need a rest for tonight's reception party. I'll send someone to pick you up at six.

B：好的。

A：I'm leaving. See you in the evening, then.

B：再见。

1—2　投资意向
A Wish to Invest

A：Hi, Mr. Roberts.

B：您好，陈先生。近来我一直在思考件事，我想告诉您我的想法。

A：I'd like to hear them. And I'll be very happy if I can help you with anything.

B: 现在西方人人都在谈论去东方投资。显然越来越多的外国公司纷纷涌入中国，而上海的浦东地区是人们投资的首选目的地之一。现在的问题不在于是否要去东方投资，而在于何时去投资为好，如何去投资为好。

A: You're absolutely right. Overseas investment in Shanghai and its surrounding areas has quadrupled in recent years. There are many reasons for this rising investment fever. Apart from the fact that China is one of the fast growing economies in the world, the Chinese central government and local governments focus a lot of their attention on opening the whole country up to the outside world, both the coastal cities and the country's interior areas. They are doing all they can to attract foreign investment. On the other hand, many institutional and individual investors overseas find it more profitable to invest directly in China than just to do trade with Chinese companies.

B: 这种偏爱的原因何在，我不太明白。请您解释一下，我愿闻其详。

A: OK. Basically, direct foreign investment in China maximizes the strengths of both parties concerned. China has massive land, abundant natural resources, huge cheap labor, low taxation, a growing consumer market, improving infrastructure and of course, a stable social and political environment with attractive investment policies. All these are rarely found elsewhere in the world. Foreign investors from developed countries or areas, on the other hand, have sufficient funds, advanced technology and managerial expertise. Direct investment in China will yield higher economic returns than import and export trade.

B: 您说得有道理。我有一些朋友有意在中国直接投资。对于最佳投资地点，您有何高见？

A: Personally, I like you to invest in the Pudong area of Shanghai. Not because it's my hometown, but it really is an ideal place for investment. If you or your friends are interested, I have a lot of investment literature for you to study. I also have heard of many very successful stories of foreign investment in China's inland areas and other coastal cities. There's really no *the* best place. There might be a better place at a given time.

B: 接下来的一个问题是,目前所许可的投资形式有哪一些?

A: Among others you can invest in a joint venture with a Chinese partner, or establish a business independently, that is, set up a company solely funded and owned by a foreign investor.

B: 两者有何不同?

A: With a joint venture, a foreign partner usually brings into the enterprise or business capital funds, machinery, advanced technology and management, while the Chinese partner supplies land, labor and a portion of the funds for the infrastructure. The business is then jointly run by both parties. As for the solely foreign-funded business, you provide all the funds and take all the benefits as well as risks. You can run the company in whatever way you prefer, within the boundary of Chinese laws, of course.

B: 您的解释使我茅塞顿开。如果我们决定在上海投资的话,我们想请您担任我们的中方顾问。希望您不要推辞。

A: It's my honor. And I'm looking forward to the early arrival of that day.

1—3 合资企业
Establishing a Joint Venture

A: I'm so happy to see you again, Mr. Roberts. May I help you in any way?

B: 您好,陈先生,离开中国已有 10 个月了。我打算同您商谈一下能否与贵公司合资兴办企业,共同生产无绳电话和移动电话。

A: That's great. Your investment proposal is a very wise decision. Our company is also seeking foreign investment in a manufacturing company for cordless and mobile phones. Your initiative is most welcome. I remember talking to you about the matter of foreign investment in China a year ago, Mr. Roberts.

B: 是的,那次您谈得很好。其结果是触发了我同贵公司合资办企业的念头。您所作的回答坦率,您所作的解释诚恳,很有说服力。现在我想搭乘中国经济快车,分享你们的经济成果好吗?

A: Of course. Welcome aboard, Mr. Roberts! Let's get down to the business of this joint venture. May I have some idea of your proposal?

B: 最近我对电信设备的市场做了一番调查。中国乃至全世界的无绳电话和移动电话的市场潜力很大。在合资企业的起步阶段,我希望有一个稳妥的速度和规模。我建议投资总额在 800 万美元之间,我想中国人喜欢这个吉利的数字。

A: Very good. Eight million is more than a lucky number; it's the right number for the initiation of this joint venture, as I understand it. But how much would your share of investment be in this partnership?

B: 我愿提供投资总额 50%的资金,其中包括建设资金、全部进口设备的费用以及来自我国内公司的工程师、技工和管理人员的费用。

A: I like the idea of a 50 to 50 investment partnership, in which case there will be a 50 to 50 distribution in business management and profits share.

B: 完全正确。

A: The problem then involves the marketing of the manufactured products. Cordless phones are in high demand in China, but we can't guarantee a 50% domestic marketing of mobile phones. Besides, we need to increase our foreign exchange reserve for the rainy day. May I suggest that you market at least 65% of the total number of mobile phones internationally? I believe you need more foreign currency than our *renminbi*.

B: 我很喜欢人民币。我听说中国的人民币不久便可成为一种可兑换的货币。不过我接受您的建议,我们负责在国际市场上推销三分之二的移动电话。

A: That's beautiful.

B: 还有两个问题需要解决。一个问题是有关我们的合作期限,另一个问题涉及企业管理人员的结构。

A: As for the term of the partnership, let's start with a 15-year term for this joint venture, and extend the contract later if both parties wish to continue the partnership. What do you say to this?

B: 非常合理。我建议成立董事会来监管公司的业务,我们以平等的伙伴关系分享权利和义务。

A: That coincides with our usual practice. Shall we hold another round of discussion next week on some technical problems in a more detailed way?

B: 好的。如同以往一样,我乐意与您合作。今天的收获很大。

A: Yes, indeed. Have a nice weekend, Mr. Roberts!

B: 我也祝您周末愉快。

句子精练
Sentences in Focus

1. I hope you wife will soon join you here. The company will pay for all the needed expenses, including her international flight.

2. We'll have a reception dinner for you tonight, and I'll send someone to pick you up at 5:30.

3. The central government focuses a lot of attention on opening the country up to the outside world in all directions, including coastal cities and interior areas.

4. Because direct foreign investment in China can maximize the strengths of all parties concerned, many overseas institutional and individual investors have found it more profitable to invest directly in China than to do trading business with Chinese companies.

5. China is known for her massive land, abundant natural

resources, cheap labor, low taxation, potential consumer market, stable social environment, attractive investment policies, and high economic returns of investment.

6. There is a variety of ways to invest in China. You may establish a joint venture with a Chinese partner, or a company solely-funded by yourself, in which you may manage your business in whatever way you prefer within the boundary of the Chinese laws, of course.

7. When establishing a joint venture, the foreign partner usually brings into the enterprise capital funds, machinery, advanced technology and management, while the Chinese partner supplies land, labor, and a portion of the funds for the infrastructure.

8. Let's get down to the business of establishing a joint venture. May I have some idea of your plan? For instance, how much would your share of investment be in this venture?

9. My suggestion for the investment share in this partnership is in the vicinity of 50 to 50, and the same applies to business management and profits share.

10. Let's say we begin with a 10-year term of a renewable partnership; we can extend our contract for another term before it expires, if both parties intend to.

11. Your idea coincides with mine.

12. Shall we hold another round of talk next week focusing on some technical problems?

13. 我为自己能受到贵方的友好邀请,与一组中国优秀的汽车专家合作共事而深感愉快和荣幸。

14. 虽然上海、天津这些沿海城市仍然是许多外国投资者的首选目标,但越来越多的美国公司却纷纷涌入中国的内地省份。

15. 我想同您商讨一下能否与贵公司合资建立一家企业,共同生产最新款式的逐行扫描 DVD 家庭影院系统。

16. 我建议成立董事会来监管公司的运作,并以平等的伙伴关系分享权利,承担义务。

第 2 单元　访谈口译
UNIT 2　Interpreting Interviews

2—1　行在美国
Travel in America

词汇预习
Vocabulary Work

据说

由汽车驱动的国家

夸张的说法

correct observation

way of life

drive-in bank / restaurant /
　church / movie

以游客的身份访美

international driver's license

行车限速

expressway

minimum speed

出公差

租车服务行业

付款方式

major credit card（e. g. , Master-
　Card，Visa，or American Ex-
　press）

deposit

special offer

passenger rail service

long distance coach

monthly pass

regulated（price）

shuttle and commuter flights

不尽如人意

subway

cab / cabby

Yellow Pages

Interpret the following interview alternatively into English and Chinese:

An interview to learn about travel and public transportation in the United States.

Q: 据说美国是一个由汽车驱动的国家,美国人实际上是一个生活在轮子上民族。你认为这是一种夸张的说法吗?

A: This is basically a correct observation, which says something about the American way of life. Americans like to do business without leaving their cars. Wherever you go, you'll see drive-in banks, drive-in restaurants, drive-in churches and drive-in movies.

Q: 如果我以游客的身份访问美国,我可以在美国境内开车吗?

A: Yes, you can. When you drive in the U. S., it's a good idea to have an international driver's license if you are a foreigner and don't have a state license. Each of the fifty states of the U. S. has its own traffic laws. Drivers are expected to know and understand the local laws even if they don't live in a particular state. You can get information when you cross the border into a different state at a tourist information center.

Q: 在中国某些道路上开车,司机必须将自己的行车速度控制在标牌规定的限速内。美国是否也有限速?

A: Yes. In most states, the speed limit on the expressway is 55 miles per hour, or about 88 kilometers per hour. On some roads, such as state or federal expressways, there is a minimum speed of 40 miles per hour, or about 65 kilometers per hour.

Q: 我作为一名出公差来美国的旅行者,可没有必要为了旅行而去买一辆车子。我想贵国一定有某种租车服务行业吧?

A: Of course we do. This country has the most developed car rental industry in the world. The two largest American car rental companies, Hertz and Avis, have offices all over the U. S., with counters at most airports and in many international cities. Other national car rental companies you can find at airports, such as Thrifty, National, Budger or Dollar, have offices in other countries too, so you may want to reserve a car through your travel agent in your own country.

Q: 那么租车时我以什么方式来付款呢?

A: In order to rent a car, you have to have a major credit card, such as MasterCard, Visa, or American Express. Without a credit card you may have to pay a very high deposit on the car. If you don't want to spend a lot of money, you may rent used cars from used car rental companies, such as Rent-A-Junker and Ugly Duckling. Their rates are often lower and they don't always demand a credit card. Sometimes they have special offers that make the total cost of renting a car even lower.

Q: 如果我没有驾照,那我怎样去其他城市呢?

A: There are three ways to get from city to city without a car. In some places, you can take Amtrak, the national passenger rail service. Or you can take a bus. Greyhound is the largest long distance coach company, which offers the monthly pass. And, of course, you can fly. There are dozens of airlines, both regional and national. Prices are not regulated, so airlines can make special offers that are sometimes cheaper than train tickets. There are also shuttle and commuter flights between some major cities that are close to each other.

Q: 听说美国城市的公共交通不尽如人意,有没有这回事?

A: Well, I have to admit that getting around a city on public transportation is generally not as easy as it is in most other countries, but it is possible. Although only a few cities have subways, most towns with a population of 50,000 or more have some kind of city bus service.

Q： 万一坐巴士或地铁到不了我想要去的地方怎么办呢？

A： You can always take a cab. You can stop a cab on the street, but that's not easy in many cities. It's actually easier to call a taxi company listed in the Yellow Pages of a telephone directory and ask them to send a cab to your door. American taxi drivers will usually expect a tip of at least 10%. In big cities like New York, cabbies expect a tip of 15%.

Q： 十分感谢您所提供的情况。

A： You're welcome.

2—2 艾滋哀之
The AIDS Epidemic

┌─────────────────┐
│ 词汇预习   │
│ **Vocabulary Work** │
└─────────────────┘

Nobel Prize winning microbiologist	ultimate solution
AIDS epidemic	massive educational campaign
plague	conceivable
on an international scale	self-defeating
leading cause	调查结果
HIV-positive	隔离
imperil	HIV virus
homosextually transmitted disease	futile
	强制性化验
put in place	voluntary and confidential testing
	better off

Interpret the following interview alternatively into English and Chinese:

An interview with a Nobel Prize winning microbiologist on the AIDS epidemic.

Q: 巴尔迪摩先生,艾滋病的传播程度有多严重?

A: AIDS is the worst plague in modern history. In the 20 years since the first reports of what we now know was AIDS, an entire generation has been born and come of age never knowing a world without the epidemic. The disease has changed the personal as well as the political — how we think and how we love, what we teach our children and what words we say in public. On an international scale, it threatens to undermine countries, particularly in Africa. AIDS is now the fourth leading cause of death globally, and the leading cause of death in Africa. Throughout the world 36 million people are HIV-positive, including 900,000 in the United States.

Q: 你所说的"危害国家生计"是指什么?

A: AIDS has stolen a generation and imperiled the future. It will cause such a significant amount of disease in the middle ages of the population that it will largely reduce the number of people available to carry out the functions of the society. In parts of Africa, it's happening already. In seven African countries, more than 20 percent of the 15- to 49-year-old population is infected with HIV. For example, Zambia cannot train teachers fast enough to replace those killed by AIDS. Within 10 years, there will be 40 million AIDS orphans in Africa.

Q: 你认为我们可以及时改变人们的基本行为,以阻止艾滋病的传播吗?

A : In time to have a significant impact, yes. I don't think we'll be perfect. People will respond differently. But for the homosexual population in San Francisco, the rate of homosextually transmitted diseases fell dramatically when a serious educational program was put in place. People were obviously willing to change their behavior when they were made to realize how severe a risk they were taking.

Q : 对于那些还未受到严重打击的群体,有何措施可以采取呢? 能否在大规模的死亡发生之前也让他们意识到问题的严重性?

A : It is certainly harder to reach people when they don't see the consequences of what they're doing right around them or when the consequences are extremely delayed. I'd guess that's been one of the problems with smokers.

Q : 怎样才能让人们意识到问题的严重性呢?

A : Drugs cannot be seen as the ultimate solution. And about $10 billion a year is needed to fight the spread of HIV. I think a massive educational campaign is the only thing conceivable at the moment that can help. Not to do it would be criminal. To argue that it's difficult and expensive and therefore we shouldn't do it would be self-defeating.

Q : 调查结果表明,公众中大部分人认为艾滋病患者应该被隔离开来。你的意见呢?

A : Quarantining will help no one. Most AIDS patients are too sick to be transmitting the virus. The virus is being spread largely by people who do not have AIDS but are infected with the HIV virus, and they may or may not even know it. Quarantining would be totally futile.

Q : 强制性化验有无作用?

A : I believe it would drive the very people you want to test underground. Voluntary, confidential testing is much more appropriate.

Q : 怎样做才能鼓励人们去接受这种令人不安的化验呢?

A : The only thing you can do is convince people that they're better off knowing than not knowing. First, because then they can take action to protect their friends and loved ones and, second, because they can begin to interpret their own symptoms and take whatever action available. AIDS is a very serious disease, but it usually reveals its presence through a variety of infections, and many of those infections can be controlled with appropriate drugs.

2—3 经营之道
Business Management

词汇预习
Vocabulary Work

business communication style

work ethic

one's prospective business contact

the "get-down-to-business-first" mentality

time-consuming

keep to

the "bottom-up, then top-down and then bottom-up" principle

top management

business practices

咄咄逼人的

straightforward

管理模式

the top-down management

efficiency

gives priority to

frustrate

fulfillment

membership

a sense of belonging in a community

individual oriented

accomplishment

dedication

利与弊

Oriental

executive

Interpret the following interview alternatively into English and Chinese:

An interview with an American manager of a Sino-American joint venture on some of the differences in business communication style and work ethic between the Chinese and the Americans.

Q: 您好，杰克逊先生。您在中国已连续工作了三年，您能否谈一下中美两国生意人在商务沟通方式上有何不同之处？

A: With pleasure. I think there are at least two differences in the way of business communication between Chinese and American businessmen. First, Chinese businessmen tend to have business negotiations in a rather indirect manner, as opposed to the more direct manner of American businessmen. The Chinese take time to learn if their prospective business contacts are really reliable, for example, by inviting them to a party and socializing with them. In contrast, The Americans act with the "get-down-to-business-first" mentality. Second, the decision-making process of Chinese companies is generally slow and time-consuming. This is because most Chinese companies keep to the "bottom-up, then top-down and then bottom-up" decision-making principle which involves many people at different levels. American companies, on the other hand, usually operate with quick decisions made by the top management. I hope American businessmen in China will understand these differences in business practices and adjust to the Chinese way.

Q: 美国式的经营之道在我们中国人看来常显得咄咄逼人。您在与中国同事的合作中有无注意到这一点？

A: Well, we are more direct and straightforward than most Chinese,

I would say, due to our different cultural traditions. I noticed that a lot of Chinese often avoid saying a clear "no" just to be polite. Sometimes my Chinese colleagues say "yes" not to express agreement, but only to show that they are listening.

Q: 我们都应该承认这些文化差异,尊重这些差异,以免产生误解。这很重要,不是吗?

A: Yes, understanding these differences, I believe, will be a first step toward establishing a firm business relationship between American and Chinese companies.

Q: 刚才您提到了中国式的决策过程,您认为这种管理模式有无优点? 将其与美国式的管理模式相比,您有何看法?

A: I would say the American-type, or the top-down, management emphasizes efficiency and competition among workers, while the Chinese-type management gives priority to careful planning and encourages cooperation among workers, and between workers and the management. Thus, while the American-type management often frustrates many workers, the Chinese-type management gives workers a joy of participation and fulfillment, and a sense of pride in their work.

Q: 谈到员工的工作态度,中国人和美国人在这方面有何不同?

A: I think most Chinese view work as essential for having membership in a community. They believe that work allows them to have the sense of belonging to a community. In other words, work is necessary for them to gain social acceptance in the society. That is why many Chinese managers and employees work so hard to maintain their positions in their companies. Also, they see work as the most important thing in life. That is, they have tried to find the meaning of life through their jobs. While the Chinese work ethic is based on social pressure and community belonging, the American work ethic seems to be more individual oriented. Traditionally, we work because it is the will of God, and we often value the results and accomplishments of work more than its process. By the way, I'm very impressed by the obvious strong sense of dedication to the jobs among the older Chinese employees.

Q: 回到我们一开始的话题，您如何评价中美两种不同经营之道的利弊?

A: It is difficult to decide which is better than which, because there are some merits and demerits to both types of management. My suggestion is that people of both countries should learn from each other. I will say that in recent years, the merits of the Chinese way, or rather, the Oriental way, of management are beginning to be recognized by an increasing number of people in the West. This more humane Oriental way of management seems to offer a great deal to the executives of our American industries.

句子精练
Sentences in Focus

Interpret the following sentences into English or Chinese:

1. This is basically a correct observation, which says something about the American way of life.

2. Each state has its own traffic laws, and a driver from another state is expected to know and understand the local laws.

3. My country has the most developed car rental industry in the world, so you may very well want to reserve a car through your travel agent in your own country if you intend to drive while traveling in my country.

4. Airfare in this country is not regulated, and airlines often make special offers in order to attract customers.

5. It's actually easier to call a taxi company listed in the Yellow Pages of a telephone directory and ask them to send a cab to pick you up at your doorstep.

6. In the 20 years since the first reports of what we now know was AIDS, an entire generation has been born and come of age never knowing a world without the epidemic.

7. A massive educational campaign is the only thing conceivable at the moment that can help; to argue that this campaign is difficult, expensive and therefore impossible would be quite self-defeating.

8. We'll have to convince people that they're better off knowing than not knowing the fact, because they can take whatever action available to treat the problem and control its infection with appropriate drugs.

9. I think Chinese businessmen tend to have business negotiations in a rather indirect manner, as opposed to the more direct style of American businessmen, who are said to work with the "get-down-to-business-first" mentality.

10. The Chinese-type management encourages cooperation among employees, between the labor and the management, and gives employees a joy of participation and fulfillment, as well as a sense of pride in their work.

11. I think most Chinese try to find the meaning of life through working in their jobs, and view work as essential for having membership in a community. Put it in another way, they regard work as a prerequisite to gain social acceptance in the community.

12. 听说美国城市的公共交通可不尽如人意,有没有这回事?

13. 司机在高速公路上开车时必须将自己的行车速度控制在标牌规定的最高限速与最低限速之间。

14. 调查结果表明,许多人对艾滋病的传播不以为然,你认为我们怎样做才能让人们意识到问题的严重性呢?

15. 美式经营之道在我们中国人看来常常显得咄咄逼人。

16. 我们应该承认我们之间的文化差异,应该尊重这些差异,以免产生误解。

参考译文
Reference Version

2—1　行在美国
Travel in America

Q : It is said that the United States is country driven by automobiles, and Americans are actually a people living on wheels. Is this an exaggeration?

A : 这种看法基本上是正确的,它反映了美国人的生活方式。美国人喜欢开车办事。你到处可以看到"免下车"银行、"免下车"餐馆、"免下车"教堂和"免下车"电影院。

Q : If I visit the United States with a tourist's visa, can I drive in the country?

A : 你可以在美国开车。如果你是外国人,又没有某州的驾驶执照,可你想开车,那你最好携带一张国际驾驶执照。美国 50 个州都有各自的交通法规。即使外州来的开车人也应知晓当地的法律。你在穿越州界时可以在新到的那个州所设的旅游信息中心打听情况。

Q : In China, drivers have to drive under a posted speed limit on some roads. Is there any national speed limit in the U. S. ?

A : 是的。大多数州的高速公路限速为每小时 55 英里,约 88 公里／小时。有些道路,如地方高速公路或州际高速公路,还规定行车时速不得低于 40 英里,约 65 公里／小时。

Q : As a visitor on a business trip, I don't need to buy a car in order to travel in America. I suppose you have some kind of car rental service, don't you?

A : 那是自然的。我国有世界上最发达的租车业。美国两家最大的租车公司 Hertz 和 Avis 在全美国都有公司办事处,在大部分机场和许多国际都市设有租车站。其他一些全国性的租车公司如Thrifty、National、Budger、Dollar 等也在其他国家设有租车办事处,所以你可以通过国内的旅行社办理租车预订事宜。

Q: How do I pay for my rental service?

A: 租车时你必须拥有一张大公司的信用卡,如"万事达"卡、"威萨"卡,或者"美国运通"卡。你若没有信用卡,也许就得付一笔高额押金。如果你不想花费太多的钱,也可以向二手车租车公司,如 Rent-A-Junker 和 Ugly Duckling 公司租上一辆二手车。这类公司的收费往往比较低,而且也不一定非要租车者用信用卡付款不可。有时它们还给顾客优惠价,使租车的费用总额更为低廉。

Q: If I don't have a license, how do I travel between cities?

A: 要是没有小汽车,你去其他城市可以搭乘三种交通工具。在有些地方,你可以乘坐全国客运火车 Amtrak。不然的话你可以坐长途汽车,"灰狗"汽车公司是美国最大的长途汽车公司,有月票出售。当然罗,你也可以坐飞机旅行。美国有数十家国内和国际航空公司,全国没有统一的票价,所以航空公司可以削价,有时机票要比火车票便宜。一些相距不远的大城市之间,也有穿梭于两地之间的航班。

Q: I heard the city public transportation system in your country is not very desirable. Is that so?

A: 这个嘛,我得承认在美国乘坐市内公交车通常没有大多数国家来得方便,但还是有车可坐。虽然有地铁的城市寥寥无几,但是人口在 5 万或 5 万以上的城镇都有某种市内巴士车服务设施。

Q: What do I do in case I can't get where I want to by bus or subway?

A: 你总可以坐出租车。虽然你可以在街上叫出租车,但在许多城市里,在街上叫出租车却不太容易。比较方便的做法通常是按电话号码簿里黄页部分所提供的号码打电话给出租车公司,让他们派车到你的所在地。美国出租车司机通常期望能得到车费 10% 以上的小费。纽约这类大城市的出租车司机期望客人给予 15% 的小费。

Q: Thank you very much for the information.

A: 不用谢。

Q : Mr. Baltimore, how serious is the AIDS epidemic?

A : 艾滋病是现代史中最糟糕的瘟疫。自从 20 多年前出现了首批有关艾滋病例的报告以来,整整一代人从出生起便生活在一个与艾滋病共存的世界里。艾滋病改变了我们的个人生活和政治生活,改变了我们的思维方式和性爱方式,改变了我们教育孩子的内容以及在公共场合言谈的内容。从国际范围来看,艾滋病将会危害国家生计。艾滋病是世界上第四大致死的病因,在非洲则是致人于死地的最大杀手。全世界已有 3,600 万人呈 HIV 阳性,其中有 90 万是美国人。

Q : What do you mean by "undermine countries"?

A : 艾滋病夺走了一代人,威胁着人类的未来。艾滋病会在中年人中间广为传播,致使劳力大量减少。在非洲的部分地区,这种局面已出现了。在 7 个非洲国家,20％以上年龄在 15 岁至 49 岁之间的人已感染了艾滋病毒。例如,赞比亚培养教师的速度已跟不上教师死于艾滋病的速度。非洲在 10 年之内将有 4,000 万艾滋病死者留下的孤儿。

Q : Do you think people's basic behavior can be altered in time to stem the AIDS epidemic?

A : 及时产生重大的效应,那是可以做到的。我认为我们不会有什么万全之策。人们会做出不同的反应。但对旧金山的同性恋群体来说,一项严肃的教育运动推出后,由同性恋传播的疾病其发生率随即大幅度降低了。当人们意识到自己是在冒多么大的风险时,他们显然会愿意改变自己的行为。

Q : What about groups not yet hard hit? Can the message get to them before massive deaths occur?

A : 当人们看不到自己的所作所为有何不良后果时,或者当不良后果久不出现时,要让人们意识到问题的严重性肯定会难得多。我想这也是瘾君子难以戒烟的原因之一。

Q : How do you reach people?

A : 药物不能被视为解决问题的最终良方。我们每年需要约 100 亿美元的资金来阻止 HIV 传播。我认为开展大规模的教育运动是目前惟一行之有效的手段。不这样去做是在犯罪。说什么因为难度大、代价高而不能这样做,则是一种自暴自弃的行为。

Q : Surveys show that a majority of the public believes AIDS victims should be quarantined. What do you think?

A : 隔离无助于任何人。大部分艾滋病患者的病太重,已无法传播病毒。病毒主要是由那些未得艾滋病但已感染上病毒的人传播的,这些人或许已经知道,或许根本还不知道自己是 HIV 带菌者。隔离是根本没有用的。

Q : Would mandatory testing help?

A : 我认为强制性化验会迫使那些你想化验的人躲避起来。自愿性化验并为化验者保密会更为妥当。

Q : How can you encourage people to go in for such a traumatic test?

A : 惟一可以做的是使人们相信知道情况总比不知道为好。首先,知道后可以采取措施保护自己的朋友和所爱的人。其次他(她)们可以开始了解自己的症状,采取一切可以采取的手段来治病。虽然艾滋病是一种非常严重的疾病,但它通常是经由各种各样传染病的侵袭才发病的,而许多传染病是可以用适当的药物加以控制的。

课文 2—3 经营之道
Business Management

Q : Hi, Mr. Jackson. You have been working in China for three years. Can you tell us how you feel about the differences in business communication style between Chinese and American businessmen?

A : 我很乐意。我认为中美两国生意人在商务沟通方式上至少有两点不同。首先,中国人在商务谈判时倾向于使用一种迂回婉转的方式,而美国人则表现出一种直截了当的作风。中国人会花时间来了解他们将要与之打交道的生意人是否靠得住,例如邀请对方参加宴会,同他们交际。与之相反,美国人则以"公务为先"的心态行事。第二,中国公司的决策过程耗时冗长。这是因为大部分中国公司遵循着一种"先自下而上,然后自上而下,然后再自下而上"的决策原则,各个层次的许多人士都介入决策过程。而美国公司通常则是经由最高管理人士的快速决策来运作的。我希望在华的美国生意人理解这些商务活动中的差异,适应中国人的经营之道。

Q: The American way of doing business often strikes us Chinese as very aggressive. Were you aware of this in your collaboration with your Chinese colleagues?

A: 这个嘛,我认为,由于我们有着不同的文化传统,所以我们同大部分中国人相比,显得较为直截了当、开门见山。我注意到许多中国人出于礼貌而经常不明确地说一声"不"。有时我的中国同事道一声"是",并不是在表示赞同,而只是表明他们在听对方说话而已。

Q: It is important for all of us to acknowledge and respect these cultural differences in order to avoid misunderstanding, isn't it?

A: 是的,我认为,理解这些差异是朝着在美国和中国公司之间建立稳固的商务关系的方向迈出的第一步。

Q: You mentioned the Chinese type of decision-making process earlier. Do you see any strengths with this type of management and how do you compare it with the American type of management?

A: 我感到美国式的管理方式,即自上而下的管理方式,注重效率,注重员工之间的竞争。而中国式的管理方式,优先考虑周密的计划,鼓励员工之间的合作,鼓励员工与管理人员之间的合作。因此,美国式的管理方式常常使许多员工感到沮丧,而中国式的管理方式能使员工有一种喜悦的参与感和成就感,对自己的工作抱一种自豪感。

Q: Talking about workers' attitude toward their work, how do the Chinese and the Americans differ in this respect?

A: 我认为,大多数中国人将工作视为能使自己成为团体一分子的必不可缺的条件。中国人相信,工作使自己有了团体归属感。换言之,中国人为了得到社会的认可,他们必须工作。这就是为何许多中国经理和员工会努力工作以保住公司职位的原因。中国人还将工作视为生活中最重要的一件事。也就是说,他们想从工作中找到生活的意义。中国人的工作观念建筑在社会压力和团体归属感基础之上,而美国人的工作观念则有更强的个体取向性。我们一向认为,我们工作是秉承了上帝的意志,我们对工作成果的重视常常高于对工作过程的重视。附带说一句,年龄较大的中国员工对自己工作有一种明显的奉献精神,我对此有很深刻的印象。

Q: Returning to where we started, how do you comment on the merits and demerits of the two different approaches to business management?

A: 很难判断孰优孰劣,因为这两种经营方式各有自己的长处与短处。我希望我们两国人民应该互相学习,取长补短。应该说近年来中国人的经营方式,更确切地说是东方人的经营方式,开始为越来越多的西方人所认识。东方人的这种人情味更浓的经营方式似乎给予我们美国产业的管理人士颇多的启迪。

句子精练
Sentences in Focus

1. 这种看法基本正确,它反映了美国人的生活方式。
2. 各州都有各州的交通法规,外州来的开车者应该了解当地的法规。
3. 我国有世界上最发达的租车业,你若打算在我国开车旅行,完全可以通过本国的旅行社办理租车预定事宜。
4. 这个国家没有统一的飞机票价,各家航空公司常常通过竞相削价来吸引更多的旅客。
5. 事实上较为方便的做法是按电话簿中黄页部分所列的出租车公司的号码打电话叫车,让他们派车上门来接你。
6. 自从20多年前出现了首批有关艾滋病例的报告以来,整整一代人从出生起便生活在一个与艾滋病共存的世界里。
7. 开展大规模的教育运动是目前惟一行之有效的手段,因此认为这种运动难度大、代价高而无法实施完全是一种自暴自弃的态度。
8. 我们应该使人们相信,知情总比蒙在鼓里好,因为了解实情后我们便可以采取一切可以采取的措施来治病,用适当的药物来控制疾病的传染。

9. 我认为中国人在商务谈判时倾向于使用一种迂回婉转的方式，而被认为在工作时具有一种"公务为先"的心态的美国人则往往表现出一种比较直截了当的作风。

10. 中国式的管理方式鼓励员工之间的合作，也鼓励劳工与管理人员之间的合作，使员工有一种喜悦的参与感和成就感，使他们对自己的工作产生一种自豪感。

11. 我认为，大多数中国人想从工作中找到生活的意义，他们将工作视为能使自己成为团体一分子的必不可缺的条件。换言之，他们认为工作是使自己得到社会认可的先决条件。

12. It is said that the public transportation of American cities is not very desirable, is it?

13. When driving on expressways, the driver must control his or her speed within the range of the posted maximum and minimum speed limit.

14. Surveys show that a majority of the public does not take a serious view of the AIDS epidemic. What do you think would be the best way to bring people to the awareness of the seriousness of the problem?

15. The American way of business practice often appears to us Chinese to be very aggressive.

16. We have to recognize and respect our cultural differences, so as to prevent any possible misunderstanding.

第3单元 礼仪性口译(英译汉)
UNIT 3 Interpreting Ceremonial Speeches English-Chinese Interpretation

3—1 故地重游
Revisiting the Old Haunt

world-renowned

diversity

dynamism

a special regard

nostalgic

memorable

utmost courtesy

extensive

overshadow

non-governmental sector

foundations

mutual benefit

good faith

strategic relationship

flourish

课文口译
Text for Interpretation

Interpret the following passage from English into Chinese:

Ladies and gentlemen,

Permit me first to thank you, our Chinese hosts, for your

extraordinary arrangements and hospitality. My wife and I, as well as our entire party, are deeply grateful.

In the short period of six days, we have gone a longer distance than the world-renowned "Long March". We have acquired a keen sense of the diversity, dynamism, and progress of China under your policies of reform and opening to the outside world.

My wife and I have a special regard and personal friendship for the people of China. Beijing is for us an old and nostalgic home. During our stay here ten years ago we spent a great deal of memorable time with the people here — working, shopping, sightseeing, and touring the city on our bicycles. During that time we never experienced anything other than the utmost courtesy and genuine friendship of the Chinese people.

Those were happy days. They were good days, important days. We were part of the dramatic process which brought us back together and set us on the road to a genuine friendly and cooperative relationship.

Our friendly and cooperative ties have become extensive, affecting all aspects of our national lives: commerce, culture, education, and scientific exchange.

I am most proud of the large number of Chinese students being educated in exchange in my country. I myself teach some of them and see the benefits that come from this exchange. At the same time we are learning valuable lessons from you.

Nonetheless, problems remain in our economic, education and strategic relations. While we are not so naive as to believe that there are no issues of difference between us, I also believe that our differences are greatly overshadowed by issues which bind us and strengthen our relationship.

As a former government leader and now a private citizen, I recognize that many of the burdens and opportunities of our relationship have now passed to the non-governmental sectors of our two societies: to individuals, our corporations, universities, research institutes, foundations, and so on. There is no doubt that our relations have reached a new stage. In this context, it is important for our two societies to search for areas of cooperation which clearly add to our mutual benefit.

My visit is a symbol of the good faith with which we seek to build up the strength of our friendship, our cultural and commercial ties and our important strategic relationship. Events of the past decade have confirmed time and time again that our friendship and cooperation will continue to flourish and yield more fruits in the days to come.

3—2　愉悦之旅
A Pleasant Trip

词汇预习
Vocabulary Work

Your Excellency
cradle of civilization
renew old friendships
establish new contacts
a constant source of encourage-
　ment
in the pursuit of

a common aspiration
endeavor
in the service of
in closing
privileged
propose a toast
cheers

课文口译
Text for Interpretation

Interpret the following passage from English into Chinese:

Respected Your Excellency,

My Chinese friends,

Thank you very much for your kind words of welcome. This is a happy and memorable occasion for me personally as well as for the members of my delegation.

To come to China, one of the very earliest cradles of civilization, is, I suppose, the dream of many people the world over. I, therefore, feel very honoured to be your guest.

In accepting Your Excellency's gracious invitation to visit this great country, I have had an excellent opportunity to renew old friendships and establish new contacts.

When we established our friendly and cooperative relations, we did so on the understanding that we would develop our friendship on the basis of mutual respect and equality, and mutual benefit. These are the principles on which we seek friendship with all peoples of the world. It is absolutely vital that all nations, big or small, strong or weak, should conduct their relations with each other on these principles.

We, therefore, welcome the interest and understanding that China has shown regarding the problems of and positions taken by small and developing countries. China's support is a constant source of encouragement to us in the pursuit of the goals of developing and maintaining the independence of our country.

It is my sincere hope that we can develop further, on the basis of mutual respect and mutual benefit, the links and the friendship that exist between our two countries. As we are both developing countries, having a common aspiration in improving the standard of life of our peoples, I look forward, in the next few days, to the opportunity of learning something from your endeavours and experience in promoting economic and social development in the service of your people.

I'd like to take this opportunity to extend to Your Excellency an invitation to visit my country, so that we will have an opportunity to return the warm welcome and generous hospitality you extended to us.

In closing, may I say again how delighted and privileged we are to be in your country. We are deeply grateful for what you have done for us since our arrival in your country.

May I propose a toast
To the health of Your Excellency,
To the health of all the Chinese friends,
To our lasting friendship.
Cheers!

3—3　欧亚合作
Euro-Asian Cooperation

词汇预习
Vocabulary Work

European Union	fishery
hereby	monetary union
equal partnership	political and economic integration
witness a rapid rise to prosperity	market share
robust economic region	a far cry from meeting demands
alliance	comparatively speaking
trade bloc	resolve differences
gross domestic product	enhance
foreign trade volume	in the interest of
tariff	thereby

Interpret the following passage from English into Chinese:

Respected Mr. Chairman,

Ladies and gentlemen,

The European Union has adopted a new strategy for Asian affairs. We hereby urge our EU members to efficiently cooperate with Asian countries to establish a constructive, stable and equal partnership between the two continents.

History has proved the necessity to expand cooperative relations between the two continents. Europe and Asia, two major cradles of human civilization, have both contributed to human progress.

Since the 1980s, Asia, and East Asia particularly, has witnessed a rapid rise to prosperity. As the world's most robust economic region the East Asia has attracted worldwide attention over the past few decades with its remarkable achievement.

In Europe, a 50-year alliance made the European Union the world's largest trade bloc in the world, with its gross domestic product and foreign trade volume both surpassing those of the United States.

In addition, EU nations have unified tariffs and established common foreign trade, agricultural and fishery policies. The EU has initially established an economic and monetary union. It has, in other words, become a region which enjoys the highest level of political and economic integration.

Trade ties between Europe and East Asia have expanded rapidly in recent years. Significantly, East Asia has replaced the United States as the EU's largest export market, with 18 percent of its exports targeted for the region.

However, the European Union continues to lag behind the

United States and Japan in terms of market share in East Asia. We realize that the current Euro-Asian economic and trade contacts are a far cry from meeting demands.

Ladies and gentlemen, Europe, North America and East Asia have emerged as the world's three major economic centers. Europe and North America have already established close ties thanks to our historical links. East Asia and North America have also established contacts via the forum of the Asian-Pacific Economic Cooperation. Comparatively speaking, ties between the European Union and East Asia remain relatively weak. Therefore, ladies and gentlemen, it is our common desire that Europe and East Asia should resolve differences through dialogues and mutual trust, enhance our cooperative relations, and form a new partnership in the interest of the peoples of our two continents.

Ladies and gentlemen, given this historic opportunity, let us work together and forge that partnership, thereby contributing to global peace, stability and prosperity.

Thank you, Mr. Chairman.

3—4 新的长征
A New Long March

词汇预习
Vocabulary Work

incomparable hospitality

splendid music

a congenial atmosphere

gracious and eloquent remarks

the wonder of telecommunications

equal dignity

free of outside interference

domination

approve

deeply rooted in the instincts of

our people	legacy
impose	destined
assess	plague
in identical fashion	rise to the heights of greatness
inconceivable	

课文口译
Text for Interpretation

Interpret the following passage from English into Chinese:

Mr. President,

On behalf of all my colleagues present here, I wish to thank you for the incomparable hospitality for which the Chinese people are justly famous throughout the world. I particularly want to pay tribute, not only to those who prepared the magnificent dinner, but also to those who have provided the splendid music.

These have been very pleasant days in China, and I'm happy that my visit should conclude in such a congenial atmosphere.

Mr. President, I wish to thank you for your very gracious and eloquent remarks. At this very moment through the wonder of telecommunications, many people are hearing what we say today. Yet, what we say here will not be long remembered. But what we do here can change the world.

So, let us start a long march together on different roads leading to the same goal, the goal of building a world structure of peace and justice in which all may stand together with equal dignity and in which each nation, large or small, has a right to determine its own form of government, its own course of development, free of outside interference or domination.

We have a social and political system which differs in many respects from your own. It is the result of different experiences and a different tradition. This system of ours does not always produce results of which we all approve. People sometimes grumble at it and criticize it. But it is a political system deeply rooted in the instincts of our people. We do not aim to impose our own ideas on other people. We believe that it is right and necessary that people with different political and social systems should live side by side. We do not assess in identical fashion all aspects of today's world — with our distinct histories, geographies and cultures it is inconceivable that we could see eye to eye on all issues — but we do agree on the fundamental need for world peace, and the equally fundamental need for all countries to determine their own fate and design their own future.

The world watches. The world listens. The world waits to see what we will do.

What legacy shall we leave our children? Are they destined to die painfully for the hatreds which have plagued the old world, or are they destined to live joyfully because we had the vision to build a new world?

This is the hour. This is the day for us to rise to the heights of greatness which can build a new and better world.

In that spirit, I ask all of you present to join me in raising your glasses to the friendship and cooperation of our two peoples which can lead to friendship and peace for all peoples in the world.

句子精练
Sentences in Focus

Interpret the following sentences from English into Chinese:

1. Permit me first of all to thank you, our host, for your extraordinary arrangements and hospitality.
2. Thank you very much for your gracious words of welcome. This is a happy and memorable occasion for me personally as well as

for all the members of my delegation.

3. To come to China, one of the early cradles of civilization, has long been my dream and therefore, I feel very honored to be your guest.

4. In accepting Your Excellency's gracious invitation to visit this great country, I have had an excellent opportunity to renew old friendships and establish new contacts.

5. I wish to thank you for the incomparable hospitality, for which the Chinese people are justly famous throughout the world.

6. We have acquired a keen sense of the diversity, dynamism, and progress of China under the policies of reform and opening to the outside world.

7. I have a special regard and personal friendship for the people of China, in which I never experienced anything other than the utmost courtesy and genuine friendship of your people.

8. Our friendly and cooperative ties have become extensive, affecting all aspects of our national lives, including industry, agriculture, commerce, culture, public health, education, and scientific and technological exchange.

9. I'm looking forward, in the next few days, to the opportunity of learning something from your endeavors and experience in promoting economic and social development in the service of your people.

10. We recognize that our differences are greatly overshadowed by issues which bind us and strengthen our relationship.

11. Our visit to your country is a symbol of the good faith with which we seek to build up the strength of our friendship, our cultural and commercial ties and our important strategic relationship.

13. It is absolutely vital that all nations, big or small, strong or weak, should conduct their relations with each other on the basis of mutual respect, and equality and mutual benefit.

14. History has proved the necessity to expand cooperative relations

between Europe and Asia, two major cradles of human civilization.

15. As the world's most robust economic region China has attracted worldwide attention with its remarkable achievement over the past two decades.

16. It is our common desire that we should resolve differences through dialogues and mutual trust, enhance our cooperative relations, and form a new partnership in the interest of the peoples of our two countries.

17. Given this rare historic opportunity, let us work together and forge our partnership, thereby contributing to global peace, stability and prosperity.

18. Let us start a long march together along different roads leading to the same goal of building a new world of peace and just, a world in which all peoples may stand together with equal dignity, and a world in which each nation has the right to determine its own course of development.

19. I'd like to take this opportunity to extend to Your Excellency an invitation to visit Canada, so that we will have an opportunity to return the warm welcome and generous hospitality you extended to us.

20. May I ask all of you present to join me in raising your glasses to the friendship and cooperation of our two peoples!

参考译文
Reference Version

3—1 故地重游
Revisiting the Old Haunt

女士们、先生们：

首先,请允许我感谢中国主人的精心安排与好客。我夫人与我,以及我团的全体人员,都深为感激。

在短暂的 6 天里,我们行程超过了举世闻名的"长征"。在改革开放政策引导下的中国,气象万千,充满活力,不断进步,这些我们都已强烈地感受到了。

我与我夫人对中国人民怀有一种特殊的敬慕之情和个人友谊。对我们两人来说,北京是我们思念的故乡。10 年前我们在此生活期间,我们与这里的人们一起度过了许多难忘的时光——我们在这里工作,购物,观光,骑自行车逛城。在那段时期中,我们所感受到的总是中国人民的高度礼貌和诚挚友情。

那是一些令人愉快的日子,一些美好的日子,一些意义重大的日子。我们参与了那富有戏剧性的转变过程,它使我们重新走到一起,使我们踏上了一条通往建立一种真诚友好与合作关系的道路。

我们友好合作关系的领域十分广泛,已深入到我们国家生活的所有方面:商业、文化、教育以及科学交流。

大批中国学生通过交流正在我国学习,我为此深感自豪。我自己也给一些学生上课,亲眼目睹了这种交流所产生的益处。与此同时,我们也从你们身上汲取宝贵的经验。

然而,在我们经济、教育以及战略关系中仍然存在着问题。一方面我们不会天真地认为,我们之间不存在着分歧,另一方面,我也认为,那些将我们联系在一起并且强化我们关系的事务,在很大程度上弱化了我们之间的差异。

作为一名前政府领导人,现在作为一名普通国民,我感到我们关系中的许多重任和机遇已转到我们两国的民间机构,如个人、公司、大学、研究院、基金会等。毋庸讳言,我们的关系已进入了一个新的阶段。在这种形势下,寻求显然可以增进互惠互利的合作领域,对我们两国来说显得很重要。

我的访问是良好诚意的象征,我们怀着这种良好诚意,希望能在友谊的基础上建立文化和商业关系,建立重要的战略关系。过去的 10 年一再证明,我们之间的友谊与合作将在未来持续发展并结出更多的果实。

3—2 愉悦之旅
A Pleasant Trip

尊敬的阁下，

中国朋友们：

我非常感谢阁下的友好欢迎词。对我本人以及代表团所有成员来说，这是愉快而难忘的一天。

访问古老文明摇篮之一的中国，我想这是世界上许多人梦寐以求的愿望。因而，我为自己能成为贵国的客人而感到荣幸。

我接受阁下的盛情邀请，访问这个伟大的国家，这使我有极好的机会重温旧情，结交新友。

我们过去建立友好合作关系时是基于这样一种认识，即我们要在相互尊重和平等互利的基础上发展我们的友谊。这些原则是我们寻求同世界各国人民建立友谊的出发点。所有国家，无论其大小强弱，都应该在这些原则的基础上处理相互间的关系，这是至关重要的。

我们因而欢迎中国关注和理解小国和发展中国家所遇到的问题以及所持的立场。中国的支持始终鼓励着我们去追求发展与保持我国独立的目标。

我真诚地希望我们能够在相互尊重、互惠互利的基础上进一步发展我们两国之间业已存在的联系和友谊。我们都是发展中国家，有着提高我们自己国民生活水平的共同愿望，所以，我期待在今后的几天里有机会向你们学习，从你们为造福贵国人民而促进经济和社会发展的奋斗和经验中学到一些东西。

我愿借此机会邀请阁下访问我国，以便我们能有机会回报你们给予我们的热情欢迎和盛情款待。

在我结束讲话之前，我想再说一遍，我们来贵国作客是多么的愉快和荣幸。对于我们抵达贵国后你们为我们所做的一切，我们深表感谢。

现在我祝酒，

为阁下的身体健康，

为所有中国朋友们的身体健康，

为我们永久的友谊，

干杯！

3—3 欧亚合作
Euro-Asian Cooperation

尊敬的主席先生，

女士们、先生们：

欧洲联盟采纳了一项新的亚洲战略。我们在此要求欧盟成员国同亚洲国家进行有效的合作，以期在欧亚两大洲之间建立一种积极、稳定与和平等的伙伴关系。

历史已证明了扩大两大洲之间合作关系的必要性。欧洲和亚洲这两个人类文明的主要发源地，对人类进步做出了贡献。

自从 20 世纪 80 年代起，亚洲，尤其是东亚，迅速成长繁荣。作为世界上最有活力的经济区域，东亚在过去数十年里以其显著的成就引起了全球的瞩目。

在欧洲，50 年的结盟使现在的欧盟成了世界上最大的贸易集团，欧盟的国内生产总值和外贸总额都已超过了美国的国内生产总值和外贸总额。

此外，欧盟各国有统一的关税，建立了共同的外贸、农业和渔业政策。欧盟正初步建立经济和货币联盟。换言之，欧盟已成为一个政治和经济一体化程度最高的地区。

近年来，欧洲与东亚之间的贸易关系迅速发展。有意义的是，东亚已取代美国成为欧盟最大的出口市场，欧盟国家出口产品的 18% 销往该地区。

然而，欧盟对东亚市场的占有率仍然继续落后于美国和日本。我们意识到，目前欧亚经贸交往已远远不能满足需要。

女士们，先生们，欧洲、北美和东亚已成为世界三大经济中心。由于历史缘故，欧洲和北美早已建立了密切的联系。东亚和北美通过亚太经济合作论坛也建立了联系。相对而言，欧盟与东亚的联系仍然比较弱。因此，女士们，先生们，欧洲和东亚通过对话和相互信任以消除分歧，增强我们的合作关系，从两大洲人民的利益出发建立新的伙伴关系，这是我们的共同愿望。

女士们，先生们，面对这一历史性的机遇，让我们共同努力，牢固建立这种伙伴关系，为世界和平、稳定与繁荣而作出贡献。

谢谢主席先生。

3—4 新的长征
A New Long March

主席先生,

我谨代表我在座的所有同事,对你们那独有的、著称于世的款待表示感谢。我不仅要特别感谢为我们准备晚宴的人们,而且还要特别感谢演奏优美音乐的人们。

我们在中国度过了十分愉快的时光,我很高兴我的访问能在如此融洽的气氛中结束。

主席先生,我要感谢您那热情洋溢、雄辩无比的演讲。此时此刻,许多人正在通过神奇的电讯设备倾听着我们的讲话。然而,我们在此所作的演讲,很快便会被人们遗忘。但是,我们在此的作为,却能改变世界。

所以,让我们沿着通往共同目标的不同的道路,一起开始新的长征。这个目标就是建立一个和平与正义的世界,在这个世界里所有人都可以站在一起享有同等的尊严,所有国家无论其大小,都有权决定自己的政府形式,选择自己的发展道路,而不受外来干涉或统治。

我国的社会制度和政治制度在许多方面都与贵国的社会制度和政治制度不同。这是我们不同的经历和不同的传统造就的。我们的制度并不总是带来大家都赞同的结果。人们有时会抱怨这种制度,批评这种制度。但是这种制度根深蒂固,已成为我国人民意识与行为的本能。我们不想把自己的思想意识强加于人。我们认为,有着不同政治制度和社会制度的人们共同相处是正确而又必要的。我们没有用同一种模式来评价当今世界的方方面面——由于我们有着截然不同的历史、地理和文化,很难想象我们会对所有问题都有一致的看法——但是我们彼此一致认为,世界和平是我们的基本需求,各国决定自己的命运、规划自己的未来也同样是我们的基本需求。

世界注视着我们,世界倾听着我们,世界拭目以待我们的作为。

我们要给下一代留下什么遗产呢? 他们是注定要痛苦地死于曾肆虐于旧世界的仇恨之中呢,还是会因为我们曾有缔造新世界的远见,而注定要愉快地生活呢?

　　时不我待,这是攀登崇高理想的高峰、创造一个更美好的新世界的时刻。

　　本着这种精神,我敬请各位与我一起举杯,为能够带给全世界人民友谊与和平的我们两国人民之间的友谊与合作而干杯。

句子精练
Sentences in Focus

1. 首先请允许我感谢东道主的精心安排与好客。
2. 我非常感谢您热情洋溢的欢迎词,对我本人以及代表团所有成员来说,这是愉快而难忘的一刻。
3. 访问中国这一古老文明的摇篮是我梦寐以求的愿望,我为自己能成为贵国的客人而深感荣幸。
4. 我接受阁下的盛情邀请,访问这个伟大的国家,这使我有极好的机会重温旧情,再交新友。
5. 对中国人民独有的、著称于世的款待我向你们表示感谢。
6. 我们都已强烈地感受到贵国在改革开放政策的引导下,气象万千,充满活力,不断进步。
7. 我对中国人民怀有一种特殊的敬慕之情和个人友谊,在这里我所感受到的是贵国人民的高度礼貌和诚挚友情。
8. 我们友好合作关系的领域十分广泛,已涉及我们国家生活的方方面面,如工业、农业、商业、文化、卫生、教育,以及科技交流等领域
9. 我期待着在今后的几天里能有机会向你们学习,从你们为造福贵国人民而促进经济和社会发展的奋斗和经验中学到一些东西。
10. 我们已注意到,那些将我们联系在一起并且强化我们关系的东西已在很大程度上弱化了我们之间的差异。
12. 我们对贵国的访问是一种良好诚意的象征,我们怀着这种良好的诚意,希望能在友谊的基础上建立文化和商业关系,建立重要的战略关系。

13. 所有国家,无论其大小强弱,都应该在相互尊重、平等互利的基础上处理相互间的关系,这一点是至关重要的。

14. 历史已证明,扩大欧亚这两大人类文明主要发源地之间的合作关系是必要。

15. 中国作为世界上最有活力的经济区域在过去 20 年里以其显著的成就引起了全球的广泛注意。

16. 通过对话和相互信任以消除分歧、增强我们的合作关系,从两国人民的利益出发建立新的伙伴关系,这是我们的共同愿望。

17. 面对这一难得的历史机遇,让我们共同努力,牢固建立起我们的伙伴关系,为世界和平、稳定与繁荣而作出贡献。

18. 让我们沿着通往共同目标的不同的道路,一起开始新的长征。这个目标就是建立一个和平与正义的新世界,在这个世界里所有人都可以站在一起享有同等的尊严,所有国家都有权选择自己的发展道路。

19. 我愿借此机会邀请阁下访问加拿大,以便使我们能有机会来回报你们给予我们的热情欢迎和盛情款待。

20. 我敬请各位与我一起举杯,为我们的友谊与合作而干杯。

第4单元 礼节性口译(汉译英)
Unit 4　Interpreting Ceremonial Speeches
Chinese-English Interpretation

4—1　新春联欢
Celebrating the Spring Festival

> ### 词汇预习
> ### Vocabulary Work

嘉宾	尽情品尝
明月当空	美酒佳肴
全体同仁	才华横溢
从百忙中拨冗光临	纯正
新春联欢晚会	无所拘束
远道而来	万事如意

> ### 课文口译
> ### Text for Interpretation

Interpret the following passage from Chinese into English：

各位嘉宾：

在这个美丽无比、明月当空的夜晚,我谨代表总经理梅女士以及公司的全体同仁,感谢各位能在一年最繁忙的季节,从百忙中拨冗光临我们的新春联欢晚会。

特别有幸的是,今晚我们请到了从加拿大远道而来的本森电子公司的朋友们。有如此杰出的贵宾与我们一起共同欢度春节,我深感自豪与荣幸。

我们尽自己之所能,并将继续竭尽全力使各位度过一个最轻松、最欢乐、最难忘的夜晚。我希望各位来宾能尽情品尝中国的传统佳肴与美酒。请不要客气。

各位还将欣赏由本公司一些才华横溢的青年员工所表演的中国味纯正的文艺节目。今晚我们会过得非常愉快。平日在公司上班时,我们中外职员几乎没有时间坐下来交谈。我希望这次晚会可以让我们有极好的机会,可以无所拘束地了解彼此的情况,增进个人之间的友谊。

女士们,先生们,我再次感谢各位嘉宾的光临。最后,我祝愿各位新年身体健康、万事如意。

4—2　圣诞晚会
At the Christmas Party

词汇预习
Vocabulary Work

董事长	令人尽兴尽致
装饰华丽	销售额
良辰佳时	务实
融洽	辉煌业绩
奉献	年终岁末之际

课文口译
Text for Interpretation

Interpret the following passage from Chinese into English:

董事长先生，

女士们、先生们：

各位圣诞快乐！

我谨代表我们一行的全体成员，感谢董事长先生的盛情邀请，使我们来到装饰得如此华丽的大厅，参加如此欢快的圣诞晚会。

圣诞节是一个十分欢愉的节日，这的确是一年中的良辰佳时。圣诞节对我们所有人都有其引人之处，那就是人间的温暖、爱恋、关怀、团聚、融洽和奉献。这就是圣诞节的精神所在。

当然，我们很喜欢这里的美酒佳肴。是的，烤火鸡的味道好极了。音乐也非常优美。要是我会跳舞的话，想必会过得更加快乐。我喜欢这里的一切，而更为重要的是，我喜欢同你们聚会，同你们交谈，增进了解，共度难忘的时光。

对于这次美好的安排，我感激不尽。晚会组织得完美无缺，令人尽兴尽致。我日后一定还会记得这次美好的聚会。

就我们融洽的商务关系而言，今年对我们所有人来说都是一个好年度。我们合资企业的销售额显著增长。我希望我们能保持这种务实的合作关系，使明年的业绩更加辉煌。

让我们在这年终岁末之际，共同举杯，祝贺这喜庆佳节。

我为有幸参加这次精彩的聚会，再次向您深表谢意。我们度过了一个美好的夜晚。

我再一次祝各位圣诞快乐！

4—3　开幕祝词
An Opening Speech

词汇预习
Vocabulary Work

宣布……开幕	国际研讨会
社区服务	筹委会

开幕式	民间组织
温哥华	宏观管理
市场经济体制	分工协作
社会福利保障体制	借鉴
政府职能	丰硕成果
政府包揽	预祝……圆满成功

课文口译
Text for Interpretation

Interpret the following passage from Chinese into English：

女士们、先生们：

我宣布，"上海社区服务国际研讨会"现在正式开幕。

首先，请允许我代表研讨会的筹委会，向参加今天开幕式的上海市政府领导、社会团体的领导、社区工作者协会的代表，以及社会各界的来宾，表示热烈的欢迎！同时向来自加拿大以及世界其他国家和地区的朋友们表示热烈的欢迎。加拿大温哥华兰戈拉社区学院对本次研讨会的成功召开给予了很大的帮助，对此我谨致以诚挚的谢意。

我国社会主义市场经济体制的建立和发展，要求我们改革和完善社会福利保障体制，从而对社区服务提出了更高的要求。随着政府职能的转变，原来由政府包揽的许多社会服务工作，有相当一部分将逐步转移到社会团体和民间组织。一方面，政府的宏观管理责任将会变得更加重大，另一方面，社会团体和民间组织需要参与更多的社区服务工作。这就提出了一个课题：政府和社会团体如何密切合作、分工协作，更好地推进社区服务事业。海外一些发达国家和地区在这方面积累了不少经验，值得我们借鉴和研究。

正是为了讨论这个课题，我们举办了这次研讨会。我相信这次研讨会对于推动中国社区服务事业的蓬勃开展，促进经济发展和社会稳定，具有积极的作用和意义。同时我也相信，在各位朋友的努力下，我们的研讨会一定能够取得丰硕的成果。

最后，我预祝研讨会圆满成功！祝愿来自海外的专家学者和全国各地的朋友们在上海生活愉快！

　　谢谢大家。

4—4　展望未来
Looking Ahead

领域	回顾过去
开拓性	展望未来
多极化	相互尊重
发展趋势	平等互利
世界格局	求同存异
泰王国	贸易歧视与制裁
衷心感谢	光辉的远景

```
课文口译
Text for Interpretation
```

Interpret the following passage from Chinese into English：

主席先生，

女士们、先生们：

　　今天，我们 25 个欧亚国家的领导人首次在此聚会。我们要在平等友好的基础上，就广泛领域里的合作以及建立新的亚欧伙伴关系，交换我们的意见。

　　这是一次具有历史意义的开拓性的会议。它反映了亚欧国家希望获得世界和平与发展、希望各洲之间进行交流与合作的共同愿望。它显示了亚洲的成长，表明了整个国际关系的巨大变化，标志着多极化的发展趋势。

我深信这次会议将对形成一个新的世界格局产生积极的影响。我愿借此机会向成功主办了这次会议的泰王国政府表示衷心的感谢。

建立一个新的亚欧伙伴关系要求我们有新的观念和新的方法。回顾过去,展望未来,我认为一个新的亚欧伙伴关系必须建筑在相互尊重和平等互利的基础上。我们应该求同存异,增进相互理解和信任,消除贸易歧视,反对贸易制裁,加强技术交流与合作。

为了增进相互理解和信任,亚洲和欧洲应该扩大和增加政治对话。就我们而言,我们愿意看到欧盟在一体化进程中前进,愿意看到欧盟保持独立和开放。另一方面,我们希望欧洲理解亚洲国家在保持政治稳定的同时,促进经济发展、扩大区域合作的意愿,支持亚洲国家为此所作的努力。

我们准备增进与亚洲和欧洲国家的合作。我们已对外贸进行了重大的改革,制定了一套相关的法律。我们已将关税降低到发展中国家的平均水平。我相信中国的改革开放和稳定会给亚欧国家的商业界带来可观的投资和贸易良机,从而为亚洲乃至全世界的和平、稳定与繁荣做出积极的贡献。

让我们为本届会议的圆满结束而共同努力。

让我们为建立一个面向新世纪的亚欧伙伴关系,为我们两大洲以及整个世界描绘光辉的远景而携起手来。

谢谢主席先生。

句子精练
Sentences in Focus

Interpret the following sentences from Chinese into English:

1. 我谨代表总经理以及公司的全体同仁,感谢各位从百忙中拨冗光临我们的新年联欢会。
2. 今晚我们请到了从伦敦远道而来的贵宾与我们一起共度中秋佳节,我为此而深感自豪与荣幸。

3. 我谨代表我们一行的全体成员,感谢董事长先生的盛情邀请,使我们有幸参加这次精彩的圣诞晚会。

4. 我感谢各位嘉宾的光临,并祝各位新年身体健康、万事如意。

5. 我希望这次晚会可以使我们有机会无所拘束地了解彼此,增进个人之间的友谊。

6. 晚会组织得完美无缺,令人尽兴尽致。对于这次美好的安排,我感激不尽。

7. 让我们在这年终岁末之际,共同举杯,祝贺这喜庆佳节。

8. 今年我们合资企业的销售额显著增长,我希望我们能继续保持这种务实的合作关系,使明年的业绩更加辉煌。

9. 现在我宣布"上海城市建设国际研讨会"现在开幕。

10. 请允许我代表筹委会的全体成员,向海内外各界来宾,表示热烈的欢迎!

11. 大会所在地的许多教育界人士对本次会议的成功召开给予了很大的帮助,对此我谨致以诚挚的谢意。

12. 这是一次具有历史意义的开拓性的会议,它对形成一个新的世界格局将产生积极的影响。

13. 我相信本届年会对于推动中国社区服务事业的蓬勃开展,促进经济发展和社会稳定,具有积极的作用和意义。

14. 一些发达国家和地区在环境保护方面积累了不少经验,值得我们借鉴和研究。

15. 回顾过去,展望未来,我认为一个新的伙伴关系必须建筑在相互尊重和平等互利的基础上。

16. 让我们求同存异,增进理解与信任,加强交流与合作。

17. 我相信中国的改革、开放和稳定会给亚太地区的商业界带来可观的投资和贸易良机,从而为亚洲乃至整个世界的和平、稳定与繁荣做出积极的贡献。

> ## 课文 4—1 新春联欢
> ## Celebrating the Spring Festival

My distinguished guests,

On this most beautiful moon-lit evening, on behalf of General Manager Ms. Mei and all my colleagues of the company, I wish to thank all the people here for taking the time off their busy schedule, at the busiest time of the year, to come to our Chinese New Year's party. We really appreciate your presence here tonight with us.

In particular, we are very fortunate tonight to have the attendance of our friends with the Benson's Electronics Company, who came here all the way from Canada. I feel very proud and honored to have such a distinguished group of guests with us, in our celebration of our Spring Festival.

We did and will continue to do our best to make this evening most relaxing, most enjoyable and most memorable for you. I hope you will have a good time tasting the traditional Chinese cuisine and drinking the unique Chinese wine to your heart's content. So help yourself.

Later on, you will enjoy the authentic Chinese entertainment performed by some talented young employees from our company. We will have a lot of fun tonight. While at work in the company, we, Chinese as well as overseas staff of the company, hardly get to sit down and talk to each other. I hope this party will give us an excellent opportunity to get to know each other better in a more informal way and increase personal friendships.

Ladies and gentlemen, I'd like to thank you again for coming to the party. And I wish everyone of you good health and the very best of luck in everything in the new year.

4—2 圣诞晚会
At the Christmas Party

Mr. Chairman,

Ladies and gentlemen,

Merry Christmas to you all!

On behalf of all the members of my group, I'd like to thank you, Mr. Chairman, for your gracious invitation for us to attend such an enjoyable Christmas party in such a magnificently decorated hall.

Christmas is a very happy and joyous occasion. It is really a wonderful time of the year. There is something in this holiday which appeals to everyone. That is, warmth, love, care, union, harmony and dedication of mankind. This is the spirit of the Christmas holiday.

Of course, we really enjoy the delicious wine and excellent food served here. Yes, the roast turkey is simply delicious. Also, the music is superb. If I were a better dancer, I could have enjoyed the party more. I like everything here, but more important, I enjoyed meeting and talking to you, getting to know you, and sharing the memorable time together.

I am deeply grateful for this nice arrangement. The party was perfectly organized and I enjoyed every minute of it. I'm sure I will remember this great occasion for many years to come.

It has been a great year for all of us in terms of our harmonious business relationship. Our joint venture has had a remarkable sales growth. I hope we will be able to maintain this practical cooperative relationship and make the coming new year a more fruitful year.

I would like to toast with you to this happy occasion at the end of the year.

Thank you very much again for this wonderful party. We had a great evening.

Merry Christmas once again to all of you!

4—3 开幕祝词
An Opening Speech

Ladies and gentlemen,

May I hereby declare open "Shanghai International Symposium on Community Service".

First of all, permit me, on behalf of the organizing committee of the symposium, to extend our warm welcome to the leaders of the Shanghai Municipal Government, leaders of social organizations, representatives of the Community Social Workers' Association and guests from various circles! Our warm welcome goes also to the friends from Canada as well as from other countries and regions. I wish to express our sincere thanks to the Langara Community College of Vancouver, Canada, whose generous help has made possible the successful commencement of this symposium.

The establishment and development of China's socialist market economy requires the reform and improvement in our social welfare and security system, which in turn places higher expectations for community services. With the transformation of governmental functions, much of the work involving social services that was initially undertaken by the government will have to be transferred gradually to social groups and non-governmental organizations. On the one hand, the government will shoulder greater responsibilities in its macro-management; and on the other hand, social groups and non-governmentabrganizations will need to involve themselves in more community services. Consequently, there has emerged an issue which concerns the ways of a close collaboration and the division of responsibilities between the government and social groups, in order to further the development of community service. Some developed countries and regions have accumulated much experience in this regard, which merits our reference and study.

It is with the purpose of sharing our views on this issue that we are hosting this symposium. I believe the symposium will prove to be constructive and significant in promoting the prosperous development of China's community service program as well as China's economic development and social stability. I also believe that our symposium is bound for abundant accomplishment through your hard work.

In conclusion, I wish the symposium a complete success. I wish our overseas experts and scholars, and Chinese friends from various parts of the country a pleasant stay in Shanghai.

Thank you all.

4—4　展望未来
Looking Ahead

Mr. Chairman,
Ladies and gentlemen,

Today, we, leaders of 25 Asian and European countries, meet here for the first time. On the basis of equality and in a friendly manner, we will exchange views on cooperation in a wide range of areas and on the building of a new Asia-Europe partnership.

It is a pioneering endeavor of historic significance. It reflects the widely-shared desire of Asian and European countries for world peace and development and for inter-continental exchanges and cooperation. It signifies the growth of Asia and the profound changes in the entire international relations, and marks a growing trend toward multi-polarity.

I am convinced that this meeting will have a positive impact on the shaping of a new world pattern. I wish to take this opportunity to express my heartfelt thanks to the Royal Government of the Kingdom of Thailand for hosting this meeting successfully.

To build a new Asia-Europe partnership calls for new concepts and new methodology. When we look back on the past experiences and look into the future, I believe that a new partnership between Asia and Europe should be constructed on the basis of mutual respect, equality and mutual benefit.

We should seek common ground while putting aside differences, enhance mutual understanding and trust, eliminate trade discrimination, oppose imposition of trade sanctions, and enhance technical exchanges and cooperation.

Asia and Europe should expand and increase political dialogues in the interest of better mutual understanding and trust. We on our part would like to see progress in EU integration and to see EU remain independent and demonstrate openness. On the other hand, we hope that Europe will understand the aspirations of Asian countries to promote economic development and expand regional cooperation while maintaining political stability, and support their efforts in this regard.

We are ready to increase our cooperation with Asian and European countries. We have carried out a major reform in foreign trade and formulated a set of related laws. We have reduced our tariffs to the average level of the developing countries. I am convinced that China's reform, opening-up and stability will provide the business community of Asian and European countries with tremendous investment and trade opportunities, thus making positive contributions to peace, stability and prosperity in Asia and the world as a whole.

Let us work together for a successful conclusion of this meeting.

Let us join hands in building an Asian-European partnership oriented toward the new century so as to shape a more splendid future for our two continents and the world at large.

Thank you, Mr. Chairman.

1. On behalf of the general manager, and on behalf of all my colleagues of the company, I wish to thank you all for taking time off your busy schedule to come to our New Year's party.

2. I feel very proud and honored tonight to have the attendance of the distinguished guests, who came here all the way from London to join us in our celebration of the Mid-Autumn Festival.

3. On behalf of all the members of my group, I'd like to thank you, Mr. Chairman, for your gracious invitation for us to attend such an enjoyable Christmas party.

4. I'd like to thank you for your presence at the party, and wish everyone good health and the very best of luck in everything in the new year.

5. I hope this party will give us an opportunity to get to know each other better in a less formal way and to increase personal friendships.

6. The party was perfectly organized and I enjoyed every minute of it. And I am very grateful for this nice arrangement.

7. I would like to toast with you to this happy occasion at the close of the year.

8. It has been a great year, a year in which our joint venture had a remarkable sales growth. I hope we will be able to maintain this practical cooperative relationship and make the coming new year a more fruitful year.

9. May I hereby declare open "Shanghai International Symposium on Urban Construction"!

10. Permit me, on behalf of the organizing committee, to extend a warm welcome to our guests of various circles, from home and abroad.

11. I wish to express our sincere thanks to the people of the local education community, whose generous help has made possible the successful commencement of this conference.

12. The conference is one of a pioneering endeavor and historic significance, one that will have a positive impact on the shaping of a new world order.

13. I am certain that this annual meeting will prove to be constructive and significant in promoting the prosperous development of China's community service program as well as China's economic development and social stability.

14. Some developed countries and regions have accumulated much experience in the field of environmental protection, and their experience certainly merits our reference and study.

15. When we look back on the past experiences and into the future, I believe that a new partnership should be constructed on the basis of mutual respect, and equality and mutual benefit.

16. Let us seek common ground while putting aside differences, enhance mutual understanding and trust, and strengthen exchange and cooperation.

17. I am convinced that China's reform, opening-up, and stability will provide the business community of the Asian-Pacific region with tremendous investment and trade opportunities, thus making positive contributions to peace, stability, and prosperity in Asia and the world as a whole.

第5单元 介绍性口译(英译汉)

UNIT 5 Interpreting Informative Speeches English-Chinese Interpretation

5—1 股票市场
The Stock Market

词汇预习
Vocabulary Work

raise money   the general public
the New York Stock Exchange   bull / bear market
publicly owned company   stock index
stockbroker   the Dow Jones Industrial Average
stock dealer   the NASDAQ Composite Index
stock trading system

课文口译
Text for Interpretation

Interpret the following passage from English into Chinese:

I'm very happy to see such a large audience. But this lecture on the stock market is meant for beginners. A stock is an ownership share in a business. Companies sell stock as a way to raise money without borrowing. People buy stock as an investment, in the hope of making a profit on an increase in the stock's price.

The stock market in the United States began in New York City in 1792. The New York Stock Exchange is the oldest financial market in the United States, and the largest stock market in the world.

The stocks of more than three thousand American and international companies are traded on the New York Stock Exchange. Together the stock represents about eighty percent of the value of all publicly owned companies in America.

Stockbrokers and dealers have been an important part of the traditional stock trading system. These financial experts are paid for their knowledge of financial markets and business. But, the Internet has made it easy for the general public to get information about companies and stocks. Many people now choose to control how their money is invested.

About fifty years ago, only five percent of Americans owned stock. They were usually very rich people trading shares with each other. Today, almost fifty percent of all Americans have stock holdings. And, sixteen percent of all stock trades take place over the Internet.

The expression used to describe such a period when the prices of most stocks are increasing is a "bull market." A "bear market" is when most stock prices are falling as investors sell stocks.

Usually, investors in the United States have bought stocks they expected to keep for many years. Over the long-term, the stock market has always increased. Short-term price decreases only affect people who sell stocks at prices lower than they paid for them. That is why during bull markets, experts tell investors to keep their stocks rather than to sell.

Recently, however, short-term trading has become more popular, especially one kind called day trading. Day traders seek to earn money from the daily changes in the price of a stock. Day trading is an extremely risky form of investing. It is possible to gain a large amount of money very quickly by day trading. Most day traders, however, lose money.

The performance of the stock market is measured by stock indexes. The Dow Jones Industrial Average follows the share prices of thirty leading industrial companies in the United States. The NASDAQ Composite Index is also a major stock index.

People usually have invested in companies that have strong earnings and a large share in their business market. But over the last few years, stocks of companies that promise future growth have had the greatest demand.

In a few years, investors should be able to trade stocks twenty-four hours a day. Seven days a week. And, in the future, financial markets around the world are expected to be linked. We just have to be a little bit more patient.

5—2 浪漫香槟
The Romantic Champagne

词汇预习
Vocabulary Work

Champagne sampling party
the release of gas
gentle, alluring fizz
candlelit dinner
Valentine's Day
akin to
driving a BMW or a Mercedes
do the trick

an allure
eponymous drink
ranked by "dosage"
fermentation
extra-brut
vintage champagne
spicy food
go especially well with

Interpret the following passage from English into Chinese:

Welcome to our Champagne sampling party. May I take a few minutes and say something about Champagne?

Champagne, for many, is simply the most romantic drink. The pop of the opening cork, the sigh of the release of gas, and the gentle, alluring fizz as the glass fills. What could go better with a candlelit dinner just for two on Valentine's Day?

Champagne is one of the world's unique flavors. The creation of a good champagne is akin to something else often associated with love and romance — fine perfume. Indeed, the link between the happy life and fizz is close. Champagne is one of the international symbols of a certain kind of pleasure. Why do people dream of driving a BMW or a Mercedes? Any car will do the trick — but some cars are about more than just getting there. And some drinks are about more than just drinking.

Few flavors in the world can match that of champagne. It is a truly unique taste, created by a complex and painstaking process. That process takes a legal minimum of 15 months. The bottles are turned every day for weeks on end. And it's in this painstaking process that makes champagne such an allure. It's about far more than just alcohol.

For me it's a wonderful thought that almost anywhere I go in the world, the flavor is waiting for me in the bottle.

While countries all over the world can produce wine, only the Champagne region of France can produce the eponymous drink. The tiny carbon dioxide bubbles in champagne allow the body to absorb the alcohol at an especially high rate. This fact makes champagne what many call "the ultimate drink," and also means that just one glass is enough to raise the romantic temperature — good news for those who don't like to drink much alcohol. Some others like champagne because it can quicken the pulse and raise the mood perfectly well.

Champagne is ranked by "dosage," the amount of sugar used during the fermentation process. The driest style, using the least sugar, is called extra-brut, but the bulk of the region's production is the very slightly sweeter brut. And the difference between non-vintage and vintage is that the former uses grapes from several different years and the latter uses grapes from just one year — but it must be a good year, and in some years no vintage champagne is made at all.

Newcomers to wine sometimes worry needlessly about matching food and wine. They shouldn't. If it feels good, just do it. Of course, spicy foods should be avoided. Oversweet dishes will also spoil the taste.

And one of the delights of Chinese food is its range — it's fairly easy to tailor a perfectly good Chinese meal that will go well with wines.

I recommend balancing oily, richer dishes, with delicate vegetable tastes. Duck goes especially well with champagne. And many of the simpler vegetables, such as bean dishes, are good too. But really it boils down to just one thing — find out for yourself.

A good wine, or a vintage champagne, is like a person you've met whose personality you don't forget. Likewise, a bottle of good champagne is nothing but the ideal companion for a delicious meal where you don't want your personality to be easily forgotten, either.

Now feel free to sample our champagne selections.

5—3 游客之居
A Place to Stay

词汇预习
Vocabulary Work

motel

lodging

ads

in any case

inn

resort

freeway

single / twin / double / queen
  size / king size bed

"long boy"

double room

waterbed

rollaway (bed)

hide-a-bed

camping

campground

trailer

the States

shelter

课文口译
Text for Interpretation

Interpret the following passage from English into Chinese:

Are you interested in knowing about finding a place to stay when traveling in the United States?

Well, if you arrive by air, you will see plenty of hotels advertised at airports. If you arrive by train or car, probably the best thing to do is look in the Yellow Pages under Hotel, Motel or Lodging. You can start by comparing the services offered in their ads. In any case, you'll have to call them and see if they have the kind of room you're looking for.

Places to stay may be called hotels, motels or motor hotels, inns, lodges or resorts. These are all similar. Motels have plenty of parking space and are usually near a freeway or highway. Inns are usually like motels. Lodges and resorts, or resort hotels, are in the mountains, on the coast, or near lakes.

Beds also go by many different names. Starting with the smallest, there are single, twin, double, queen and king size ones. "Long boys" are for exceptionally tall people. At some hotels, queen beds are the smallest size used, so a double room has two of them. Some hotels even offer their guests waterbeds. A rollaway can be moved into a room to sleep an extra person. Hide-a-beds are sofas that fold out to make beds.

People who prefer camping to staying in hotels will have a hard time in American cities, because most of them don't have campgrounds nearby. You can camp in state and national parks, though, which generally have facilities for both tents and trailers.

It is my sincere wish that you will have a good time touring the States, and you will find a nice roof to shelter yourself.

5—4 教堂之游
A Tour around the Cathedral

词汇预习
Vocabulary Work

the Washington National Cathedral	shaped like a cross
the Episcopal Church	bell tower
the Cathedral Church of Saint Peter and Saint Paul	windows set high in the walls
	sunlight spilling across the floor
hectare	religious service

Interpret the following passage from English into Chinese:

What we see now is the Washington National Cathedral. The Washington National Cathedral is one of the largest and most famous religious centers in the United States. It belongs to the Episcopal Church. The official name of the building is the Cathedral Church of Saint Peter and Saint Paul. But everyone calls it the National Cathedral because people of all religions are welcome to pray there.

The National Cathedral was built with money from private citizens. The work started in 1907, and the Cathedral was not completely finished until 1990. The first stone was laid in the presence of President Theodore Roosevelt. Every President of the United States since then has attended services or visited the Cathedral. It was built on 7,000 hectares of land on one of the highest places in the city. It looks like many of the great religious centers built in Europe about 800 years ago. The building is shaped like a cross or the letter T. In the center is a bell tower 91 meters high. Two more towers stand at the bottom of the cross.

Two hundred windows are set high in the walls of the National Cathedral. Most are made of many pieces of colored glass. They color the sunlight as it enters the building and spills across the floor. Some windows have flower designs. Others have images from Christian stories or from American heroes. In one window is a rock that was brought back from the moon.

The National Cathedral also celebrates American heroes. It has statues of Presidents George Washington and Abraham Lincoln, for example. And more than 150 famous Americans are buried there. They include President Woodrow Wilson, business leader Andrew

Mellon and writer Helen Keller.

The Washington National Cathedral is open to all people for many religious events throughout the year. The Cathedral also holds Christian religious services, family activities, weddings, funerals, concerts and educational programs for children.

Now you have thirty minutes to look around.

句子精练
Sentences in Focus

Interpret the following sentences from English into Chinese:

1. I'm very happy to see such a large audience, but this lecture on cloning technology is meant for beginners.

2. People buy stock as an investment, in the hope of making a profit on an increase in the stock's price.

3. The stocks on the New York Stock Exchange represent about eighty percent of the value of all publicly owned companies in America.

4. The Internet has made it easy for the general public to get information about financial investment.

5. The performance of the stock market is measured by stock indexes, such as the Dow Jones Industrial Average and the NASDAQ Composite Index.

6. Few flavors in the world can match that of champagne, which is a truly unique taste, created by a complex and painstaking process.

7. One of the delights of Chinese food is its range — it's fairly easy to tailor a perfectly good Chinese meal that will go well with wines.

8. A good wine, or a vintage champagne, is like a person you've met whose personality you don't forget.

9. A bottle of good champagne is nothing but the ideal companion

for a delicious meal where you don't want your personality to be easily forgotten.

10. Places to stay while traveling in this country go by different names, such as hotels, motels or motor hotels, inns, lodges or resorts.

11. A rollaway can be moved into a room to sleep an extra person, and a hide-a-bed is a sofa that folds out to make a bed.

12. People who prefer camping to staying in hotels will have a hard time in the cities, because most of these cities don't have campgrounds nearby.

13. Built with money from private citizens, the Washington National Cathedral is one of the largest and most famous religious centers in the United States.

14. The colored glass windows color the sunlight as it enters the building and spills across the floor.

15. The Washington National Cathedral is open to all people for many religious events throughout the year, and also holds many religious services, family activities, weddings, funerals, concerts and educational programs for children.

参考译文
Reference Version

5—1 股票市场
The Stock Market

　　我很高兴能见到这么多的听众。不过这只是一个普及性的讲座。股票是指对某个公司的份额拥有。公司出售股票作为一种不需借款而筹资的方式。人们购买股票作为一种投资,希望通过股价上涨而获利。

　　美国的股票交易所于1792年诞生于纽约。纽约股票交易所是美国最古老的金融市场,同时也是世界上最大的股票市场。

3,000多家美国公司和国际性公司的股票在纽约股票交易所进行交易,总股价约占全美上市公司总市值的80%。

股票经纪人和交易商是传统的股票交易系统的一个重要组成部分。这些金融专家凭借其对金融市场及商务的专业知识而取得报酬。但是,因特网的出现使普通老百姓易于获得有关公司和股票的信息。现在很多人愿意自我管理投资的方式。

大约50年前,只有5%的美国人拥有股票,他们通常是一些很富有的人,相互进行股票交易。今天,几乎50%的美国人持有股票,而且16%的股票是在因特网上交易的。

描述大多数股票的价格处于上涨期的术语是"牛市",而因投资者纷纷抛售股票致使大多数股票价格下跌则意味着已进入"熊市"。

通常,在美国的投资者购买那些他们期望多年持有的股票。股票的长期行情总是上涨的。短期的价格下跌只会影响那些以低于买入价抛售股票的人。那就是为什么在"牛市"时,专家劝告投资者持有股票而不要抛售股票。

然而,近来短期交易变得越来越普遍,尤其是一种叫做当日交易的方式越来越流行。当日交易者希望从股票价格每日变化的股市中赢利。当日交易是一种风险极大的投资方式,当日交易有可能快速赚大钱,但是大部分当日交易者都是赔钱的。

股票市场的行情是以股票指数来衡量。道·琼斯工业平均指数追踪美国30家主要工业公司的股价行情。纳斯达克综合指数也是一个主要的股票指数。

人们通常投资于那些具有较强赢利能力而且占有很大市场份额的公司。但近年来,需求量最大的股票是那些发展前景看好的公司的股票。

再过几年,投资者将能一周7天、一天24小时地进行股票交易。而且,未来的全球金融市场都将连网交易。让我们耐心等一段时间吧。

5—2 浪漫香槟
The Romantic Champagne

欢迎光临我们的香槟品酒会。请允许我简单介绍一下香槟。

对许多人来说,香槟是最浪漫的饮料。开启酒瓶时软木塞的嘭然声,气体释放时的咝咝声,倒入酒杯时诱人的嘶嘶声,还有什么可以配得上两人世界的情人节烛光晚宴呢?

香槟是世界上口味独特的饮料之一。一瓶上等香槟的效果好似一瓶洋溢着爱和浪漫气息的上乘香水。的确如此,幸福生活和气体饮料密切相关。香槟是国际上示意某种欢乐的标志。人们为什么梦寐以求能拥有一辆宝马或奔驰这类好车? 任何车都可以当作坐骑到达某地,但是有些车的作用不仅仅限于到达某地。同样,有些饮料的作用不仅仅在于饮用。

世界上几乎没有哪一种饮料的口味可以与香槟的口味相媲美。香槟确实口味独特,这种口味是通过复杂而艰辛的酿造过程而获得的。按规定这一酿造过程历时至少 15 个月,其间连续数周每瓶香槟天天都要翻转。正是这一艰辛的制作过程才赋予了香槟如此诱人的魅力。香槟的意义已远远超出了酒的意义。

对我来说,无论我来到世界何方,天南地北几乎都有香槟相待,一想到此,令人心满意足。

虽然世界各国都能酿酒,但是只有法国香槟地区才能酿造出这种同名汽酒。香槟里的那些二氧化碳小气泡使人体能够以极快的速度吸收酒精。这就是为什么许多人将香槟称之为"极品饮料"的原因,同时也说明了为什么仅仅一杯香槟就足以让浪漫气氛升温,这对那些不愿多喝酒的人来说香槟可是个好选择。另外一些人喜欢香槟是因为它可以很有效地加快脉搏跳动,振奋情绪。

香槟按其在发酵过程中所含糖份的"剂量"分类。最干的香槟含糖量最低,叫做"偏酸型",法国香槟地区生产的香槟主要为稍带甜味的微甜酸酒。普通香槟和精制香槟的不同之处在于前者使用不同年份的葡萄酿制,而后者使用同一年份的葡萄酿制——但是必须是一个好年份,有些年份则连一瓶精制香槟都酿造不出来。

初尝葡萄酒者有时不知道如何选择下酒菜,这种担心实在没有必要。如果感觉好吃,就开怀大吃。当然,辛辣的食物还是应该避免,过甜的菜肴也会破坏口味。

中国菜的美味之一是其种类繁多的菜式,我们很容易选择一种与饮用葡萄酒相得益彰的菜肴。

我建议将油腻味重的食物与清淡爽口的素食搭配起来。鸭子特别适合做香槟的下酒菜,许多更为简易的素菜如豆类菜都是不错的选择。当然,其实只有一条标准,那就是自己喜欢就是好的。

遇到一瓶上等葡萄酒,或者说一瓶精制香槟,就像遇到一个个性令你难以忘怀的人。同样,一桌美味佳肴,配以一瓶上等香槟助兴,你的个性也会给客人留下难以忘怀的深刻印象。

下面请各位尽情品尝我们所选的香槟精品。

5—3　游客之居
A Place to Stay

各位是否想了解一下在美国旅行时如何寻找住所?

好的,如果你坐飞机来,可以在机场看到大量介绍旅馆的广告。如果你坐火车或汽车来,你也许最好查阅一下电话簿黄页部分里刊登在"旅馆"、"汽车旅馆"或"公寓房间"栏目下的广告。你可以先将各家旅馆在它们的广告上所列的服务项目作一比较。当然,无论你作何种选择,都得打电话给你感兴趣的旅馆,了解一下有无你想要的那种房间。

旅舍种类繁多,有旅馆、汽车旅馆、客栈、度假胜地小旅店、度假胜地宾馆等。通常客栈与汽车旅馆相似。度假胜地小旅店和度假胜地宾馆坐落在山中、海边,或与湖泊为邻。

旅馆里的床亦名目繁多。从尺寸最小的床说起,有"单人床"、"对床"、"双人床"、"大号床"以及"加阔床"。"长小伙子床"是一种专为个子特别高的人而准备的床。有些旅馆里的"大号床",其尺寸可能是这类床的最小号,这样可以在双人房里同时放入两张"大号床"。有些旅馆甚至还为客人准备了"水床"。"滚动式折叠床"可随时推入房内,为客人加铺。"暗床"则是一种沙发式折叠床,将其摊开,可作床用。

对于那些宁愿露宿户外而不愿睡在旅馆里的人来说,美国城市可不是他们的乐园,因为大多数城市没有邻近的野营地。当然,游客可以在州辖公园和国家公园宿营，通常州辖公园和国家公园都有便于安放帐篷和拖车式移动房屋的配套设施。

我衷心希望各位在美国游有所乐，居有其屋。

5—4　教堂之游
A Tour around the Cathedral

现在我们所看到是华盛顿国家大教堂。华盛顿国家大教堂是美国规模最大、最负盛名的宗教中心之一，隶属主教派教会。该建筑的正式名称是圣彼得和圣保罗大教堂。但是人们叫它国家大教堂，是因为它欢迎任何教派的人到这里祈祷。

国家大教堂是由私人赞助建造的。工程开始于 1907 年，直到 1990 年才全部竣工。奠基石是西奥多·罗斯福总统在场时放置的。从那以后，每一任美国总统都参加过这里举行的宗教礼仪活动或参观过大教堂。大教堂建于城市最高处之一的一块土地上，占地面积为7,000 公顷。大教堂看起来就像欧洲许多建于约 800 年前的宗教大中心，形状像个"十"字，或像字母"T"，中心是一座高达 91 米的钟楼，另外两座塔楼坐落在十字的底部处。

200 扇窗高高地嵌入在国家大教堂的墙上，大多数窗都由许多块彩色玻璃拼成，射入的阳光被窗玻璃染成各种颜色，洒落在大教堂的一侧地上。有些窗带有花卉图案，有些窗的画面则是有关基督教的故事或美国历史英雄的形象。一扇窗上还有一块采自月球的石头。

国家大教堂还用于纪念美国英雄。例如，大教堂里安放着乔治·华盛顿总统和亚伯拉罕·林肯的塑像。另外还有 150 多位美国名人安眠于此地，其中包括总统伍德罗·威尔逊、商界领袖安德鲁·梅隆和作家海伦·凯勒。

华盛顿大教堂全年对举办各种宗教活动的所有人士开放。大教堂还举办基督教宗教活动、家庭活动、婚礼葬礼、音乐会和儿童教育活动。

现在给你们 30 分钟自由观赏。

1. 我很高兴能见到这么多的听众。不过这只是一个克隆技术的知识普及性讲座。

2. 人们购买股票作为一种投资,希望通过股价上涨而获利。

3. 纽约股票交易所的股票总股价约占全美上市公司总市值的80%。

4. 因特网的出现使普通老百姓易于获得有关金融投资的信息。

5. 股票市场的行情是以股票指数来衡量,例如道·琼斯工业平均指数和纳斯达克综合指数。

6. 世界上几乎没有哪一种饮料的口味可以与香槟的口味相媲美,这种独特的口味是通过复杂而艰辛的酿造过程而获得的。

7. 中国菜的美味之一是其种类繁多的菜式,我们很容易选择一种与饮用葡萄酒相得益彰的菜肴。

8. 遇到一瓶上等葡萄酒,或者说一瓶精制香槟,就像遇到一个个性令你难以忘怀的人。

9. 一桌美味佳肴,配以一瓶上等香槟助兴,你的个性会给客人留下难以忘怀的深刻印象。

10. 在这个国家旅行时可供住宿的旅舍种类繁多,有旅馆、汽车旅馆、客栈、度假胜地的小旅店和宾馆等。

11. 滚动式折叠床可随时推入房内,为客人加铺,而暗床则是一种沙发式折叠床,摊开后可作床用。

12. 对于那些宁愿露宿户外而不愿睡在旅馆里的人来说,城市可不是他们的乐园,因为大多数城市没有邻近的野营地。

13. 由私人赞助建造的华盛顿国家大教堂是美国规模最大、最负盛名的宗教中心之一。

14. 彩色玻璃窗将射入的阳光染成各种颜色,洒落在大教堂的一侧地上。

15. 华盛顿大教堂全年对举办各种宗教活动的所有人士开放,还举办许多宗教活动、家庭活动、婚礼葬礼、音乐会和儿童教育活动。

第 6 单元　介绍性口译（英译汉）

UNIT 6　Interpreting Informative Speeches
Chinese-English Interpretation

6—1　传统节日
Traditional Holidays

> ### 词汇预习
> ### Vocabulary Work

烹调	中秋节
鱼肉满架	满月
象征意义	月饼
农历	蜜饯
端午节	豆沙
放逐	蛋黄
忠臣	海鲜
糯米粽子	家禽
祭祀	饺子
亡灵	八宝饭
龙舟比赛	米羹

Interpret the following passage from Chinese into English：

我很高兴有机会向各位介绍中国的主要传统节日。

同世界其他地区一样，节日在中国是人们勤于烹调、饱享口福的时候。菜市场鱼肉满架，购物和烹调成了人们的主要活动。但是除了节庆膳食在数量和质量上与平日不同之外，一些历史悠久、具有象征意义的特色食物也是节日必不可缺的伴侣。

例如，农历五月五日的端午节是为了纪念被昏庸君主贬官放逐而抱石投江自尽的古代诗人和忠臣屈原。最初人们将以竹叶包扎好的糯米粽子投入屈原自尽的那条江，以祭祀亡灵。今天，人们在端午时节举行龙舟比赛，而粽子则由活生生的人来享用。

农历八月十五日的中秋节是观赏满月的日子。圆圆的月亮象征着圆满，进而象征着家庭团聚。中秋节的特制食品是一种圆形的月饼，内含核桃仁、蜜饯、豆沙或蛋黄等食物。

春节是中国的农历新年，春节的日期按农历而定，通常出现在公历2月前半期的某一天。大吃大喝历来是春节的主要内容。除了常见的海鲜、家禽和肉类之外，人们还要按各自的地方习俗烹制一些传统菜肴，例如北京的饺子、上海的八宝饭和广州的米羹。全国各地都可以见到形态各异、口味不一的年糕。"年糕"这个词里的"糕"字与"高"谐音，寓意来年"节节高"。

6—2　集团公司
An Ambitious Conglomerate

竭诚欢迎　　　　　　　　各界人士

集科、工、贸、旅游、娱乐于一体	拓展市场
物贸中心	提供全方位的服务
房地产开发公司	经营范围
娱乐总汇	商务咨询
中澳合资纺织制品有限公司	商务投资考察
年销售额	景点
国家旅游局批准	投资开发项目
国家认可的	工艺品
外国商社	招商
三资企业	

课文口译
Text for Interpretation

Interpret the following passage from Chinese into English：

　　海华(集团)公司竭诚欢迎海内外各界人士以各种形式参与本公司的各项业务运作。

　　海华(集团)公司是一个集科、工、贸、旅游、娱乐于一体的跨地区、跨行业、跨所有制的大型(集团)公司。海华(集团)公司下设研究所、物贸中心、百货商店、房地产开发公司、娱乐总汇、旅游公司、中澳合资纺织制品有限公司、沪港合资机械有限公司等40余家公司。拥有资产5亿多元,员工6千多人,年销售额达18亿元。

　　海华(集团)公司所属的海华商务国际旅游公司(简称为"海华商旅")是经国家旅游局批准的商务旅行社,是经营国际、国内、出入境、票务等旅游业务的专业公司。公司拥有一支经国家认可的英、日、德、法、韩等语种齐全的翻译导游队伍。公司经营管理海华(集团)公司的票务中心,拥有出租车队和航空售票处,拥有铁路、轮船票务服务站,为国内外宾客提供便捷服务。

　　"海华商旅"服务于上海几千家外国商社和三资企业。我们的宗旨是拓展国内外商务旅游市场,以旅游促商务,为改善上海的投资环境提供全方位的服务。

"海华商旅"的主要经营范围包括：

—— 经营国内外旅游业务；

—— 提供国内外商务咨询；

—— 安排国际商务、文化交流；

—— 安排国内外商务投资考察；

—— 组织旅游设施、景点的投资开发项目；

—— 设计和营销旅游工艺品；

—— 兼营商务礼仪以及各种形式的招商投资活动。

"海华商旅"以优良的服务态度、优惠的旅游价格，竭诚与客户建立互惠互利的合作关系，坦诚相待，共同发展商务旅游事业。

6—3 出版王者
A Super-Publisher

词汇预习
Vocabulary Work

新闻出版署	制版
国际新闻局	入境口岸
高级编辑	出版物
排版	展示会
印刷厂	幻灯片
旅游指南	音像制品
小说	缩微胶卷
古典文学	激光视盘
专业教科书	电脑可读光盘

Interpret the following passage from Chinese into English：

欢迎各位来访中国国际出版集团的总部大楼。

中国国际出版集团是中国最大的外语出版、印刷和发行单位,其前身是与中华人民共和国同时诞生的中央人民政府新闻出版署国际新闻局。

集团现有职工 4,000 名,其中包括 100 名外国专家和一大批高级编辑、记者和翻译,拥有排版、印刷和发行的最新技术与设备。

我们与北京外语印刷厂合作负责出版 7 份杂志,这些杂志以 36 种不同的语言编写,内容涉及贸易、国家政策和中国文化。

集团所辖的 11 家出版社以 20 种不同的语种推出各类图书,内容包括政治、经济、艺术、汉语、医学、文化习俗,以及儿童读物、旅游指南、小说、古典文学和专业教科书。

我们的制版与印刷设备堪称一流,可以用 50 种不同的语种进行印刷。我们与中国国家图书贸易公司合作,建立了一张遍布世界 182 个国家和地区的发行网络。

我们在上海、厦门、烟台、无锡和桂林都设有分局。几乎在所有的书店、旅馆、入境口岸、机场和旅游景点都能看到我们的出版物。我们还在许多海外图书及出版展示会上展出我们的出版物。此外,我们还可以提供以其他形式出现的中国出版物,例如手工艺品、图片、幻灯片、音像制品、缩微胶卷、激光视盘、电脑可读光盘等。

6—4 丝绸之路
The Silk Road

丝绸之路   追溯

朝廷使者	佛教
西域	伊斯兰教
河西走廊	石榴
塔里木盆地	香水
帕米尔山区	历史文物
阿富汗	散居
伊朗	少数民族
伊拉克	天方夜谭
叙利亚	敦煌
地中海	吐鲁番
丝绸织物	领略自然景观的魅力
火药	欣赏古代艺术家高超的工艺
造纸术	品尝地方风味小吃
印刷术	

课文口译
Text for Interpretation

Interpret the following passage from Chinese into English：

欢迎各位参加"丝绸之路游"。为期两周的游览将成为您一生中最难忘的经历之一。

丝绸之路的历史可以追溯到公元前 2 世纪,当时一名中国官员、朝廷的使者张骞沿着这条连接亚欧两大洲的贸易通道出使西域。这条通道源于长安城(即今日的西安),一路穿越陕西省、甘肃省境内的河西走廊、新疆的塔里木盆地、帕米尔山区、阿富汗、伊朗、伊拉克以及叙利亚,最后抵达地中海的东岸,全程 7 千公里,其中有 4 千多公里的路段在中国境内。

15 世纪前的一千多年里,中国通过这条通道给西域各国带去了丝绸织物、火药、造纸术和印刷术。同时,这条通道也从国外给我们引进了佛教、伊斯兰教,以及葡萄、核桃、石榴、黄瓜、玻璃、香水等产品。因为中国丝绸是沿着这条道进入西方国家的,所以欧洲学者将此道称作

"丝绸之路"。

丝绸之路沿途的大批历史文物、引人入胜的自然风景以及富有情趣的地方文化,使这一长途远游成了世界上最精彩的旅游节项目之一。在丝绸之路的中国段,沿线散居着许多少数民族,他们对来自世界各地的游客都以礼相待,热情好客。这里的食物和工艺品不同于中国中部的食物和工艺品。这里民间传说,如同天方夜谭一般神奇,听来别有一番情趣。

我社安排的"丝绸之路游",始于西安古城,止于新疆的乌鲁木齐,其间我们还要游览兰州、敦煌以及吐鲁番。沿线您可以领略自然景观的魅力,欣赏古代艺术家高超的工艺,品尝地方风味小吃,结识当地居民。这次游览一定会给您留下可与家人和朋友共享的美好回忆。

句子精练
Sentences in Focus

Interpret the following sentences from Chinese into English:
1. 中国农历五月五日的端午节旨在纪念古代诗人屈原。
2. 中秋节的特制食品是一种内含核桃仁、蜜饯、豆沙或蛋黄等食物的圆形的月饼,圆象征着圆满,进而象征着家庭团聚。
3. 春节是中国的农历新年,其日期按农历而定,通常出现在公历 2 月前半期的某一天。
4. 大饱口福历来是春节的主要内容,除了常见的海鲜、家禽和肉类之外,人们还要按各自的地方习俗烹制一些传统菜肴。
5. 我们竭诚欢迎海内外各界人士以各种形式参与本公司的各项业务运作。
6. 本公司是一个融科、工、贸、旅游、娱乐于一体的跨地区、跨行业、跨所有制的大型(集团)公司,公司拥有固定资产 3 亿 8 千万元,年销售额达 15 亿元。
7. 华兴商务国际旅游公司拥有一支经国家认可的主要语种齐全的翻译导游队伍。
8. 我们的宗旨是拓展国内外商务旅游市场,以旅游促商务,为客户提供全方位的服务。

9. 公司以优良的服务态度、优惠的旅游价格,竭诚与客户建立互惠互利的合作关系,坦诚相待,共同发展商务旅游事业。

10. 出版集团所辖的各出版社以不同的语种推出各类图书,内容包括政治、经济、艺术、语言、医学、文化习俗、古典文学和专业教科书。

11. 我们已建立了一张遍布世界各地 100 多个国家和地区的发行网络。

12. 连接亚欧两大洲的贸易通道"丝绸之路"全程长达 7 千公里,其历史可以追溯到公元前 2 世纪。

13. 我社安排的"丝绸之路游",始于西安古城,止于新疆首府乌鲁木齐,沿线游客们可以领略自然景观的魅力,欣赏古代艺术家高超的工艺,品尝地方风味小吃,结识当地居民。

14. 丝绸之路沿途的大批历史文物、引人入胜的自然风景以及富有情趣的地方文化,使"丝绸之路游"成了世界上最精彩的旅游节项目之一。

参考译文
Reference Version

6—1 传统节日
Traditional Holidays

I'm very happy to have the opportunity to talk to you about major traditional Chinese holidays.

Like in the rest of the world, holidays in China are a time for serious cooking and delighted eating. Grocery markets are well stocked with all kinds of fish and meat and shopping and cooking become major activities. But in addition to the quantitative and qualitative differences apparent in holiday meals, some special traditional foods and their symbolic significance are indispensable on these occasions.

The Dragon Boat Festival on the 5th day of the 5th lunar month (around early June) is celebrated in memory of Qu Yuan, an ancient poet and loyal minister who drowned himself while in exile from a corrupt court. *Zongzi*, a kind of glutinous rice dumplings wrapped in bamboo leaves, were originally prepared as sacrificial offerings for Qu Yuan's departed soul and dropped into the river where he drowned himself. Today, however, dragon boat races are held during the festival and the *zongzi* are consumed by the living.

The Mid-autumn Festival which occurs on the 15th day of the 8th lunar month (around mid-September) is an occasion for viewing the full moon. The round moon is a symbol for completeness, and by extension, family reunion. The specialty of the day is the *yuebing* (mooncake), a round pastry filled with nuts, candied preserved fruits, bean paste, duck egg yolks, etc.

The Spring Festival, the Chinese lunar New Year, is celebrated according to the lunar calendar, and generally occurs some time in the first half of February. Customarily, lavishly consuming food and drink is a major activity. In addition to the popular seafood, poultry and meat, regional custom dictates the preparation and consumption of traditional favorites, for example, *jiaozi* (boiled dumplings) in Beijing, *babaofan* (a steamed sweet glutinous rice pudding) in Shanghai, and the soup of small rice-balls (cooked with pork and chicken) in Guangzhou. Throughout China, *niangao* (literally meaning the "year cake", a thick steamed pudding of glutinous rice flour) is made in a great variety of shapes and flavors. The character *gao* in the word *niangao* is homonymous with the word "high", suggesting "growing up and prospering" in the new year.

6—2　集团公司
An Ambitious Conglomerate

Haihua (Group) Corporation sincerely welcomes personalities of all walks of life at home and abroad to join, in whatever form, the partnership with the corporation in its business operations.

Haihua (Group) Corporation is a large cross-regional, cross-trade and cross-ownership (group) corporation which integrates scientific research, manufacturing industry, trade, and tourist and entertainment services. The 40-odd-member Haihua family consists of a research institute, a materials trading center, a department store, a real estate development company, an entertainment concourse, a tourist company, a Sino-Australian jointly-funded textile manufacturing company limited, a Shanghai-Hong Kong jointly-funded machinery company limited, etc., with the combined capital assets in the amount of 500 million *yuan*, over 6,000 employees and an annual turnover of 1.8 billion *yuan*.

Haihua International Business Travel Company, which is subordinate to Haihua (Group) Corporation, is a business travel agency approved by the Chinese National Tourism Administration. This is a professional company whose scope of business ranges over international, domestic, in- and out-bound travel, and ticket-booking services. The company takes pride in its state-certified professional tourist guides and interpreters proficient in English, Japanese, German, French, Korean, and other foreign languages. The company manages the ticket-booking center of Haihua (Group) Corporation. It has a fleet of taxis, an airline ticket office, and rail and water passenger transportation ticket service booths, providing convenient and prompt services for overseas and domestic customers.

HIBT (Haihua International Business Travel Company) also provides services for thousands of foreign business establishments as well as foreign-funded enterprises in Shanghai. We work under the principle of expanding our business travel markets at home and abroad, promoting business activities with the tourist development and offering an all-round service so as to improve the investment environment in Shanghai.

HIBT's business scope covers the following areas:

— Conducting domestic and overseas tourist services;

— Providing consultancy services for domestic and overseas business activities;

— Arranging international business and cultural exchanges;

— Arranging domestic and overseas investigation tours for business investment;

— Organizing investment projects in manufacturing tourist facilities and developing scenic spots;

— Designing and marketing tourist handicraft products;

— Undertaking services for business ceremonies and various types of tender invitation projects.

Known for its excellent service and reasonable charges, HIBT does its best to establish cooperative relations with all its interested clients on the basis of mutual benefit, and to develop business tourism in an honest partnership.

6—3　出版王者
A Super-Publisher

Welcome to the head office of the China International Publishing Group.

The China International Publishing Group is the largest foreign language publishing, printing and distribution establishment in China. Its predecessor was the International Press Bureau of the Central People's Government Press and Publication Administration, set up at the same time as the founding of the People's Republic of China.

Today the group employs over 4,000 staff members, including 100 foreign experts and a large group of senior editors, journalists and translators, working with the latest technology and equipment for composition, printing and distribution.

We are also responsible, through the partnership with the Beijing Foreign Languages Printing House, for producing seven magazines in 36 different languages documenting trade, state policies and Chinese culture.

The group's 11 publishing houses put out books in 20 different languages on political science, economics, art, Chinese language, medicine, cultures and customs, as well as children's books, tour guidebooks, novels, classical literature, and academic textbooks.

Our first-class plate-making and printing equipment enables us to print texts in 50 different languages. We have a distribution network with the China International Book Trading Corporation covering 182 countries and regions throughout the world.

Our branch bureaus operate in Shanghai, Xiamen, Yantai, Wuxi and Guilin. Visitors can find our publications at nearly every book-store, hotel, port-of-entry, airport and tourist attraction. We also display our publications at many overseas book and publishing exhibi-tions. In addition, we can provide access to Chinese publications in the form of handicrafts, prints, slides, audio and video tapes, micro-film, video compact and laser disks, CD-ROMs, etc.

6—4 丝绸之路
The Silk Road

Welcome to the Silk Road Tour! You will find this two-week trip one of your most memorable experiences in your life.

The Silk Road dates back to the second century B. C. when a Chinese official and envoy of the royal court Zhang Qian embarked on his business trip to Xiyu (meaning western countries) following this trade thoroughfare linking Asia and Europe. Originating from Chang'an (the present-day Xi'an), the route traversed Shaanxi Prov-ince, the Hexi Corridor in Gansu Province, the Tarim Basin in Xin-jiang, the Pamir mountain region, Afghanistan, Iran, Iraq and Syria, ending at the eastern shores of the Mediterranean. More than 4,000 of its 7,000 kilometers were in China.

For over a thousand years up till the 15th century, China brought its silk cloth and goods, gunpowder, and paper making and printing techniques to the West via this road. This road, in return, introduced into China Buddhism and Islam as well as grapes, walnuts, pomegranates, cucumbers, glass, perfume and other products from the outside world. Because China's silk reached the West along this road, European scholars came to call it the "Silk Road".

A wealth of historical relics, fascinating scenery and interesting local cultures along the Silk Road makes this long trip one of the world's most exciting tourist attractions. Many Chinese ethnic minorities scatter along the Chinese portion of the road, all courteous and hospitable to visitors from the rest of the world. The food and crafts in the region are different from those in central China. And the folklore is simply exotic and colorful.

The Silk Road Tour our travel agency offers will start from the ancient city of Xi'an and ends at Urumqi of Xinjiang. The tour will also cover Lanzhou, Dunhuang and Turpan. All along the route, you will take pleasure in the charms of the natural landscape, appreciate the superior workmanship of ancient artists, enjoy local delicacies and meet local people. The trip will certainly leave you sweet memories that you will share with your family and friends.

句子精练
Sentences in Focus

---

1. The Dragon Boat Festival on the 5th day of the 5th month of China's lunar calendar is set aside and celebrated in memory of the ancient poet Qu Yuan.

2. The mooncake, a special food of China's Mid-autumn Festival, is a round pastry filled with nuts, candied preserved fruits, bean paste, duck egg yolks, etc., symbolizing completeness and

perfection, and by extension, family reunion.

3. The Spring Festival, or the Chinese lunar New Year, is celebrated according to the lunar calendar, and generally occurs some time in the first half of February.

4. Lavishly consuming food and drink is customarily a major activity during the Spring Festival season. In addition to the popular seafood, poultry and meat, regional custom dictates the preparation and consumption of some traditional favorite dishes.

5. We sincerely welcome personalities of all walks of life at home and abroad to join, in whatever form, the partnership with the corporation in its business operations.

6. Ours is a large cross-regional, cross-trade and cross-ownership (group) corporation which integrates scientific research, manufacturing industry, trade, and tourist and entertainment services; the company has fixed capital assets of 380 million *yuan* and an annual turnover of 1. 5 billion *yuan*.

7. Hua Xing International Business Travel Company is staffed with a team of state-certified professional tourist guides and interpreters proficient in all major languages of the world.

8. We operate under the principle of expanding our business travel markets at home and abroad, promoting business activities with tourist development and providing our clients with an all-round service.

9. This company does its best to establish cooperative relations with all its clients on the basis of mutual benefit, and develop business tourism in an honest partnership.

10. The group's publishing houses put out publications in different languages on a variety of subjects including political science, economics, art, languages, medicine, cultures and customs, classical literature, and academic textbooks.

11. We have a distribution network covering well over 100 countries and regions throughout the world.

12. The 7,000-kilometer-long "Silk Road", whose history dates back to the second century B. C. , is a trade thoroughfare linking Asia and Europe.

13. "The Silk Road Tour" that we offer follows a route beginning from the ancient city of Xi'an and ending at Urumqi of Xinjiang, along which the tourist will take pleasure in the charms of the natural landscape, appreciate the superior workmanship of ancient artists, enjoy local delicacies and meet local people.

14. A wealth of historical relics, fascinating scenery and interesting local cultures along the Silk Road makes this trip one of the world's most exciting tourist attractions.

第7单元 说服性口译(英译汉)

UNIT 7 Interpreting Persuasive Speeches English-Chinese Interpretation

---

7—1 应试之灾
The Examination-oriented Education

词汇预习
Vocabulary Work

unacceptable burden

examination and selection

at the tender age of

effectively

least receptive to learning

sit exams

penalty

death sentence

subject

compulsory system

authority

end up as a failure

motion

课文口译
Text for Interpretation

Interpret the following passage from English into Chinese:

Mr. Chairman,

Ladies and gentlemen,

    The greatest wish of every caring and responsible society is to do something important and meaningful to improve the lives of its children. The most obvious way of doing this is to free childhood from the unacceptable burden of examinations and selection created by our educational system.

At the tender age of 13 or 14, children are selected and pushed into examination classes which will effectively decide their futures. Then, at the age in their lives when most of them are least receptive to learning, they are forced to sit exams where the penalties for failure are as final as death sentence.

The lives of secondary school children are ruled by these exams in this country. Some schools do offer a wide range of interesting subjects, but only for those who have already been labeled as failures. So parents continue to push, pull, threaten and force their children through exams, or search anxiously for schools with "high standards" to do the pushing and forcing for them, because this is what our universities demand.

But is there any need for all that? Why do we put such pressure on our young people at a time when the brain is biologically at its least receptive? And we know that if children took the wrong course at the age of 14, then their lives could be ruined. So why do we choose this period in their lives as the time to make or break them?

If the pressures of selection at 16 were removed, secondary education could become a different process altogether. From about 13 onwards children could be free to study if they choose; or they could choose to study for part of the time only. They could spend exactly as long as they wanted doing the subjects they wanted to do. If they wanted to spend half the day in the art rooms or doing drama, that would be their decision.

Children complain that their classes are boring, their textbooks are boring, and their teachers are boring. However, the voice of the children is rarely heard; and all too often, when they have to write, they simply write what they know the teacher wants to read.

I am deeply convinced that children under a less compulsory system would actually learn more and be more cooperative with adults and authority in general. I am sure they would be happier and more creative, and therefore more useful to the society. We shouldn't have to spend so much time threatening 13 and 14 year-olds that if they don't study all day, every day, they will end up as failures for the rest of their lives.

Therefore, ladies and gentlemen, I'm sure you will agree that you have no choice but to agree with today's motion. The system that exists today is certainly harmful to our children and therefore must be changed.

Thank you.

7—2 广而"误"之
The Effects of Misleading Advertising

denounce	pervasive
commercials	conventional
adolescent	attribute
vulnerable	wrinkle
prime target	blemish
take advantage of	conform to the norm / ideal
in the guise of	artificial image
designer jeans or sneakers	desperate
status	go to great lengths to do something
femininity	thing
masculinity	cosmetics

in need of alteration

disguise

ironically

weight-reduction

detrimental

nutrition

vitality

taboo

placed in a double bind

virginal

seductive

depict

课文口译
Text for Interpretation

Interpret the following passage from English into Chinese:

I'm speaking to denounce a disease with our modern society, that is, the sex role of misleading advertisements and commercials.

Advertising affects all of us throughout our lives. Adolescents, especially female adolescents, are particularly vulnerable, however, because they are new and inexperienced consumers and are the prime targets of many advertisements.

Advertisers are fully aware of their role and do not hesitate to take advantage of the insecurities and anxieties of young people, in the guise of offering solutions. A cigarette provides a symbol of independence. A pair of designer jeans or sneakers conveys status. The right perfume or beer resolves doubts about femininity or masculinity.

No politician or educator is more pervasive or persuasive than advertising. It teaches us to be consumers, to value material things above all else, to feel that happiness can be bought, that there are instant solutions to life's complex problems, and that products can fulfill us and meet our deepest human needs. The value of a person, especially the value of a young woman, depends upon the products used.

For a woman, conventional beauty is her only attribute. She is supposed to have no lines or wrinkles, no scars or blemishes. She is thin, generally tall and long legged, and above all young. All "beautiful" women in television commercials conform to this norm. The image is artificial and can only be achieved artificially. Desperate to conform to an ideal and impossible standard, many women go to great lengths to manipulate and change their faces and bodies. More than a million dollars is spent every hour on cosmetics in this country. A woman is conditioned to view her face as a mask and her body as an object, as things separate from and more important than her real self. She is constantly in need of alteration, improvement, and disguise. She is made to feel dissatisfied with and ashamed of herself, whether she tries to achieve "the look" or not.

Ironically, the heavily advertised products, such as cosmetics and weight-reduction drinks, are even detrimental to physical attractiveness. There is very little emphasis in the media on nutrition and exercise and other important aspects of health and vitality.

Adolescent females are also discouraged from growing up and becoming adults. Growing older is the great taboo. Although boys are allowed and encouraged to become mature adults, girls are encouraged to remain little girls, to be passive and dependent, never to mature. Somehow placed in a double bind, they are supposed to be sexy and virginal, experienced and naive, seductive and pure.

Misleading advertisements and commercials depict a world in which love and passion are reserved solely for products, in which sexuality becomes a commodity, and in which young women are the worst victims.

7—3 共创未来
The Future Is Ours to Build

| 词汇预习 |
| Vocabulary Work |

beckon   industrious
acknowledge   frugal
ideology   horizon
institution   salute
minimize   vitality
dwell on   optimism
distinctly   mighty
heritage   break down barriers
dignity   suspicion
revere elders   bond
potential   shared optimism
dawning

| 课文口译 |
| Text for Interpretation |

Interpret the following passage from English into Chinese:

Ladies and gentlemen,

History beckons again. We have begun to write a new chapter for peace and progress in our histories, with America and China going forward hand-in-hand.

We must always be realistic about our relationship, frankly acknowledging the fundamental differences in ideology and institutions between our two societies. Yes, let us acknowledge those differences; let us never minimize them; but let us not be dominated by them. I have not come to China to hold forth on what divides us, but to build on what binds us. I have not come to dwell on a closed-door past, but to urge that Americans and Chinese look to the beautiful future. I am firmly convinced that, together, we can and will make tomorrow a better day.

We may live at nearly opposite ends of the world. We may be distinctly different in language, customs, and political beliefs; but on many vital questions of our time there is little distance between the American and Chinese people.

Indeed, I believe if we were to ask citizens all over this world what they desire most for their children, and for their children's children, their answer, in English, Chinese, or any language would likely be the same: We want peace. We want freedom. We want a better life. Their dreams, so simply stated, represent mankind's deepest aspirations for security and personal fulfillment. And helping them make their dreams come true is what our jobs are all about.

We have always believed the heritage of our past is the seed that brings forth the harvest of our future. And from our roots, we have drawn tremendous power from faith and freedom. Our passion for freedom led to the American Revolution. We know each of us could not enjoy liberty for ourselves unless we were willing to share it with everyone else. And we knew our freedom could not be truly safe, unless all of us were protected by a body of laws that treated us equally.

Trust the people — these three words are not only the heart and soul of American history, but the most powerful force for human progress in the world today.

Like China, our people see the future in the eyes of our children. And, like China, we revere our elders. To be as good as our fathers and mothers, we must be better.

Over a century ago, Grant, who was then a former president,

visited your country and saw China's great potential. "I see dawn-ing," Grant wrote, "the beginning of a change. When it does come, China will rapidly become a powerful and rich nation ... The popula-tion is industrious, frugal, intelligent, and quick to learn. "

Today, China's economy crackles with the dynamics of change. Unlike some governments, which fear change and fear the future, China is beginning to reach out toward new horizons, and we salute your courage.

We Americans have always considered ourselves pioneers, so we appreciate such vitality and optimism. Today, I bring you a message from my countrymen: As China moves forward on this new path, America welcomes the opportunity to walk by your side.

I see America and our Pacific neighbors going forward in a mighty enterprise to build strong economies and a safer world. For our part, we welcome this new Pacific tide. Let it roll peacefully on, carrying a two-way flow of people and ideas that can break down bar-riers of suspicion and mistrust, and build up bonds of cooperation and shared optimism.

The future is ours to build.

7-4　继往开来
The New Beginning of an Old Story

词汇预习
Vocabulary Work

fellow citizens	slave-holding society
the peaceful transfer of authority	flawed and fallible people
oath	grand and enduring ideal
affirm old tradition	scapegoat

a call to conscience

commitment

civic duty and family bonds

a saint of our times

uncounted, unhonored acts of decency

never yielding

课文口译
Text for Interpretation

Interpret the following passage from English into Chinese:

Distinguished guests and my fellow citizens, the peaceful transfer of authority is rare in history, yet common in our country. With a simple oath, we affirm old tradition and make new beginnings.

I am honored and humbled to stand here, where so many of America's leaders have come before me, and so many will follow.

We have a place, all of us, in a long story — a story we continue, but whose end we will not see. It is the story of a new world that became a friend and liberator of the old, a story of a slave-holding society that became a servant of freedom, the story of a power that went into the world to protect but not possess, to defend but not to conquer.

It is the American story — a story of flawed and fallible people, united across the generations by grand and enduring ideals.

The grandest of these ideals is an unfolding American promise that everyone belongs, that everyone deserves a chance, that no insignificant person was ever born. Americans are called to enact this promise in our lives and in our laws. And though our nation has sometimes halted, and sometimes delayed, we must follow no other course.

While many of our citizens prosper, others doubt the promise, even the justice, of our own country. The ambitions of some Americans are limited by failing schools and hidden prejudice and the circumstances of their birth. And sometimes our differences run so deep, it seems we share a continent, but not a country.

We do not accept this, and we will not allow it. Our unity, our union, is the serious work of leaders and citizens in every generation.

America, at its best, is a place where personal responsibility is valued and expected. Encouraging responsibility is not a search for scapegoats; it is a call to conscience. And though it requires sacrifice, it brings a deeper fulfillment. We find the fullness of life not only in options, but in commitments. And we find that children and community are the commitments that set us free.

Our public interest depends on private character, on civic duty and family bonds and basic fairness, on uncounted, unhonored acts of decency which give direction to our freedom.

Sometimes in life we are called to do great things. But as a saint of our times has said, every day we are called to do small things with great love. The most important tasks of a democracy are done by everyone.

What you do is as important as anything government does. I ask you to seek a common good beyond your comfort; to defend needed reforms against easy attacks; to serve your nation, beginning with your neighbor. I ask you to be citizens, not subjects; responsible citizens, building communities of service and a nation of character.

Americans are generous and strong and decent, not because we believe in ourselves, but because we hold beliefs beyond ourselves. When this spirit of citizenship is missing, no government program can replace it. When this spirit is present, no wrong can stand against it.

Never tiring, never yielding, never finishing, we renew that purpose today, to make our country more just and generous, to affirm the dignity of our lives and every life.

句子精练
Sentences in Focus

Interpret the following sentences from English into Chinese:

1. With a simple oath, we affirm old tradition and make new beginnings.

2. I'm speaking to denounce a disease with our modern society, that is, the sex role of misleading advertisements and commercials.

3. A caring and responsible society should do something important and meaningful to improve the lives of its children, rather than create heavy academic and psychological burdens for the children at their tender age of 12, and force them to sit exams where the penalties for failure are as final as death sentence.

4. I am deeply convinced that children under a less compulsory system would actually learn more; they would be more creative and cooperative with adults and authority in general.

5. In the world today, no political speech or academic lecture is more pervasive or persuasive than advertising.

6. Female adolescents are particularly vulnerable to, and have been the prime targets of, many advertisements and commercials.

7. Advertisers are fully aware of their role and do not hesitate to take advantage of the insecurities and anxieties of young people, in the guise of offering them solutions to any problems conceivable.

8. A consequence of advertising is that it conveys the message that the value of a person is dependent upon the value of products used, and that it makes us feel that happiness can be bought, that there are instant solutions to life's complex problems, and that products can fulfill us and meet our deepest human needs.

9. All "beautiful" women in television commercials conform to the norm by which one is supposed to be thin, generally tall and

long-legged, and have no lines or wrinkles, and no scars or blemishes.

10. Desperate to conform to an ideal and impossible standard, many women, under the influence of advertising, go to great lengths to manipulate and alter their faces and bodies, as if they were things separable from and more important than their real selves.

11. Ironically, the heavily advertised products, such as cosmetics and weight-reduction drinks, are even detrimental to physical attractiveness.

12. Misleading advertisements and commercials depict a world in which love and passion are reserved solely for products, in which sexuality becomes a commodity, and in which young women are the worst victim.

13. We must frankly acknowledge the fundamental differences in ideology and institutions between our two societies.

14. I have come to China not to hold forth on what divides us, but to build on what binds us, not to dwell on a closed-door past, but to urge us look to the beautiful future.

15. I have always believed the heritage of our past is the seed that brings forth the harvest of our future.

16. Today, China's economy crackles with the dynamics of change, and you are beginning to reach out toward new horizons, and we salute your courage.

17. Let the Pacific tide roll peacefully on, carrying a two-way flow of people and ideas that can break down barriers of suspicion and mistrust, and build up bonds of cooperation and shared optimism.

18. We find the fullness of life not only in options, but in commitments.

19. Our public interest depends on private character, on civic duty and family bonds and basic fairness, on uncounted, unhonored acts of decency which give direction to our freedom.

参考译文
Reference Version

> ### 7—1　应试之灾
> ### The Examination-oriented Education

主席先生，

女士们、先生们：

　　对于每一个富有爱心与负责精神的社会，其最大的愿望莫过于为改善儿童的生活而做重要的、有意义的事。将这种愿望付诸实践的最显然的做法便是去除儿童的考试与选拔负担，这种负担源于我们的教育制度，令人难以接受。

　　年仅十三四岁的孩子被选进将要决定他们前途的应试班学习。尔后，就在他们中间的大部分人处于一生中的学习接受能力最糟糕的时候，却被迫参加考试，而对考试失败者的惩罚如同死刑一般，使人永世不得翻身。

　　在我们这个国家，中学生的命运受到这些考试的摆布。虽然一些学校确实也开设了大批有趣的课程，然而这些课程只是为那些早被定为失败者的学生开设的。所以家长不停地采用强推、硬拉、威胁、强迫等手段将他们的孩子推上考场，或者急不可耐地寻找"高水准"的学校代为行使督战之责，因为这样做符合我们大学的要求。

　　但这样做有无必要呢？我们为什么要在人脑处于接受能力最低的生理发育阶段对我们的年幼者施加这种压力呢？而且我们也知道，如果孩子在 14 岁时选错了路子，那么他们的一生可能会毁掉。既然如此，我们为何要选择在他们一生中的这个时期试图造就他们或压垮他们呢？

　　如果孩子在 16 岁时所面临的选拔压力能予以免除的话，那么中学教育可能会完全改观。从 13 岁起，孩子可以自由选择是否学习，或者可以选择半日制的学习。他们可以完全按照自己的意愿，想学多久就学多久。如果他们想在美术课或戏剧课花上半天时间，他们自己可以自行决定这么做。

孩子们抱怨课程乏味、课本乏味、教师乏味。然而,他们的诉说声却几乎无人听见。当他们不得不写些东西时,他们只是迎合教师的口味,写一些教师想看的内容,这种情况已是司空见惯的了。

　　我深信,在强制性程度较低的制度下,孩子实际学到的东西会更多,他们通常能更好地同成人和领导合作。我敢肯定,他们会更加幸福,更富有创造力,因而对社会的作用也就更大。我们不应该花那么多的时间对十三四岁的孩子大加威胁,对他们说要是不整天学习、不每天学习的话,他们的结果只能是一辈子失败。

　　因此,女士们,先生们,我相信你们也会认为除了赞同今天的提议之外,已别无选择。现行的教育制度肯定对我们的孩子有害,所以必须予以改变。

　　谢谢各位。

7—2　广而"误"之
The Effects of Misleading Advertising

　　我在此发表演讲,谴责现代社会的一大弊病,那就是误导性广告的性别效应。

　　我们所有人在其一生中无时不受广告的影响。少年,尤其是少女,新近涉足消费市场,经验不足,是广告的主要对象,所以特别容易受到广告的侵袭。

　　广告商们充分意识到自己的作用,他们毫不迟疑地利用年轻人的不稳定性和渴求性,主动充当解难的智者。一支烟象征着独立,一条名牌牛仔裤或一双名牌旅游运动鞋给人以身份。恰当的香水或啤酒使人对女性气质或男性气概不再生疑。

　　没有哪一个政治家或教育家具有广告那么强的渗透力和说服力。广告教我们成为消费者,广告告诉我们"万般皆下品,惟有物质高",广告让我们感到幸福是可以花钱购买的,生活中的复杂问题都有手到病除的良方,产品可以使我们充实,可以满足我们人类最深层次的需求。一个人的价值,尤其是一个年轻女性的价值,取决于所用产品的价值。

　　对一名女子来说,标准美是她的惟一标志。她的皮肤应天生丽质,没有皱纹,没有疤痕,没有瑕疵。她的身材应该清瘦苗条,通常高挑个,双腿修长,其中青春年少则是首要条件。所有在电视广告中出现的"花容玉貌"般的倩女均都符合这个标准。这种形象是人为的,只可能人为地塑造。许多妇女极度渴求达到一个理想的而又无法达到的标准,她们尽其所能来摆布和修改自己的容貌体态。这个国家每小时花费在化妆品上的钱超过100万元。女子已习与性成地视自己的脸蛋为面具,视自己的身体为物品,是一种脱离了原型而又高于原型的东西。女子自身需要经常不断地予以修正、改良与伪装。无论她是否想获得那般"花容玉貌",都已被塑造为那种自我不满、自我惭愧的人。

具有讽刺意义的是,诸如化妆品和减肥饮料这些被广告大肆渲染的产品对人体的魅力甚至是有害的。媒体对营养、锻炼以及其他一些与健康和活力有关的重要因素则很少强调。

少女自然成长也不被看好。年纪增长是大忌。虽然男孩可以成为一名成熟的男子,并且还受到鼓励,但对女孩的要求却是妙龄永驻,唯唯诺诺,依附顺从,永不成熟。不知何故,对她们的要求总有两面性,既要求她们性感多情,又要求她们冰清玉洁,既要求她们老到练达,又要求她们少不更事,既要求她们风骚冶艳,又要求她们质朴无华。

在被误导性的广告所描绘的世界里,爱恋和激情全然为产品拥有,性成了商品,其中年轻女子则成了最大的牺牲者。

7—3 共创未来
The Future Is Ours to Build

女士们、先生们:

今天历史又在召唤。美中两国携手并进,已开始在我们的历史上为和平与进步谱写新的篇章。

我们必须始终现实地看待我们的关系,坦率地承认我们两个社会之间在意识形态和制度上的根本差异。是的,让我们承认这些差异,让我们永远不要轻视这些差异,但是我们不要被这些差异所压倒。我来中国不是为了评说那些将我们分隔开来的东西,而是为了强化那些将我们维系在一起的东西,不是为了回顾闭关锁国的过去,而是为了敦促我们两国人民展望前程似锦的未来。我坚信我们能够,而且也一定会,共同建设美好的未来。

我们可以生活在近乎世界的两端,我们可以有两种截然不同的语言、习俗和政治信仰,但是在我们这个时代的许多至关重要的问题上,我们两国人民之间几乎没有距离。

我的确相信,假若我们去问一下世界上的所有公民,他们最希望留下什么东西给他们孩子,给他们孩子的孩子,那么他们的回答无论是用英语、汉语还是其他语言来表达,都可能是一致的:我们要和平,我们要自由,我们要更美好的生活。他们这些言简意赅的愿望,代表着人类对安全以及满足个人意愿的最深切的要求。我们所要做的是去帮助他们实现自己的愿望。

我们一向认为,我们的历史传统是未来丰收的种子。我们一开始便从信仰和自由中汲取了巨大的力量。我们对自由的渴望导致了美国革命。我们明白,除非我们愿意同其他人一起分享自由,否则我们自己便无法享受自由。我们明白,除非我们大家都受到在其面前人人平等的法律的保护,否则我们的自由便不可能有真正的保障。

相信人民——这四个字不仅是美国历史的精髓,同时也是今日世界上人类进步的最强大的动力。

同中国人一样,我国人民看待未来也是着眼于下一代的利益。同中国人一样,我们也尊敬长辈。若要像前辈那样出色,我们就必须胜于前辈。

一个多世纪前,当时已卸任的美国前总统格兰特访问了贵国。他看到中国蕴藏着巨大的潜力。"我看到黎明的曙光,"格兰特写道,"我看到变革的端倪。变革一旦出现,中国将迅速成为一个强盛而富裕的国家……中国人民勤奋、节俭、聪颖、接受能力强。"

今天,中国经济突飞猛进,日新月异。与一些惧怕变革、惧怕未来的国家不同,中国开始迈向新的高度,为此我们向你们表现出这种勇气致敬。

我们美国人一向视自己为开拓者,所以我们赞赏你们的活力和乐观精神。今天,我给你们带来了我国同胞的口信:中国在这条新的道路上向前迈进,我们美国喜有机会同中国并肩前进。

我看到美国与其太平洋的邻国正在一项伟大事业中向前迈进,努力建设强大的经济和更为安全的世界。就我们而言,我们欢迎这股太平洋的新浪潮。让这股浪潮平顺地滚滚向前,促进人民和思想的双向交流,以打破猜忌和不信任这两大障碍,建立合作关系,树立共有的乐观精神。

未来靠我们去构筑。

7—4　继往开来
The New Beginning of an Old Story

尊敬的来宾们,同胞们,政权的和平移交虽在历史上实属罕见,但在我国却不足为奇。我们以简单的誓言肯定老传统,开创新未来。

我站在这里感到荣幸和谦卑,有许多美国领导人走在我的前面,还会有很多人相继而来。

在我们国家漫长的传奇历程中我们有自己的位置,我们所有人都有自己的位置,我们将继续延续这个历程,然而我们将看不到它的尽头。这是一个新世界继往开来的历程,一个由拥有奴隶的社会转变为崇尚自由的社会的历程,一个强国保护世界而非占有世界、捍卫世界而非征服世界的历程。

这就是美国的传奇历程,一个并非完美无缺的民族的传奇历程,一个世世代代被伟大而永恒理想团结在一起的民族的传奇历程。

这些理想中最伟大的理想是展现在世人面前的美国诺言,即人人都有位置,人人都有机会,无人微不足道。美国人有责任在生活和法律中实践这一诺言。虽然我们国家有时停滞不前,有时彷徨拖延,但是我们决不选择其他道路。

在许多国人获得成功的同时,也有一些人对我们国家的这个诺言,甚至对我们国家本身的公正,表示怀疑。衰退的学校教育、潜在的偏见以及出生的环境限制了一些美国人的进取抱负。有时候我们的分歧深得好似我们分属同一大陆上的不同国家。

我们不接受这种状况,我们不允许这种状况的存在。我们的团结,我们的联合,是每一代领导人和国民的严肃使命。

最理想的美国是一个尊重并期盼个人责任心的国家。鼓励承担责任不是寻找替罪羊,而是对良知的呼唤。尽管这样做需要付出代价,但能带来更深的成就感。生活的充实不仅在于做出选择,而且还在于承担义务。我们感到,致力于儿童和社会事业使我们获得了自由。

我们的公共利益依赖于个人品格,依赖于公民职责、家庭纽带及基本公平原则,依赖于将我们引向自由的无数的默默无闻的高尚行为。

生活中有时我们被召唤去从事伟业。但是,正如我们这个时代的一位圣人所说,我们每天都被召唤以极大的爱心去做琐碎小事。一个民主政体中的最重要的使命是靠大家来完成的。

你们的作为同政府的作为同样重要。我请求你们为大众谋利而不计较个人安逸,捍卫所需的改革而不被随意攻击,报效祖国从帮助邻居做起。我请求你们做公民而不做臣民,做富有责任性的公民,建设有奉献精神的社区、有高尚品格的国家。

美国人慷慨、坚强、正直,这不是因为我们自我笃信,而是因为我们的信念超越了自我。这种公民精神一旦失去,政府的任何规划都无法取而代之。这种精神只要存在,任何邪恶都无法与之较量。

今天我们再次重申这样的宗旨:我们将永不疲倦、永不屈服、永不停止地使我们的国家变得更公正、更慷慨,矢志维护我们的人生尊严,矢志维护我们每个人的人生尊严。

句子精练
Sentences in Focus

1. 我们以简单的誓言肯定老传统,开创新未来。
2. 我在此发表演讲,谴责现代社会的一大疾病,那就是误导性广告的性别效应。
3. 一个富有爱心与负责精神的社会应该为改善儿童的生活做一些重要的、有意义的事,而不是在年仅 12 岁的孩子身上增加沉重的学习和心理负担,迫使他们参加那种只许成功不可失败的考试,对考试失败者来说,他们所面对的只能是一种不可更改的死刑判决。
4. 我深信,孩子在强制性程度较低的教育制度下所学到的东西会更多,他们会更富有创造力,通常也能更好地同成人和领导合作。
5. 在当今世界,没有什么政治性的演说或学术性的讲座会具有像广告那么强的渗透力和说服力。
6. 少女是广告的主要对象,她们特别容易受到广告的侵袭。

7. 广告商们充分意识到自己的作用，他们毫不迟疑地利用年轻人的不稳定性和渴求性，扮演万能智者的角色。

8. 广告的一个不良后果是它传递了这样一种信息，即一个人的价值取决于所用产品的价值，广告让我们感到幸福是可以花钱买来的，让我们感到生活中的复杂问题都有手到病除的良方，让我们感到产品可以使我们充实，可以满足我们人类最深层的需求。

9. 所有在电视广告中出现的"倩"女均都符合这样一种标准：一名女子应该身材苗条，高挑个，双腿修长，她的皮肤应该天生丽质，没有皱纹，没有疤痕，没有瑕疵。

10. 广告效应使许多妇女极度渴求自己能达到一个理想的而又无法达到的标准，她们尽其所能来摆布和改变自己的容颜和体态，似乎容颜和体态可以与自身分割开来，并且比自身更为重要。

11. 具有讽刺意义的是，诸如化妆品和减肥饮料这类被广告大肆渲染的产品其实对人体的魅力是有害的。

12. 在被误导性的广告所描绘的世界里，爱恋和激情全然是产品的附庸，性别成了商品，其中年轻女子则成了最大的受害者。

13. 我们必须坦率地承认我们两个社会之间在意识形态和制度上的根本差异。

14. 我来中国不是为了评说那些将我们分隔开来的东西，而是为了强化那些将我们维系在一起的东西，不是为了回顾闭关锁国的过去，而是为了敦促我们去展望前程似锦的未来。

15. 我一向认为，我们的历史传统孕育着未来的丰收。

16. 今天，中国经济突飞猛进，日新月异。你们开始迈向新的高度，为此我们向你们表现的这种勇气致敬。

17. 让这股太平洋的浪潮平顺地滚滚向前，促进人民的双向交流，促进思想的双向交流，以打破猜忌和不信任这两大的障碍，建立合作关系，树立共有的乐观精神。

18. 生活的充实不仅存在于做出选择，而且还在于承担义务。

19. 我们的公共利益依赖于个人品格，依赖于公民职责、家庭纽带及基本公平原则，依赖于将我们引向自由的无数的默默无闻的高尚行为。

第8单元 说服性口译(汉译英)

UNIT 8 Interpreting Persuasive Speeches
Chinese-English Interpretation

8—1 第二文化
Acquiring a Second Culture

> **词汇预习**
> **Vocabulary Work**

生活方式	蕴蓄
含义	抽象
价值观	外族文化
信仰	开阔
思维方式	礼仪规范
日常活动	目标语
从广义上说	恰当得体
物质／精神文化	举止

> **课文口译**
> **Text for Interpretation**

Interpret the following passage from Chinese into English:

　　文化是指一个民族的整体生活方式。这一简单定义的含义使文化包括了这样一些内容,即一个民族的风俗、传统、社会习惯、价值观、信仰、语言、思维方式以及日常活动。文化还包含了文明史。从广义上说，有两种文化，即物质文化和精神文化。物质文化是具体的、可见的，而精神文化则比较蕴蓄、比较抽象。

由于人类语言是文化的直接表现，所以第二语言的学习涉及了第二文化的学习。第二语言教师应该引导学生注意并了解他们所学语言的文化内容。包括理解外族文化的价值观，掌握外族文化的礼仪，了解外族文化与本族文化之间的差异。

随着学生外语学习的深化，他们会增进对所学语言民族的文化特征的认识。这种开阔了的文化认识可以涉及文化的所有方面：外族人的生活方式，以及外族社会的地理、历史、经济、艺术和科学等。我们知道，每个民族的文化有不同于其他民族文化的礼仪规范。因此，学生在上外语课时应该学习操目标语的民族那些恰当得体的礼仪规范，学习如何理解陌生的文化习俗，学习在与外族人交际时应有的言谈举止。

8—2　环境保护
Environmental Protection

保护环境	综合整治
双重任务	大规模
从国情出发	国土控管
基本国策	宣传环保知识
经济持续发展	植被
污染防治	退耕还林
生态环境	退耕还草
协调	封山绿化
行之有效的	道德
履行国际义务	行为准则

任重而道远　　　　　　　　　　　一如既往

Interpret the following passage from Chinese into English：

女士们、先生们：

中国作为一个发展中国家，面临着发展经济与保护环境的双重任务。从国情出发，中国在全面推进现代化的过程中，将环境保护视为一项基本国策，将实现经济持续发展视为一项重要战略，同时在全国范围内开展污染防治工作和生态环境保护活动。

自改革开放以来，中国国民生产总值的年均增长率为 10% 左右，同时环境恶化的状况已基本得到了控制，在许多地区还得到了改善。实践证明，我们协调经济发展与环境保护两者之间关系的做法是行之有效的。

中国作为国际社会中的成员，在努力保护自己环境的同时，还积极参与国际环保事务，促进国际环保合作，并认真履行了国际义务。所有这些都充分表明了中国政府和人们保护全球环境的诚意和决心。

中国为保护自己的环境作了哪些努力呢？中国环境保护的形势又如何呢？概括说来，我们做了以下几件事：

　　—— 选择持续发展的实施战略；

　　—— 逐步改进法律和行政制度；

　　—— 预防与控制工业污染，综合整治城市环境；

　　—— 大规模地进行国土控管和农村环保；

　　—— 保护生态环境，保护植被，退耕还林，退耕还草，封山绿化；

　　—— 加速环境科技的开发；

　　—— 在人民中宣传环保知识，提高人们对环保道德与行为准则的认识；

　　—— 采取强有力的措施促进环保工作的国际合作。

女士们，先生们，人类在解决环境与发展问题中仍面临着大量的难题，任重而道远。中国将一如既往，与其他国家合作，为保护我们的生存环境,为人类的幸福和繁荣,为造福下一代而奋斗。

　　谢谢。

8—3　迎接挑战
Meeting the Challenge

词汇预习
Vocabulary Work

调整	拜金主义
转轨	公益事业
计划 / 市场经济体制	传统美德
人口老龄化	受到冲击
保健 / 退休 / 福利制度	都市化
产业结构调整	出路
就业	孕育
服务性行业	世界经济一体化

课文口译
Text for Interpretation

Interpret the following passage from Chinese into English：

　　这个世界每天都在变化。世界正在不断地调整自己。变化是当今最流行的字眼。我们正处在一个从工业化社会向服务和信息社会的转轨过程之中。

　　同样,中国也在发生变化,也在调整自己。中国正处在建立和完善社会主义市场经济体制的改革进程中。中国社会正在改革中变化,在变化中进行改革。中国社会的变化,使许多问题得到解决,同时也产生了一些新的问题。其中有四个问题对人民的现在甚至未来的影响作用最大。

1. 人口老龄化。老人和高龄老人的数量在增加,儿童的比例——尤其是在城市中——在减少。这将影响我国的经济发展,威胁我国保健制度、退休制度以及其他一些福利制度的健康发展。

2. 就业问题。不断推进的产业结构调整限制了就业。服务性行业的增多,对高技术劳动力需求的不断增长,国际国内日益激烈的竞争压力,农村人口大量流入城市,这些对现阶段以及未来的就业,对全面提高生活水平的可能性,都构成了严重的威胁。

3. 对家庭和儿童构成的威胁。我国离婚率相对增长,整整一代青年人在独生子女家庭的环境中成长,人们频繁的职业和居住地的变动等等,这些都给家庭和儿童造成了威胁。

4. 对传统社会价值观的挑战。中国社会中的拜金主义,对自我的日益关注以及对公益事业的淡漠使中国的许多传统美德受到冲击。

这些问题的存在值得我们每个人重视,因为它们会影响到我们每个人的生活质量。这些问题渊源于经济和社会条件的变化,它们是全国性、甚至是世界性的问题。这些问题伴随着都市化和现代化的进程而产生。我们无法回避这些问题,惟一的出路在于学会如何处理它们。

然而,不断变化着的社会不仅给我们带来了问题,也给我们带来了机会。变化可以被认为是不断产生的挑战和危机,而挑战在我们看来则是建设更好社会的机遇。汉语中"危机"这个词由两个字组成——"危"和"机"。因此,"危机"也孕育着机会。中国的社会变更给社会带来了许多问题,同时也给人们带来了更多的机遇。在世界经济日趋一体化的今天,让我们迎接挑战,拥抱机遇,承担责任,共同建设更美好的明天。

8—4　习武健身
Practicing Martial Art for Your Health

词汇预习
Vocabulary Work

武术宫　　　　　　　　　　健身

减肥   杂技
填写登记表   顶尖 / 身怀绝技 / 无懈可击的
会员卡   武林高手
古代格斗术   优秀教头
习武   价格从优
中国武术协会   货物齐全
扣人心弦的表演   激光视盘

课文口译
Text for Interpretation

Interpret the following passage from Chinese into English：

欢迎各位来北京武术宫习武健身。我可不想劝说任何人，也不打算说服任何人，因为健身是每个人自己的事，是为将来作投资。

当然啰，如果您在寻找可以健身、减肥、结交朋友以及了解中国文化的场所，您找对了地方。您只需在这里填写一张登记表，再拿一张会员卡即可。这些事只需几分钟即可办完。

您在这里可以欣赏古代格斗术，您也可以在这里习武。由中国武术协会创立的武术宫为您准备了精彩的、扣人心弦的表演节目——您除了可以观赏武术家的表演外，还可以观赏京剧节目和杂技表演。

倘若您想有一种身入其境的体验，中国武术协会将随时派出最好的教学人员，我们这里有中国顶尖的武林高手、身怀绝技的优秀教头和无懈可击的武术表演家。

无论您身居何处，您若想在自家门前学习武术，中国武术协会都可派出一流教员，指导个人或团体皆可。

如果您在市场上寻购武器器具或资料、中国武术协会也为您准备好了一切，价格从优。我们还有货物齐全的书店，出售您感兴趣的一切有关中华武术的图书资料、录像带和 DVD 激光视盘。

女士们，先生们，这里是您的理想之地，我们愿为您效劳。

句子精练
Sentences in Focus

Interpret the following sentences from Chinese into English：

1. 文化是指一个民族的整个生活方式，即一个民族的风俗、传统、社会习惯、价值观、信仰、语言、思维方式以及日常活动。

2. 每个民族的文化有不同于其他民族文化的礼仪规范。

3. 由于人类语言是文化的直接表现，所以可以说，第二语言学习涉及对所学语言的民族文化特征的认识和理解。

4. 中国作为一个发展中国家，面临着发展经济与保护环境的双重任务。

5. 中国在全面推进现代化的过程中，不仅将实现经济持续发展视为一项重要战略，同时也将生态环境的保护视为一项基本国策。

6. 中国作为国际社会中的一员，认真履行国际义务，积极参与国际环保事务，促进国际环保合作。

7. 我们必须在人民中宣传环保知识，提高人们对环保道德与行为准则的认识。

8. 我们在解决环境与发展问题中仍面临着大量的难题，任重而道远。

9. 中国将一如既往，与其他国家合作，为保护我们的生存环境，为人类的幸福和繁荣，为造福下一代而奋斗。

10. 我们正处在一个由工业化社会向服务与信息社会转轨的过程中。

11. 中国正处在一个摆脱僵硬的计划经济体制，建立和完善社会主义市场经济体制的改革进程中。

12. 人口老龄化将影响我国的经济发展，威胁我国的保健制度、退休制度以及其他一些福利制度的健康发展。

13. 不断推进的产业结构调整使服务性行业增多，使高科技以及熟练劳动力的需求增长。

14. 拜金主义、对自我的日益关注以及对公益事业的淡漠使中国许多传统美德受到冲击。

15. 这些问题渊源于经济和社会条件的变化，是都市化和现代化所带来的问题。

16. 不断变化着的社会不仅给我们带来了问题,也给我们带来了机会。

17. 在世界经济日趋一体化的今天,让我们迎接挑战,拥抱机遇,承担责任,共同建设更美好的未来。

18. 您在这里可以欣赏精彩的、扣人心弦的武术表演,也可以观赏京剧节目和杂技表演。

19. 我不想说服任何人去习武健身,因为这是个人的事,是人们为将来所做的投资。

参考译文
Reference Version

8-1 第二文化
Acquiring a Second Culture

Culture means the total way of life of a people. This simple definition implies that culture refers to the customs, traditions, social habits, values, beliefs, language, ways of thinking and daily activities of a people. It also includes the history of civilization. In the broad sense, there are two types of culture, that is, material culture and spiritual culture. Material culture is concrete and observable, while spiritual culture implicit and abstract.

Because human language is a direct manifestation of culture, learning a second language involves learning a second culture. For the teacher of a second language, he or she should make sure to develop the students' awareness and knowledge of the culture of the target language they are learning. This includes understanding the values of the target culture, acquiring a command of the etiquette of the target culture and understanding the differences between the target culture and the students' own culture.

As students progress through a foreign language program, it is expected that they will increase their awareness of the cultural characteristics of the speakers of the language under study. This broadened cultural knowledge may touch on all aspects of culture: the people's way of life as well as the geographic, historical, economic, artistic, and scientific aspects of the target society. We know that each culture has different etiquette patterns. And therefore, in a foreign language course, students should learn the appropriate etiquette patterns expected of the people living in the country where the target language is spoken. Students should also learn how to interpret unfamiliar cultural conventions and how to act appropriately when communicating with the persons of the foreign culture.

8—2 环境保护
Environmental Protection

Ladies and gentlemen,

As a developing country, China is confronted with the dual task of developing the economy and protecting the environment. Proceeding from its national conditions, China has, in the process of promoting its overall modernization program, made environmental protection one of its basic national policies, regarded the realization of sustained economic development as an important strategy and meanwhile, carried out throughout the country campaigns for pollution prevention and treatment as well as ecological environmental protection.

Over the years since its adoption of reform and opening policy, China's gross national product has achieved a sustained average annual growth of around 10 percent, while its environment has basically ceased from deteriorating, and proved in many areas. The end-results of our work have shown that China's endeavor in striking a balance between economic development and environmental protection has been effective.

As a member of the international community, China, while making great efforts to protect its own environment, has taken an active part in international environmental protection affairs to promote international cooperation in environmental protection, and earnestly fulfilled her international obligations. All these have given full expression to the sincerity and determination of the Chinese government and people to protect the global environment.

What efforts has China made to protect its own environment? What is the situation of environmental protection in China? Briefly, here is what we have been doing to protect our environment:

— Choosing a sustainable development strategy for implementation;

— Improving the legal and administrative systems step by step;

— Preventing and controlling industrial pollution and comprehensively working on the improvement of the urban environment;

— Carrying out territorial control and rural environmental protection on a large scale;

— Protecting ecological environment, protecting vegetation, returning cultivated land to forests or pastures, and closing off hillsides to facilitate afforestation;

— Accelerating the development of environmental science and technology;

— Popularizing environmental protection knowledge among the people and raising their awareness of environmental ethics and code of conduct; and finally

— Taking vigorous action to promote international cooperation in environmental protection.

Ladies and gentlemen, mankind still faces a great many difficulties in solving the problems of the environment and development, and there is a grand task to perform and a long way to go. China will, as it did in the past, cooperate with other countries of the world and strive for the protection of the environment for human survival, for the happiness and prosperity of humanity, and for the benefits of our children.

Thank you.

This world changes everyday. This world is in constant readjustment of itself. Change is the most popular word today. We are in the process of changing from the industrial society to a service and information society.

Likewise, China is changing and readjusting itself. China is in the process of reforming itself, establishing and improving a socialist market economy. The Chinese society is changing in the process of reforming and reforming in the process of change. During this process, many problems have been resolved and meanwhile new problems have surfaced, among which the following four problems, in particular, are exerting the heaviest impact on China today and possibly on China tomorrow.

1. The aging of the population. The population of the old and very old citizens is climbing, while the proportion of children — particularly urban children — in the whole Chinese population is declining. This will obstruct the development of our national economy, and threaten the sound development of our health care system, retirement system and other benefits systems.

2. Threatened employment. The continuous industrial restructuring places a stricter requirement on the entry into new jobs as well as on employees' vocational qualifications. The growth of the service sector, the increasing demand for skilled workers, the pressure resulting from the intensifying competition at home and abroad, the problems resulting from the rural population migrating into cities, all pose a grave threat to the employment prospects at present and in the future, as well as to an overall improvement of the lives of the peo-

ple.

3. Problems threatening families and children. The relative growth of divorce rate, a whole generation of youngsters growing up with the one-child-family background, people's frequent changes of their jobs and residence, etc. , all these combine to pose problems for families and children.

4. Challenges to traditional social values. The phenomenon of money worship and obsession in our society, a growing concern with self interests and neglect of public welfare exert negative impact on people's attitude towards many Chinese traditional virtues.

These problems merit the immediate attention and concern of every one, because they will affect the life of each of us. Arising from the changed economic and social conditions, these problems have nationwide and even world-wide consequences. During the process of urbanization and modernization, these problems are inevitable and there's no way for us to avoid any contact with them. The only way out of the worsening situation is for us to learn to deal with them.

On the other hand, the perpetually changing society brings us not just problems, but opportunities as well. Change can be viewed as something that constantly generates challenge and crises, and challenge, in our view, is the opportunity to build a better society. The word of crisis in Chinese is one with two characters, *wei* and *ji*, meaning respectively danger and opportunity. Thus, *weiji* entails opportunities. Social changes in China create problems for the society and meanwhile more opportunities for the people. In the economic globalization today, let us meet challenges, embrace opportunities, shoulder responsibilities and work together to make tomorrow a better day.

8—4 习武健身
Practicing Martial Art for Your Health

Welcome to the Beijing Martial Art Palace to practice martial art for body-building. But I have no intention of persuading anyone, and am not prepared to convince anyone, either. You know, exercising for your health and fitness is a matter of personal choice; it's an investment for one's future.

Of course, if you're looking for a place where you can build up your body, reduce your weight, make new friends and learn about Chinese culture, this is the very place for you. All you need to do is fill out a form and get a membership card. It takes only a few minutes.

Here you enjoy and learn this ancient form of combat. The Palace, a creation of the Chinese Martial Art Association, puts on fabulous performances to thrill the visitor — not only martial artists in action but also Peking Opera and acrobatics shows.

If you want to get in on the action yourself, the Chinese Martial Art Association has the best teaching team available any time upon request: nothing less than the best professional martial artists, excellent coaches with unique skills and perfect martial art performers in China, gathering under one roof.

If you prefer to learn the art on your own home turf, the Chinese Martial Art Association will send its first-class coaches to train you or your group, no matter where you live.

If you are in the market looking for martial art equipment or literature, the Chinese Martial Art Association is well supplied with all that you need, at excellent prices. We also have a well-stocked bookstore selling printed information, videotapes and DVD disks on everything you are interested in knowing about Chinese martial art.

Ladies and gentlemen, this is the place for you, and we are here for you.

1. Culture refers to the total way of life of a people, that is, the customs, traditions, social habits, values, beliefs, language, ways of thinking and daily activities of a people.

2. The culture of a nation has a set of etiquette patterns that distinguishes it from those of other cultures.

3. Because human language is a direct manifestation of culture, we may very well say that learning a second language involves the recognition and understanding of the characteristics of the national culture of the target language community.

4. As a developing country, China is confronted with the dual task of developing its economy and protecting its environment.

5. In the process of promoting its overall modernization program, China has not only regarded the realization of sustained economic development as an important strategy but also made environmental protection one of its basic national policies.

6. As a member of the international community, China has earnestly fulfilled its international obligations, and taken an active part in the affairs of international environmental protection, and promote international cooperation in environmental protection.

7. We must popularize knowledge about environmental protection among the people and raise their awareness of environmental ethics and the code of conduct.

8. We still face a great many difficulties in solving the problems of the environment and development—a grand task to perform and a long way to go.

9. China will, as it always did, cooperate with other countries of the world and strive for the protection of the environment for human survival, for the happiness and prosperity of humanity, and for the benefits of our children.

10. We are in the process of transforming from an industrial society to a service and information society.
11. China is in the process of an economic reform, freeing itself from the rigid planned economy and at the same time establishing and improving a socialist market economy.
12. The aging of the population will obstruct the development of our national economy, and threaten the sound development of our health care system, retirement system and other welfare and benefits systems.
13. The continuous industrial restructuring increases the number of service trades and intensifies the demand for high technology and skilled workers.
14. The phenomenon of money worship and obsession, a growing concern with self-interests, and neglect of public welfare exert negative impact on people's attitude towards many Chinese traditional virtues.
15. Arising from the changed economic and social conditions, these problems are inevitable in the process of urbanization and modernization.
16. The perpetually changing society brings us not only problems, but also opportunities.
17. In the economic globalization today, let us meet challenges, embrace opportunities, shoulder responsibilities, and work together to make tomorrow a better day.
18. Here you will not only enjoy fabulous and exciting performances by martial artists, but also Peking Opera and acrobatics shows.
19. I have no intention of persuading anyone, nor am I prepared to convince anyone, either, for practicing martial art for your health and fitness is a matter of personal choice, and an investment for one's future.

第 9 单元　学术性口译(英译汉)

Unit 9　Interpreting Academic Speeches English-Chinese Interpretation

9—1　语言系统
The Linguistic System

词汇预习
Vocabulary Work

mutually unintelligible

in broad outlines

approach (a problem)

be intimately familiar with

a finite set of rules

an infinite set of sentences

comprise

acquire (a language)

related in an arbitrary fashion

linguistic knowledge
　/ competence

linguistic behavior / performance

unique

species

creative aspect

well-formed (sentence)

generate

课文口译
Text for Interpretation

Interpret the following passage from English into Chinese:

There are as many as three thousand languages which are spoken today. These languages are very different one from another. Indeed, it is primarily the fact that they are so different as to be mutually unintelligible that allows us to call them separate languages. A speaker of one of them, no matter how skillful and fluent, cannot communicate with a speaker of another unless one of them, as we say, "learns the other's language." Yet these differences, great as they are, are differences of detail — of the kinds of sounds used and the ways of putting them together. In their broad outlines, in their basic principles, and even in the way they approach certain specific problems of communication, languages have a great deal in common.

We are all intimately familiar with at least one language, yet few of us ever stop to consider what we know about it. The words of a language can be listed in a dictionary, but not all the sentences, and a language consists of these sentences as well as words.

Speakers use a finite set of rules to produce and understand an infinite set of sentences. These rules comprise the grammar of a language, which is learned when you acquire the language. The grammar of a language includes the sound system, how words may be combined into phrases and sentences, and the way in which sounds and meanings are related.

The sounds and meaning of words are related in an arbitrary fashion. That is, if you had never heard the word "grammar", you would not, by its sounds, know what it meant. Language, then, is a system that relates sounds with meanings, and when you know a language, you know this system.

This linguistic knowledge, or linguistic competence, is different from linguistic behavior, known as linguistic performance. If you woke up one morning and decided to stop talking, you would still have the knowledge of your language. If you do not know the language, you cannot speak it; but if you know the language, you may choose not to speak.

Language is a tool of communication. But if language is defined merely as a system of communication, then language is not unique to humans. We know birds, bees, crabs, spiders, whales, and most other creatures communicate in some way. However, there are certain characteristics of human language not found in the communication systems of any other species. A basic property of human language is its creative aspect — a speaker's ability to combine the basic linguistic units to form an infinite set of "well-formed", or grammatical, sentences, most of which are novel, never before produced or heard. The grammar of human language can generate infinite messages, a property unique to the human species.

9—2　人机之争
Two Kinds of Brain

词汇预习
Vocabulary Work

complexity	straightforward
mammalian	programmed to do something
neurons	gene
cell	potentialities
interconnect	in terms of
in a vastly complicated network	equivalent
intricacy	duplicate
rather than	a point of concern
on-off device	rival

Interpret the following passage from English into Chinese:

Good afternoon, ladies and gentlemen, I would like to thank you for inviting me to talk about the subject of the difference between a brain and a computer.

The difference between a brain and a computer can be expressed in a single word: complexity.

The large mammalian brain is the most complicated thing, for its size, known to us. The human brain weighs three pounds, but in that three pounds are ten billion neurons and a hundred billion smaller cells. These many billions of cells are interconnected in a vastly complicated network that we can't begin to interpret as yet.

Even the most complicated computer man has yet built can't compare in intricacy with the brain. Computer switches and components number in the thousands rather than in the billions. What's more, the computer switch is just an on-off device, whereas the brain cell is itself possessed of a tremendously complex inner structure.

Can a computer think? That depends on what you mean by "think." If solving a mathematical problem is "thinking," then a computer can "think" and do so much faster than a man. Of course, most mathematical problems can be solved quite mechanically by repeating certain straightforward processes over and over again.

It is frequently said that computers solve problems only because they are "programmed" to do so. They can only do what men have them do. One must remember that human beings also can only do what they are "programmed" to do. Our genes "program" us and our potentialities are limited by that "program."

Our "program" is so much more enormously complex, though, that we might like to define "thinking" in terms of our creativity in literature, art, science and technology. In that sense, computers certainly can't think. Surely, though, if a computer can be made complex enough, it can be as creative as we. If it could be made as complex as a human brain, it could be the equivalent of a human brain and do whatever a human brain can do.

But how long will it take to build a computer complex enough to duplicate the human brain? Perhaps not as long as some think. Long before we approach a computer as complex as our brain, we will perhaps build a computer that is at least complex enough to design another computer more complex than itself. This more complex computer could design one still more complex. The point of concern is that mankind is not only creating a servant, but also a threatening rival.

9—3 生物革命
The Biological Revolution

词汇预习
Vocabulary Work

biotechnological

hatch

womb

implanted electrodes

artificial hormones

envision

just over the horizon

new breakthrough

genome

portend

scenario

vivacious

introspective

extrovert

stem cell

regenerate

Alzheimer's disease

embryo

physical endurance

unequivocally

abiding   neurological
a period of debility   mental deterioration
dementia   in a vegetative state

Interpret the following passage from English into Chinese:

Respected Mr. President,

Dear faculty and students,

Thank you for inviting me to talk about the emerging biological revolution.

In his book *Brave New World*, published in 1932, Aldous Huxley predicted a big biotechnological revolution about to take place: the hatching of people not in wombs but in test tube; the drug which gave people instant happiness; the sensation which was simulated by implanted electrodes; and modification of behavior through the administration of various artificial hormones. With 70 years separating us from the publication of this book, we can see that Huxley's technological predictions are startlingly accurate. Many of the technologies that Huxley envisioned are already here or just over the horizon. But this revolution has only just begun. New breakthroughs in biomedical technology are announced daily; achievements such as the completion of the human genome project portend much more serious changes to come.

According to Huxley, the most significant threat posed by contemporary biotechnology is the possibility that it will alter human nature and thereby move us into a "posthuman" stage of history. This is important because human nature exists and defines us as a species with a stable continuity. It is what defines our most basic values. Medical technology offers us in many cases a devil's bargain:

longer life, but with reduced mental capacity; freedom from depression, together with freedom from creativity or spirit. It will blur the line between what we achieve on our own and what we achieve because of the levels of various chemicals in our brains.

Consider the following three scenarios, all of which are distinct possibilities that may unfold over the next generation or two.

The first has to do with new drugs. We know human personality is plastic. Psychotropic drugs can affect traits like self-esteem and the ability to concentrate. Stolid people can become vivacious; introspective ones extroverts; you can adopt one personality on Wednesday and another for the weekend.

In the second scenario, advances in stem cell research allow scientists to regenerate virtually any tissue in the body, so that life expectancies are pushed well above 100 years. If you need a new heart or liver, you just grow one inside the chest cavity of a pig or cow; brain damage from Alzheimer's and stroke can be reversed. The only problem is that there are many subtle aspects of human aging that the biotech industry hasn't quite figured out how to fix: people grow mentally rigid and increasingly fixed in their views as they age. Worst of all, they just refuse to get out of the way, not just of their children, but their grandchildren and great-grandchildren.

In a third scenario, people will screen embryos before implantation so as to optimize the kind of children they have. If someone doesn't live up to social expectations, he tends to blame bad genetic choices by his parents rather than himself. Human genes have been transferred to animals and even to plants to produce new medical products; and animal genes have been added to certain embryos to increase their physical endurance or resistance to disease. These will have serious and unexpected consequences.

We don't have to await the arrival of human genetic engineering to foresee a time when we will be able to enhance intelligence, memory, emotional sensitivity, and sexuality, as well as reduce aggressiveness and manipulate behavior in a host of other ways.

The medical profession is dedicated to the proposition that anything that can defeat disease and prolong life is unequivocally a good thing. The fear of death is one of the deepest and most abiding human passions, so it is understandable that we should celebrate any advance in medical technology that appears to put death off. But people worry about the quality of their lives as well — not just the quantity. Ideally, one would like not merely to live longer but also to have one's different faculties fail as close as possible to when death finally comes, so that one does not have to pass through a period of debility at the end of life.

While many medical advances have increased the quality of life for older people, many have had the opposite effect by prolonging only one aspect of life and increasing dependency. Alzheimer's disease — in which certain parts of the brain waste away, leading to loss of memory and eventually dementia — is a good example of this, because the likelihood of getting it rises proportionately with age. At age 65, only one person in a hundred is likely to come down with Alzheimer's; at 85, it is one in six. The rapid growth in the population suffering from Alzheimer's in developed countries is thus a direct result of increased life expectancies, which have prolonged the health of the body without prolonging resistance to this terrible neurological disease.

We could find ways to preserve bodily health but would fail to put off age-related mental deterioration. Stem cell research might yield ways to grow new body parts. But without a parallel curer for Alzheimer's, this wonderful new technology would do no more than allow more people to persist in vegetative states for years longer than is currently possible.

The consequences of medical advances might be the world in which people routinely live to be 120, or even up to 150, but the last decades of life in a state of childlike dependence on caretakers.

We're still trying to make sense of what is happening.

Thank you again for my privilege of speaking at this famous university.

9—4 信息时代
The Information Age

词汇预习
Vocabulary Work

commodity	profit margin
imperative	dealer
implication	corporate
foreign exchange rate	market player
stock market	transact
have the edge on	key factor
competitor	influential
boom	electronic dealing
coverage of breaking news	broking
proprietary knowledge	attendance

课文口译
Text for Interpretation

Interpret the following passage from English into Chinese:

My topic today is "Information — A Valuable Commodity".

Let us take a look at the most important commodity in the world — information. The advancement of communication technology has given us the ability to know and understand what is going on in any part of the world at any given time. It has become imperative for us to understand the implications of economic and political change and the impact that this has on foreign exchange rates and the stock market. Financial institutions have put great emphasis on developing technology that will enable us to have the edge on our competitors in terms of analyzing the global information and distributing this to our customer base.

The growth in the number of independent news companies combined with improved telecommunication has led to a boom in the level of coverage of breaking news and a drop in the cost of obtaining that information. Thus, the proprietary knowledge that was previously possessed by dealers is now generally available to non-bank financial institutions and corporations. This change immediately has led to a narrowing in the profit margin being made from customer business and greater competition among dealers for that business.

Customers have been marketed more intensely by an increasing number of financial institutions. The corporate customer now receives more information analysis and opinion from such a wide range of market players that they themselves have more information available to them than some of the lesser financial institutions. The general response of customers to this huge flow of information led to an increase in the level of business transacted as they seek to take advantage of market opportunities.

The dramatic increase in information flow has been a key influential factor in the financial market over the last 20 years.

My next lecture will focus on electronic dealing and broking, and their impact on the marketplace. Your attendance is most welcome.

句子精练
Sentences in Focus

Interpret the following sentences from English into Chinese:

1. Although the languages of various regions are so different that they are mutually unintelligible, they have a great deal in common in their basic principles, and in the way they approach certain specific problems of communication.

2. One of the wonders about language and language use is that with a finite set of rules speakers can produce and understand an infinite set of sentences.

3. The creative aspect of human language is not found in the communication system of any other species. That is, human beings have the ability to combine basic linguistic units to form an infinite set of grammatical sentences, most of which are novel, never before produced or heard.

4. The difference between a human brain and a computer can be expressed in a single word: complexity.

5. The many billions of brain cells are interconnected in a vastly complicated network that we can't begin to interpret as yet.

6. While the computer switch is just an on-off device, the brain cell is itself possessed of a tremendously complex inner structure.

7. Our gene "program" is so much more enormously complex that we might like to define "thinking" in terms of our creativity in literature, art, science and technology.

8. The point of concern is that while programming the computer, mankind is not only creating a servant, but also a threatening rival.

9. What I want to focus on is the principles that underlie computer programming.

10. New breakthroughs in biomedical technology are announced

daily; achievements such as the completion of the human genome project portend much more serious changes to come.

11. We don't have to await the arrival of human genetic engineering to foresee a time when we will be able to enhance intelligence, memory, emotional sensitivity, as well as manipulate behavior in a host of other ways.

12. While many medical advances have increased the quality of life for older people, many have had the opposite effect by prolonging only one aspect of life and increasing dependency.

13. We could find ways to preserve bodily health but would fail to put off age-related mental deterioration.

14. Stem cell research might yield ways to grow new body parts, but without a parallel curer for Alzheimer's, this wonderful new technology would do no more than allow more people to persist in vegetative states for years longer than is currently possible.

15. I should thank you for the privilege of speaking here and for ensuring me such an attentive audience.

16. The advancement of telecommunication technology has given us the ability to know and understand what is going on in any part of the world at any given time.

17. It has become imperative for us to understand the implications of economic and political change and the impact that this has on the market of stocks, securities and futures.

18. The dramatic increase in information flow has been a major influential factor in the financial market over the last decade.

参考译文
Reference Version

> ### 9—1　语言系统
> ### The Linguistic System

今天人们所说的语言达三千种之多。这些语言之间有很大的差异。实际上,正因为这些语言互不相通,我们才将它们叫做独立的语言。操其中一门语言者,无论其熟练程度和流利程度有多高,都无法同操另一门语言者交谈,除非他们中间有一人如同我们所说的那样"学会了另一人所说的语言"。语言之间虽然有着这些巨大的差异,却也是一些细微、具体的差异,如语音类别以及语音组合方式的差异。从语言的概貌、基本原则,甚至对一些具体的交际问题的处理方法上看,语言有着诸多的共同点。

虽然我们人人至少通晓一门语言,但很少有人会静心思考一下自己对所操语言的语言知识又了解了多少呢。语言的词汇可以在词典中列出,但并非所有句子都能为词典所收入,而语言是由词和句子构成的。

说话者可以运用一组数量有限的规则来表达与理解数量无限的句子。这些规则组成了语言的语法体系,你在习得语言的同时学到了语法。语法包括音系、组词成短语或句子的规则以及语音与语义之间联系的规则。

词音与词义的联系是任意划定的。这就是说,倘若你从未听到过"语法"这个词,你便无法单从这个词的发音上知晓它的词义。因此,语言是一种将语音与语义联系在一起的体系。当你会讲某种语言时,你便有了这个体系的知识。

这种语言知识(或者叫做语言能力),有别于语言行为(或者叫做语言操作)。某天早晨你醒来后决定不说话,你仍然具有你所操语言的知识。如果你没有这种语言知识,你便不会说这门语言。但是如果你有这种语言知识,你却可以选择不说这门语言。

语言是交际的工具。但是如果语言的定义仅仅是一种交际系统，那么语言便不是人类的专有品。我们知道大部分生物如鸟、蜜蜂、蟹、蜘蛛、鲸等，都有某种交际方式。然而，人类语言的某些特征却为任何其他物种的交际系统所缺乏。人类语言的一个基本属性是创造性，即说话者的语言创造能力，也就是说，说话者能够将语言的基本单位组合起来，生成无限多的符合语法规范的句子，而大部分生成的句子却是说话者自己从未说过或从未听到过的新句子。人类语言的语法系统可以生成无限多的信息，这就是人类所特有的物种属性。

9－2　人机之争
Two Kinds of Brain

下午好，女士们，先生们，我感谢你们邀请我来谈一下大脑与电脑的区别问题。

大脑与电脑的差别可以用三个字来表明，即"复杂性"。

哺乳动物硕大的脑子就其体积而言是我们所知道的最为复杂的东西。人脑的重量为 3 磅，而这 3 磅却包含着 100 亿个神经元以及 1,000 亿个更小的细胞。千百亿个大脑细胞互为串联，形成了一张我们还无法开始解释的极为复杂的网络。

就复杂性来说，世界上已生产出的最为复杂的电脑也无法与大脑的复杂性相提并论。电脑的开关和元件其数量只有数千个，而不是数千亿个。此外，电脑的开关只是一个离合装置，而大脑细胞却有着极其复杂的内部结构。

那么电脑能否思考？这取决于你所说的"思考"指的是什么？如果解决数学问题属于"思考"，那么电脑可以思考，而且思考的速度远比人来得快。当然，大部分数学问题可以通过一遍又一遍地重复一些简易的操作过程，非常机械地予以解决。

我们经常听到人们说，电脑会处理问题是因为电脑设有能让其处理问题的程序，它们只能按人的指令行事。我们应该知道，人类也设有程序，人类也同样按照所编制的程序行事。我们的基因给我们编写了"程序"，我们的所作所为无不受到那个"程序"的限制。

我们大脑的"程序"复杂之极，我们或许可以从我们在文学、艺术、科学和技术上的创造力这个角度给"思维"下定义。从这个意义上说，电脑肯定无法思维。当然啰，如果电脑可以制作得具备足够的复杂性，它们也可以有同我们人类一样的创造性。假若电脑可以制作得同人脑一样复杂，电脑便可成为人脑的同类，可以做人脑所能做的一切。

那么制造出一台复杂的足以复制人脑的电脑还需多久？或许不会像一些人认为得那么久。远在我们动手制造一台同我们大脑一样复杂的电脑之前，我们也许会制造一台电脑，其复杂性大到足以使其设计出一台比自己更为复杂的电脑的程度。这台更为复杂的电脑还可以设计出另外一台复杂程度高于自己的电脑。问题在于人类不仅在制造仆人，同时也在制造威胁自己生存的竞争对手。

9—3 生物革命
The Biological Revolution

尊敬的校长先生，
各位老师和同学：

感谢你们邀请我来谈一下正在发生的生物革命。

奥尔德斯·赫胥黎在其 1932 年出版的《美妙的新世界》一书中预言了一场即将发生的生物技术大革命。赫胥黎预示，人类可以在试管里而不是在子宫里孕育，药物可以即刻给人以快感，植入体内的电极可以给人以刺激，输入不同的人造荷尔蒙可以改变人的行为。此书问世70 年后，我们看到赫胥黎对技术发展的预言是如此之惊人的精确，所预言的许多技术已经诞生或即将诞生。但是这场革命还只是刚露面。在生物医学技术领域里，每天都有新的突破。人类基因组项目的完成预示了将要出现的更为重大的变革。

赫胥黎认为，当代生物技术对人类构成的最严重的威胁是有可能改变人性，从而把我们带入"后人类"的历史阶段。赫胥黎的预警很重要，因为人性确实存在，人性界定着我们这个具有稳定延续性的物种，同时又界定着我们最基本的价值观。医学技术在许多方面给我们提供了一种魔鬼的交易：我们虽然延长了寿命，但是脑力却减退了。我们虽可免患忧郁症，但是也失去了创造力和灵气。我们无法区分哪些成就是我们自身努力的结果，哪些成果是由我们大脑里化学物质的含量造就的。

我们不妨考虑一下以下三种未来一两代人可能会遇到的情形。

第一种情形与使用新药有关。我们知道,人的个性具有很强的可塑性。精神药物可以影响人们的自尊性和注意力这类特性。呆板的人可以变得活泼,内向的人可以变得外向,你甚至可以隔三差五变换自己的个性。

第二种情形与干细胞研究有关。干细胞研究的成果使科学家能够再生人体的几乎所有组织,从而把人的寿命延长到一百多岁。如果你需要一个新心脏或新肝脏,你只要在猪或牛的胸腔内培育一个即可。老年痴呆病或中风造成的脑损伤可以治愈。所存在的问题是,人类因衰老而产生的许多微妙问题,生物技术界还未能找到医治的良方,例如随着年龄的增长,人们的头脑日益僵化,思想日益顽固。最糟糕的是,他们对子女不愿松手,甚至还要管束孙辈和重孙辈的生活。

第三种情形涉及人们在胚胎移植前对胚胎的择优筛选。如果某个人有违社会的期望,这个人不会归咎自己,而会责怪父母未能选好良种。人类基因已被植入动物甚至植物以生产新的药物,动物基因也被植入某些人类胚胎以增强体力或抗病能力,这种转基因的做法都将产生严重的、难以预料的后果。

我们无须等待人类基因工程的降临便可预测到,未来某时我们将通过各种方法来提高自身的智力、记忆力、情绪敏感性和性功能,同时也可降低自己的进取性,控制自己的行为。

医学界决意坚持这样一种主张,即任何一种能够攻克疾病、延年益寿的东西无疑都是好东西。对死亡的恐惧是人类最深刻、最持久的情感之一,所以我们欢庆任何一种看来能延迟死亡的医学技术成果都是可以理解的。但是,人们所关心的不仅是生命的长短,而且还担心生活的质量。理想的状况是,人们不仅希望活得更长久,而且也希望自己的各种身心功能尽可能持续到生命的最后一刻,以免在人生的末年度过一段衰弱的时光。

虽然医学方面取得的很多成果提高了老年人的生活质量,但是,另外一些成果却产生了相反的作用,即在延长生命的某个方面的同时却也强化了依赖性。老年痴呆症就是一个很好的例子,患者大脑的某些部位的功能衰退导致记忆丧失,最终出现了痴呆,而老年痴呆症的患病几率正是随着年龄的增长而增长。在 65 岁的人群中,患病的几率可能只是 1‰,而在 85 岁人群中则上升为 6 比 1,即 6 人中就有一人可能患病。因此,在发达国家中导致老年痴呆症患者急剧增多的直接原因就是延年益寿,身体健康的时间延长了,但是抵抗这种可怕的神经疾病的能力却未随之增长。

我们可以找到保持身体健康的方法,但无法推迟与老龄有关的脑力衰退。干细胞研究可能会找到新器官的培育途径。但是,如果我们没有同时找到医治老年痴呆症的良方,这种奇妙的新技术无非只是让更多的人在植物状态下苟活更长的时间罢了。

医学进步带来的结果可能是,人类都可以活到 120 岁,甚至活到 150 岁,但在生命的最后几十年中只能像孩童那样依赖护理人员。

我们还在努力理解所发生的一切。

再次感谢你们给我如此殊荣来到这所名牌大学发表演讲。

9—4　信息时代
The Information Age

我今天的题目是"信息——贵重的商品"。

我们来看一下信息这个世界上最重要的商品。通讯技术的进步使我们能够了解并理解世界上任何一个地方、任何一个时间里所发生的事。理解经济和政治变化的含义以及这些变化对外汇兑换率和股票市场的影响对我们来说已是绝对必要的。金融机构注重发展技术,这使我们能够在分析全球性信息以及在我们的客户圈内传播这些信息方面战胜竞争对手。

独立新闻公司的大量增加,加之通讯手段的改善,使能导致行情下跌的新闻其传播覆盖程度大为提高,使获取这类信息的成本下降。因此,原属经纪人独家拥有的知识,今天那些非银行金融机构和公司企业通常都能得到。这种变化致使经纪人原本可从客户身上赚取的利润额为之下降,同时也加剧了经纪人之间的商战。

越来越多的金融机构争取客户的营销手段也越来越强化。现在公司客户可以从如此之多的市场竞争玩家那里得到更多的信息分析与见解资料,所以这些客户本身就拥有多于那些规模较小的金融机构所拥有的信息。由于客户希冀利用市场提供的机会,他们对这种信息巨大流动现象的普遍反应导致了成交量的提高。

信息流动量的剧增是过去 20 年中左右金融市场的一个重要因素。

我在下一期的讲座里将着重讨论电子交易与电子经纪及其对市场的影响,欢迎各位届时光临。

句子精练
Sentences in Focus

1. 虽然不同地区的语言因差异巨大而互不相通,然而从语言的基本原理以及对一些具体的交际问题的处理方法上看,它们却有着许多共同之处。

2. 语言与语言使用的奇妙处之一在于,说话者可以运用一组数量有限的规则来表达和理解数量无限的句子。

3. 人类语言的创造性为任何其他物种的交际系统所缺乏,也就是说,人类能够将语言的基本单位组合起来,生成无限多的符合语法规范的句子,而大部分生成的句子却是说话者自己从未说过或从未听到过的新句子。

4. 人脑与电脑的差别可以用三个字来表明,即"复杂性"。

5. 千百亿个大脑细胞相互串联在一起,形成了一张我们还无法开始解释的极为复杂的网络。

6. 电脑的开关仅仅是一个离合装置,而大脑细胞却有着极其复杂的内部结构。

7. 我们的基因"程序"更为复杂,所以我们或许可以从我们在文学、艺术、科学和技术上的创造力这个角度给"思维"下定义。

8. 问题在于人类在给电脑编制程序时不仅在制造仆人,同时也在制造威胁自己生存的竞争对手。

9. 我想着重谈一下电脑编程的指导原则问题。

10. 在生物医学技术领域里,每天都有新的突破,人类基因组项目的完成预示了将要出现的更为重大的变革。

11. 我们无须等待人类基因工程的降临便可预测到,未来某时我们将通过各种方法来提高自身的智力、记忆力、情绪敏感性,控制自己的行为。

12. 虽然医学方面取得的很多成果提高了老年人的生活质量,但是,另外一些成果却产生了相反的作用,即在延长生命的某个方面的同时强化了依赖性。

13. 我们可以找到保持身体健康的方法,但无法推迟与老龄有关的脑力衰退。

14. 干细胞研究可能会找到新器官的培育途径,但是如果我们没有同时找到医治老年痴呆症的良方,这种奇妙的新技术无非只是让更多的人在植物状态下苟活更长的时间罢了。

15. 感谢你们给我如此殊荣在此发表演讲,同时也感谢你们为我请来了如此专心致志的听众。

16. 电信技术的进步使我们能够了解并理解世界上任何一个地方在任何一个时间里所发生的事。

17. 理解经济和政治变化的含义以及这些变化对股票、证券和期货市场的影响对我们来说已是绝对必要的了。

18. 信息流动量的剧增是过去 10 年中左右金融市场的一个重要因素。

第 10 单元　学术性口译(汉译英)

UNIT 10　Interpreting Academic Speeches
Chinese-English Interpretation

10—1　文化冲突
On Cultural Clashes

冲突	顽疾
融合	泛滥
文明圈	极端个人主义
儒教	自我约束性
伊斯兰教	集体责任感
对抗	温厚儒雅
摩擦	地球村
仿效	泾渭分明
文化认同感	互补
盛行	和睦共处

课文口译
Text for Interpretation

Interpret the following passage from Chinese into English：

主席先生:

能有机会在研讨会上以"文化冲突与融合"为题进行发言,我谨向您表示感谢。

约翰逊博士在他的讲话中提出了"冲突论"的见解。约翰逊博士的理论是建筑在这样一种观点之上的:他认为在后冷战时期,全球冲突源于文化冲突,而文化冲突的焦点集中在宗教和信仰的不同,而非意识形态的不同,也不是国与国之间在经济与政治上的对抗。他认为同属一个文明圈的国家将在冲突中聚合在一起,信奉儒教和伊斯兰教的国家将站在一条战线上,与西方国家和世界其他地区形成对抗。我对这样一种观点深感不安。

约翰逊博士的冲突论表明了许多西方国家对东亚,尤其是对中国近年来经济持续增长的一种失望而又焦虑的心情,同时也反映了人们对西方文明前途的一种与日俱增的困惑感和信心缺乏症。

我们承认不同文化之间的巨大差异,这些差异有时可能会引起摩擦。然而,将这种摩擦夸大其词为世界政治冲突和战争是一种误导,是很危险的。倘若这种冲突论对决策产生影响作用,其危险性便越大。

一些西方人士认为,其他国家的现代化意味着对西方经济、政治和社会制度与价值观念的仿效。我认为,现代化不意味着西方化。事实上,亚洲的经济成功使亚洲人民觉悟起来,产生了文化认同感。他们开始重新思考西方的社会与政治模式是否适用于他们本国,他们是否应该建立起自己的社会与政治发展模式。

我认为,西方模式只是通往现代化的一种途径,全然不是惟一的途径,或许很可能不是一条最佳途径。中国以及其他一些亚洲国家的经济成功不是简单模仿现代西方文明的结果;恰恰相反,我们的成功代表了一种新文化的诞生,它代表了一种集东西方传统的优点之大成的新价值体系。

我赞同许多东亚学者的观点,东方文明可以医治盛行于西方世界的一些顽疾。西方世界个人自由的泛滥导致了极端个人主义、性关系混乱以及过度的暴力行为,对此我们决不可视而不见。相反,东方社会的自我约束性、集体责任感以及温厚儒雅的传统倒可以消除西方社会的许多恶疾。

在这个信息时代,世界已缩小为一个地球村。这个地球村里,不再有什么泾渭分明的东方世界和西方世界，我们是生活在同一个社区里的邻里。因此，我们彼此之间无需相互冲突。我们之间的关系是一种友好合作、平等互补的关系。我们应该相互理解，相互学习，和睦共处。

我的发言到此结束，谢谢主席先生。

10—2　语用能力
Communicative Competence

词汇预习
Vocabulary Work

起着推波助澜的作用	任意性的
自言自语	遣词造句
宠物	语气
属性	场合
概念	上下文
语音	

课文口译
Text for Interpretation

Interpret the following passage from Chinese into English：

　　人们聚在一起，无论做什么总离不了说话。我们生活在语言的世界里。我们对家人说话，对亲属说话，对朋友说话，对同事说话，我们还对陌生人说话。我们面对面地说话，我们在电话里说话，我们回答时还要说话。电视机和收音机在言语海洋里起着推波助澜的作用。除了睡觉之外，我们很少有不说话的时候，我们甚至在睡梦中也会说话。有些人在睡眠时会大声说话。我们还会自言自语，有时对宠物说话，有时则对自己说话。我们是这个星球上惟一能说话的动物。

拥有语言,确切地说是拥有创造性的语言,较之任何其他属性更能将人类同其他动物区别开来。要理解人就必须理解那种使我们成为人的语言。

懂一种语言使你可以说这门语言,你说的话也可以被其他懂这种语言的人听懂。这意味着你能够发出表示某种概念或意义的声音,能够听懂或解释其他人发出的声音。因此,懂得一种语言不仅指了解这种语言包含了哪些语音,而且还指了解语音与意义的关系。

你如果不懂某种语言,别人用这种语言对你说话时发出的声音你基本上无法理解,这是因为大部分语音与语义之间的关系是任意确定的。

懂得一种语言能使你遣词造句。懂得一种语言意味着你能够说出前人未说过的话,也能听懂在此之前无人说过的话。语言学家称这种能力为语言运用的创造属性。

懂得一种语言包括懂得哪些句子在某种场合中使用是恰当的。这就是说,语言的使用受到场合或上下文的约束。当一个人对另外一个人说话时,他会根据不同的对象使用不同的词汇和语气。当一个人说出一句话时,同样这句话在不同的场合、对不同的听众可以包含不同的内容。

10－3　中国书法
Chinese Calligraphy

词汇预习
Vocabulary Work

中国书法	隶书
文化遗产	楷书
山不在高,有仙则名。	行书
水不在深,有龙则灵。	草书
甲骨铭文	象形字
青铜器	夸张
篆书	旅游资源

石碑　　　　　　　　　　曲阜孔庙

悬崖峭壁　　　　　　　　泰山岱庙

匾额　　　　　　　　　　高僧

厅堂卷轴对联

Interpret the following passage from Chinese into English：

　　我很高兴有机会向诸位介绍中国书法这一宝贵的文化遗产及其对中国旅游业的贡献。

　　中国有句古话是这样说的："山不在高，有仙则名；水不在深，有龙则灵。"中国书法好似山上之仙、水中之龙。

　　中国书法同其他书写形式有很大区别。汉字在其漫长的发展史中演化成许多不同的艺术形式，其中包括甲骨铭文、青铜器铭文、篆书、隶书、楷书、行书和草书。

　　许多汉字属象形文字，常可从字的形状揣知其义。无论是刀刻书法还是笔墨书法都可以通过字形的夸张取得艺术效果。

　　因此书法一直是一门研究艺术。千百年来中国书法家倾注了大量的心血研究书法艺术的形式、规则及理论。他们的成果对朝鲜、日本和东南亚国家的汉字书法家产生了巨大的影响。这些国家的书法家经常不断地访问中国，探索书法艺术。

　　汉字的传统书法并未受到外界的影响，这是我国的一大旅游资源。中国大多数旅游区都有不可胜数的铭文石碑（其中许多是刻在悬崖峭壁上的铭文）、匾额和厅堂卷轴对联。以石碑闻名遐迩的桂林七星岩内各个朝代的铭文随处可见。

　　旅游区的古代书法遗迹皆以碑林和石刻为主。例如建于 1091 年的"西安碑林"，碑林区还留有大量的周（公元前 11 世纪 — 公元前 256 年）秦（公元前 221 — 公元前 206 年）时期的石刻作品。

　　对于那些有兴趣把书法作为一种艺术形式来研究的人士来说，曲阜孔庙和泰山岱庙里的石碑是必看无疑的。两处都存有数百件书法风格各异的石刻碑匾。

中国历史上许多诗人和高僧在浪迹名山时皆墨撒悬崖峭壁，以此抒发感情。所幸的是，他们的许多作品均被完好地保存了下来。除了石碑岩崖作品外，在丝绸和纸张上行文留字则是更为常见的书法形式。

汉字书法无论以何种形式出现都将继续吸引着海外游客。

10—4 社区服务
Community Service

词汇预习
Vocabulary Work

街道委员会	2010 年远景目标纲要
里弄居民委员会	发展不平衡
民政部	不足之处
社会福利	非政府组织
推广	奉献
蓬勃展开	切合时宜
"十五"计划	学术报告

课文口译
Text for Interpretation

Interpret the following passage from Chinese into English：

女士们、先生们：

我很高兴能够参加本届社区服务国际学术研讨会，并作发言。

社区服务是当今各国普遍关注的一个问题。它不但是社会稳定的措施之一，而且是社会进步与发展的需要。社区服务对于解决某些社会问题，改善人民生活，促进精神文明建设都有着重要的作用。

过去我国在较长时间内没有使用"社区服务"这个名称,但是在实践中做了许多服务于社区居民的工作,例如我国许多城市的街道委员会和里弄居民委员会所做的许多工作,属于社区服务工作。

改革开放以来,尤其是自国家民政部在总结城市社会福利改革经验的基础上,肯定和推广社区服务的经验以来,社区服务在全国范围内蓬勃展开。我国的国民经济和社会发展"十五"计划和 2010 年远景目标纲要明确提出要积极发展社会福利事业和社区服务。可以预期,社区服务将引起全社会的普遍关注,并将有一个新的发展。

当然,我国社区服务的发展还很不平衡,还有许多不足之处和薄弱环节。这些问题的解决,除了政府加强领导予以解决之外,非常需要社会各方面以及非政府组织的积极努力,需要广大群众的直接参与,做出奉献。这既是过去实践的经验总结,又是今后工作的努力方向。

我国社区服务起步较晚,经验不足。参加这次研讨会的欧美社区服务学者,以及来自东南亚国家和地区的朋友们给我们带来了宝贵的经验和意见,他们所作的学术报告对进一步促进和改善我国的社区服务工作,必将产生积极的影响。

句子精练
Sentences in Focus

Interpret the following sentences from Chinese into English:
1. 我对全球冲突源于文化冲突这样一种观点深感不安。
2. 这种观点反映了人们对西方文明的前途怀有一种与日俱增的困惑感。
3. 亚洲的经济成功使这个地区的人民觉悟起来,对自己的聪明才智与创造力有了新的认识,他们开始重新思考西方的社会模式与政治模式是否适用于他们本国。
4. 东亚的经济成功代表了一种新文化的诞生,代表了一种集东西方传统优点之大成的新价值体系的诞生。
5. 我赞同许多东亚学者的观点,东亚社会的自我约束性、集体责任感以及温厚儒雅的传统可以医治盛行于西方世界的许多顽疾。

6. 在这个信息时代,世界已缩小为一个地球村,我们彼此之间无需冲突,我们之间的关系是一种友好合作、平等互利、和睦相处的关系。

7. 我们创造性地运用语言的能力较之任何其他人类的属性更能将我们同动物区别开来。

8. 懂得一门语言还包括懂得哪些句子在某种场合中使用是恰当的,这就是说,语言的使用受到场合或上下文的约束。

9. 中国有句古话是这样说的:"山不在高,有仙则名;水不在深,有龙则灵"。

10. 许多汉字属象形文字,人们常可从字的形状揣知其义。

11. 汉字在其漫长的发展史中演化成许多不同的艺术形式,其中包括甲骨铭文、青铜器铭文、篆书、隶书、楷书、行书和草书。

12. 千百年来中国许多书法家潜心研究书法艺术的形式、规则及理论。

13. 以石碑闻名遐迩的桂林七星岩内各个朝代的铭文随处可见。

14. 对于那些有兴趣把书法作为一种艺术形式来研究的人士来说,曲阜孔庙和泰山岱庙是必游之地。

15. 中国历史上许多诗人和高僧在浪迹名山时皆撒墨于悬崖峭壁上,他们以此来抒发自己的感情。

16. 社区服务不但是社会稳定的一种措施,同时也是社会进步与发展的需要。

17. 我国社区服务起步较晚,发展还很不平衡,还有许多不足之处和薄弱环节需要克服。

18. 各位专家学者所作的学术报告对促进和改善我们的工作,必将产生积极的影响。

参考译文
Reference Version

10—1 文化冲突
On Cultural Clashes

Mr. Chairman,

Thank you for giving me the opportunity to speak at this seminar on the topic of "The Clash and Fusion of Cultures".

In his speech, Dr. Johnson put forward his "clash theory". Dr. Johnson's theory is based on his argument that in this post-Cold War era, global clashes result from clashes between cultures centering on different religions or beliefs, instead of differences in ideology or state-to-state economic and political confrontation. He believes that countries belonging to the same civilization rim will unite in the clash and the Confucian and Islamic countries will stand together to form confrontation between the West and the rest of the world. I'm very concerned with this view.

Dr. Johnson's clash theory suggests a sense of frustration and anxiety among many Western countries toward the sustained economic rise of East Asia, especially in China, in recent years. It also reflects people's growing confusion and lack of confidence about the future of the Western civilization.

We acknowledge huge differences between different cultures, which may occasionally give rise to friction. However, it is misleading and very dangerous to magnify such friction into world political clashes and wars. And it will be even more dangerous if the clash theory finds its way into the job of policy making.

Some Westerners believe that modernization in other countries means emulating the Western economic, political, and social systems and values. I argue that modernization does not mean Westernization. As a matter of fact, the economic success in Asia has given rise to an awakening recognition of Asians' cultural identity. They have begun to reconsider whether the Western social and political model is suitable to them and whether they should initiate their own social and political development models.

I argue that the Western model is one of the ways to modernization, but it is by no means the only way, or, quite possibly, not the best way. China and some other Asian countries' economic success is not a result of a simple imitation of modern Western civilization; quite on the contrary, our success represents the emergence of a new culture, a new value system that incorporates the strengths of both Oriental and Western traditions.

I share the same view with many East Asian scholars that the Oriental civilization can heal some of the prevailing, stubborn Western ills. We should not turn a blind eye to the fact that individual freedom has gone overboard in the West, resulting in extreme individualism, sexual promiscuity and excessive use of violence. By contrast, self-discipline, corporate responsibility and pacific tradition of East Asia can offset many Western vices.

At this age of information, the world has shrunk as a global village in which there will be no clear-cut worlds of the East and the West any more, but a world of one community with neighboring families. Therefore, we do not necessarily have to come into clash with each other. Our relationship is one of friendly cooperation, equality and mutual complementarity and therefore, we should understand and learn from each other, and live in harmony.

Thank you for your attention. And thank you, Mr. Chairman.

10—2　语用能力
Communicative Competence

Whatever else people do when they come together, they talk. We live in a world of language. We talk to our family members, our relatives, our friends, our colleagues and total strangers. We talk face to face and over the telephone, and respond with more talk. Television and radio further swell this torrent of words. Hardly a moment of our waking lives is free from words, and even in our dreams we talk. Some of us talk aloud in our sleep. We also talk when there is no one to answer. Sometimes we talk to our pets and sometimes to ourselves. We are the only animals on the planet of Earth that talk.

The possession of language, or rather, the language with a creative aspect, more than any other attribute, distinguishes humans from other animals. To understand our humanity we must understand the language that makes us human.

When you know a language, you can speak and be understood by others who know that language. This means you have the capacity to produce sounds that signify certain concepts or meanings and to understand or interpret the sounds produced by others. Therefore, knowing a language does not only mean knowing what sounds are in that language, but also means knowing how to relate sounds and meanings.

If you do not know a certain language, the sounds spoken to you will be mainly incomprehensible, because the relationship between speech sounds and the meanings they represent is, for the most part, an arbitrary one.

Knowing a language enables you to combine words to form phrases, and phrases to form sentences. Knowing a language means being able to produce new sentences never spoken before and to understand sentences never heard before. Linguists refer to this ability as the creative aspect of language use.

Knowing a language includes knowing what sentences are appropriate in particular situation. That is to say, language use is situation-dependent or context-dependent. When one speaks to someone else, he or she may use different words and tones to different people. When one utters a sentence, this same sentence may mean different things in different situations and to different audiences.

10—3 中国书法
Chinese Calligraphy

I am very pleased to have the opportunity to talk about Chinese calligraphy, a highly-valued Chinese cultural heritage, and its contribution to Chinese tourism.

An ancient Chinese saying goes that "Any mountain can be famous with the presence of an immortal, and any river can be holy with the presence of a dragon. " Chinese calligraphy is like an immortal in a mountain and a dragon in a river.

Chinese calligraphy is very different from other forms of writing. During their long history of development Chinese characters have evolved and been written into many different artistic styles, including the inscriptions on bones or tortoise shells and on ancient bronze objects, the seal character, official script, regular script, running script and cursive script.

Many Chinese characters are pictographs and often the meaning of a particular character is apparent in the pictorial form of the character. Calligraphy, whether done with a knife or brush, can be rendered in ways that exaggerate the form, consequently yielding effects of artistic beauty.

Calligraphy, therefore, has been traditionally a subject of artistic study. Down through the centuries Chinese calligraphers have devoted substantive attention to studying the forms, laws and theories pertinent to the art of calligraphy. Moreover, their works have significantly influenced calligraphers of Chinese characters in Korea, Japan and Southeast Asian countries. People from these countries regularly visit China in search of calligraphic art.

Traditional Chinese calligraphy has not been influenced by the outside world. As a result, it constitutes a tourist resource. Most of the Chinese tourist areas have numerous inscribed tablets, including inscriptions on precipices, horizontal inscribed boards and couplets written on the scrolls hung on the pillars of halls. The Seven-Star Cave of Guilin, widely known as a sea of stelae, contains everywhere inscriptions from various dynasties.

Ancient calligraphy relics found in tourist areas primarily consist of tablet forests and stone cuts, for example, the Xi'an Tablet Forest which was built in 1091 and a large number of stone cuts included from the periods of Zhou (11th century BC — 256 BC) and Qin (221 BC — 206 BC).

The stelae in Qufu's Confucius Temple and Mount Tai's Dai Temple are undoubtedly visitors' choice for those interested in studying calligraphy as an art form. Each location contains several hundred tablets inscribed with various styles.

Historically, many poets and senior monks wrote inscriptions on precipices to express their feelings when they visited famous mountains. Fortunately, many of their works have been well preserved. In addition to stone tablets and inscriptions on mountain precipices, calligraphy has also been practiced as more popular forms of art with silk and paper.

Whatever the form, calligraphy of Chinese characters will continue to exert a magnetic influence on tourists to China.

10—4　社区服务
Community Service

Ladies and gentlemen,

I am very pleased to attend and speak at the current session of the International Symposium on Community Service.

Community service is an issue that has received wide attention across the world. Community service is not only a measure to ensure social stability, but also a need for social progress and development. It plays an important role in providing solutions to some social problems, improving people's lives and promoting the construction of healthy values and moral conduct among the citizens.

In spite of the fact that for a long time in the past, there was no such term as "community service" in China, much work was done to provide a variety of service to residents of a community, such as the work of residential district and neighborhood committees in many

Chinese cities.

China's nationwide community service drive has progressed in a vigorous manner ever since the country's initiation of her reform and opening-up program, particularly since the Ministry of Civil Administration acknowledged and decided to popularize the successful experiences involving community service, on the basis of summarizing the work of reform in the urban social welfare system. China's "Outline of the Tenth Five-year Plan for National Economic and Social Development and the Long-range Objectives for the Year 2010" explicitly proposed to actively develop social welfare and community service. It is expected that popular awareness will be aroused to community service in China, which, in turn, will facilitate a new round of development of China's community service.

Of course, the development of our community service is by no means a balanced one. Much work need be done to strengthen quite a number of weak links. The success in resolving these problems depends largely on, apart from a stronger governmental leadership, concentrated endeavors on the part of various social groups and non-governmental organizations, and the direct participation and dedication of the citizens. This conclusion is not only something that was derived from our past experience, but also points to the direction of our future work.

We are aware of the fact that China's community service has a short history and suffers a lack of experience due to its late initiation. We are very fortunate, however, to hear at this symposium the valuable experience and opinions from the participating European and North American scholars in community service as well as from our friends from South-East Asian countries. Their presentations are sure to exert a positive impact on the furtherance and improvement of China's community service.

1. I am deeply concerned with the view that global clashes result from clashes between different cultures.
2. This view reflects people's growing confusion about the future of the Western civilization.
3. The economic success in Asia has given rise to Asians' awakening recognition of their own wisdom and creativity. They have begun to reconsider whether the Western social and political model is applicable favorably to their own countries.
4. East Asia's economic success represents the emergence of a new culture, a new value system that incorporates the strengths of both Oriental and Western traditions.
5. I share the same view with many East Asian scholars that the Oriental civilization with its self-discipline, corporate responsibility and pacific tradition can offset many stubborn ills prevailing in the West.
6. At this age of information, the world has shrunk into a global village in which we do not necessarily have to come into clash with each other, and in which our relationship is but one of friendly cooperation, of equality and mutual benefits, and of peaceful and harmonious coexistence.
7. Our creative use of language, more than any other human attribute, distinguishes ourselves from animal species.
8. Knowing a language includes knowing what sentences are appropriate in a particular situation. That is to say, language use is situational, or context-dependent.
9. An ancient Chinese saying goes that "Any mountain can be famous with the presence of an immortal, and any river can be holy with the presence of a dragon. "

10. Many Chinese characters are pictographs; often the meaning of a particular character is apparent in the pictorial form of the character.

11. During their long history of development Chinese characters have evolved and been written into many different artistic styles, including inscriptions on bones or tortoise shells and ancient bronze objects, the seal character, official script, regular script, running script and cursive script.

12. Over the centuries Chinese calligraphers have devoted substantive attention to the study of the forms, laws and theories that are pertinent to the art of calligraphy.

13. Wherever you go in the Seven-Star Cave of Guilin, widely known for its stelae, you are likely to see a lavish number of inscriptions from various dynasties.

14. Qufu's Confucius Temple and Mount Tai's Dai Temple are undoubtedly visitors' choice for those who are interested in studying calligraphy as an art form.

15. Historically, many poets and senior monks wrote inscriptions on precipices to express their feelings when they visited famous mountains.

16. Community service is not only a measure to ensure social stability, but also a need for social progress and development.

17. China's community service has a late start and its development is by no means balanced; therefore, much work need be done to offset the problems and strengthen the weak links.

18. The presentations given by various scholars and specialists at this conference are sure to exert a positive impact on the furtherance and improvement of our work lying ahead.

第 11 单元　商务性口译（英译汉）

UNIT 11　Interpreting Business Speeches
English-Chinese Interpretation

11—1　企业文化
Entrepreneurial Culture

词汇预习
Vocabulary Work

the Enron case

a nimble and flexible outfit

the exception rather than the rule

academics

a paragon of management virtue

stodgy

paramount

distill a lesson

debacle

acclaim

initiative

the usual corporate checks
　and balances

unethical means

too much leeway

seniority-based salaries

highly leveraged compensation

mentor

entrepreneurship

hands-off management

a runaway train

课文口译
Text for Interpretation

Interpret the following passage from English into Chinese:

Ladies and gentlemen,

Good afternoon. Today I'll focus on the importance of entrepreneurial culture, drawing on the lesson from the Enron case.

For most of the 1990s, CEOs at Old Economy companies struggled to turn slow-moving organizations into nimbler, more flexible outfits. The truth is, real transformations are the exception rather than the rule. Changing the core values, the attitudes, and the fundamental relationships of a vast organization is overwhelmingly difficult. That's why an army of academics and consultants descended on Enron in the late 1990s and held it up as a paragon of management virtue. Enron seemed to have transformed itself from a stodgy regulated utility to a fast-moving enterprise where performance was paramount.

If only that were true. Enron tumbled down. Many of the same academics are now busy distilling the cultural and leadership lessons from the debacle. Their conclusion so far: Enron didn't fail just because of improper accounting or alleged corruption at the top. It also failed because of its entrepreneurial culture — the very reason Enron attracted so much attention and acclaim. Too much emphasis on earnings growth and individual initiative, coupled with a shocking absence of the usual corporate checks and balances, turned Enron's entrepreneurial culture from one that rewarded aggressive strategy to one that increasingly relied on unethical means. In the end, too much leeway was given to young, inexperienced managers without the necessary controls to minimize failures.

Jeffrey K. Skilling assumed Enron CEO in early 2001. His recipe for changing the company was right out of the New Economy playbook. Layers of management were wiped out. Hundreds of outsiders were recruited and encouraged to bring new thinking to a tradition-bound business. The company abolished seniority-based salaries in favor of more highly leveraged compensation that offered huge cash bonuses and stock option grants to top performers. Young people, many just out of undergraduate or MBA programs, were handed extraordinary authority, able to make $5 million decisions without higher approval.

In larger companies like IBM, even though there is a movement toward youth, there are still enough older people around to mentor them. At Enron, you had a bunch of kids running loose without adult supervision.

The new entrepreneurial culture encourages the "loose and tight" environment. The idea is to combine tight controls with maximum individual authority to allow entrepreneurship to flourish without the culture edging into chaos.

At Enron, however, the pressure to make the numbers was often overwhelming. The environment was ripe for abuse. Nobody at corporate was asking the right questions. It was completely hands-off management. It was a runaway train.

I'd like to stop here and take your questions.

11-2 认识债券
Getting to Know Bonds

词汇预习
Vocabulary Work

appeal

the repayment of the loan in full
  at maturity

capital appreciation

high return

in a nutshell

diversification in investment

equities

unduly

immediate yield

polarized between growth
  and security

opt for

corporate bonds

credit rating agency   assign ratings to

Moody's and Standard & Poors   liquidity

课文口译
Text for Interpretation

Interpret the following passage from English into Chinese:

How many of you buy bonds? More and more people show great interest in bonds investment.

A major appeal of investing in bonds is that they provide investors with a steady stream of income and guarantee the repayment of the loan in full at maturity.

Bonds also appeal to investors because of their scope for capital appreciation. Take for instance a fall in interest rates, in this case bonds which were issued when interest rates were high will become increasingly valuable and as the bond price rises, this provides profit for bond sellers.

In addition, if interest rates had fallen significantly over a period of time, economic growth would be stimulated as lower borrowing costs and savings rates would encourage businesses to invest and households to consume. In such a low interest-rate environment, it may still be good for investors to consider investing some money in bonds because they will be able to achieve a higher return than cash deposits.

In a nutshell, an investor should consider investing in bonds as an alternative for the purpose of diversification in investment.

As a bond pays a regular interest, it may be suitable for investors, such as retirees, who require a regular income over a specific time.

Equities and government bonds are well suited to some investors. Younger investors will benefit from equity capital growth because they are generally investing for the longer term and not unduly concerned with the lack of immediate yield. Investors concerned with avoiding risk will be prepared to accept the relatively low yields now available on government bonds.

But many investors fall somewhere between these two extremes. In recent years, financial markets have become increasingly polarized between growth and security. Investors looking for medium and low-risk are increasingly turning to the corporate bond market as an alternative to equities and government bonds. Corporate bonds offer an ideal alternative to equities and government bonds, providing some of the benefits of each. With corporate bonds, an investor can opt for a lower risk exposure than with equities but a higher income yield than with government bonds.

The main disadvantage of corporate bonds is that an investor only indirectly participates in the company's success, through its credit-worthiness, but otherwise will not benefit from corporate expansion in the way that equity holders will. On the other hand, absolute risk is lower than for equities because coupon payments cannot be waived and, in the event of a default, bondholders are ranked highly among creditors.

However, corporate credit-worthiness is a key factor in assessing the value and risk of corporate bonds. Credit rating agencies play an important role in this process. The two main agencies are Moody's and Standard & Poors. They assign ratings both to entities issuing bonds and to specific corporate bond issues. This gives investors a guide as to their credit quality, which indicates possible risk.

Liquidity is also an important factor. Investors should be generally aware that corporate bonds, even in mature markets such as the United States and Britain, have fairly limited secondary markets. That is to say, unlike equities or government bonds, they cannot always be sold easily to other investors.

Although corporate bonds carry more risk than government

bonds, that risk can be controlled to a large extent by credit analysis and other checks on the issuer and the terms of the bond. In return, investors have the opportunity to achieve a good cash income.

Buy stocks or bonds? Make your own decision.

11—3 硅谷之贵
The Unique Silicon Valley

magnet

the epoch-making European
　Renaissance

the bygone age

preeminence

prototype

exalt

stigma

the sine qua non

initial capital

high flyer

ethos of team work

esprit de corps

icon

college dropout

discernible

phenomenal success

proliferate

dot. com company

traumatic experience

setback

cutting-edge

课文口译
Text for Interpretation

Interpret the following passage from English into Chinese:

What makes Silicon Valley so successful and unique?

Silicon Valley is a magnet to which numerous talented engineers, scientists and entrepreneurs from overseas flock in search of fame and fast money and to participate enthusiastically in a technological revolution whose impact on mankind will surely surpass the epoch-making European Renaissance and Industrial Revolution of the bygone age.

With the rapid spread of the Internet and the relentless technological innovations generated through it, the information era is truly upon us, profoundly influencing and changing not only our lifestyle, but also the way we work, do business, think and communicate with others.

It is noteworthy that close to 50% of its skilled manpower, including engineers, scientists and entrepreneurs, come from Asia. Prominent among them are Indians, Chinese and Singaporeans. They include such illustrious names as Vinod Khosla who co-founded Sun Microsystems, Jerry Yang of Yahoo fame and Singaporean Sim Wong Hoo.

Many countries have, or are in the process of creating, their own "Silicon Valley." So far, none has as yet threatened the preeminence of the U. S. prototype. What makes Silicon Valley such a unique entity? I think there are several crucial factors.

First and foremost, it has the largest concentration of brilliant computer professionals and the best supporting services in the world, and easy access to world-class research institutions, like Stanford University, which continually nurture would-be geniuses which the industry needs in order to move forward. Without these advantages, the Valley would be a different place.

Secondly, it actively encourages, or even exalts, risk-taking. Hence, failure holds no terror and there is no stigma attached to a failed effort. On the contrary, they will try even harder next time round. Such never-say-die approach is the sine qua non for the ultimate triumph in entrepreneurship and technological breakthrough.

A third decisive factor is the vital role of venture capitalists who willingly support promising start-ups with urgently needed initial capital to get them started. Some would even give failed entrepreneurs a second chance if convinced that a fresh concept might lead to eventual success.

It is a common practice for start-ups to offer generous share options to employees in order to attract the right talent into their folds. This is a powerful incentive to motivate the staff to do their utmost and to share in the company's prosperity if it reaches its goal. Many regard this as the foundation of a successful enterprise.

Those that have become high flyers, such as Netscape, Intel, Cisco and Yahoo, have turned many of their employees, including support staff like secretaries, into dot. com millionaires overnight, often at the relatively young age of 20s or 30s.

The valley's professionals are among the most hardworking people anywhere. A 15-hour day and 7-day week is not uncommon, especially during the start-up stage. They would give up social life, and curtail their family life too, in order to pursue the pot of gold at the end of the rainbow. It is this single-minded pursuit of excellence, supported by strong ethos of teamwork and esprit de corps, that sustain them until their mission is accomplished.

Paper qualification, though useful, is not a be all and end all. More weight is given to a candidate's proven abilities and aptitude for the job. This is amply demonstrated by industry icons like Apple's Jobs and Wozniak and Microsoft's Gates, all college dropouts who might not have emerged in a qualification-conscious community.

While racial prejudice no doubt still exists in the United States, it is hardly discernible in the Valley. What counts most is one's vision and track record, and not one's nationality, skin color or creed. This, together with its multiracial society, informal lifestyle and agreeable climate, lures foreigners to its shores.

Its phenomenal success has led to a worldwide fever to proliferate dot. com companies, both as a prestigious symbol and a quicker way to wealth. In consequence, many bright young people have given up their secure jobs to join in the race. But the reality is that, because of its high-risk nature, for every success story there are hundreds who will fall by the wayside.

However, with the collapse of the U. S. NASDAQ share index, the share options held by numerous paper dot. com millionaires have become virtually worthless in these changed circumstances. Those who could not take the hit, as it were, left their employment feeling disillusioned.

Be that as it may, the majority in the Valley views this traumatic experience only as a temporary setback for the industry. They are sanguine that its longer-term prospects remain bright as the ultimate potential of the information age has not yet run its full course. They are confident that it will flourish well into this century provided it maintains its cutting-edge in science and technology.

11—4 专利法规
On Patent Laws

patent laws
online bookseller Amazon-dot-com
public consultation
domain
allegedly
abuse

one-click purchasing option
advent
coincidence
mimic
lobby

Interpret the following passage from English into Chinese:

Today, we, pioneers and leaders of electronic commerce, are meeting here to call for changes in US patent laws. We believe such changes are needed to deal with new business models related to the growth of the Internet.

I share the same view with Jeff Bezos, chief executive of online bookseller Amazon-dot-com. Mr. Bezos argued in an open letter that current patent laws could end up harming all kinds of businesses if the laws were not adapted to new business methods used in e-commerce.

I think US Patent laws are designed to protect the commercial rights of people who have invested in new products, systems or methods. Hereby I propose that the period of protection offered by patents should be cut from 17 years to about 4 years. I also propose a one-month period of public consultation before patents are issued. The purpose of these changes is to ensure that patented business models and software are more quickly released into the public domain.

Amazon was once under criticism for allegedly abusing current laws by patenting business methods that are so general in scope they should be available to everyone. Two examples include Amazon's patent for the so-called one-click purchasing option on its World Wide Web site and its program for paying other web sites that refer customers to the Amazon site.

From my experience of working with Hi-Technology companies in California's Silicon Valley, the biggest problems arise when existing patent protections for business methods are combined with the Internet.

When you combine the ability to patent business methods with the advent of the Internet you have a very interesting coincidence. The Internet, because it is brand new, provides a new way of doing just about everything. You can have electronic shopping carts on the Internet that mimic the shopping carts in the real world. But because it is in a new environment, a new medium, that is sufficiently novel to obtain a patent on that idea.

If changes in the patent laws are going to have any real impact, they must be made soon, before too many more new business method patents are issued. Some of my colleagues in the industry have already begun lobbying lawmakers to make the changes. But we have to be a little bit more patient because it will take at least two years for any changes proposed now to be approved by lawmakers and established as law.

句子精练
Sentences in Focus

Interpret the following sentences from English into Chinese:
1. Today I'll focus on the importance of entrepreneurial culture, drawing on the lesson from a few outstanding cases.
2. The truth is, really successful transformations are the exception rather than the rule.
3. Changing the core values, the attitudes, and the fundamental relationships of a vast organization is overwhelmingly difficult.
4. Too much emphasis on earnings growth and individual initiative, coupled with a shocking absence of the usual corporate checks and balances, turned the company's entrepreneurial culture from one that rewarded aggressive strategy to one that increasingly relied on unethical means.
5. The new entrepreneurial culture encourages the "loose and tight" environment. The idea is to combine tight controls with maxi-

mum individual authority to allow entrepreneurship to flourish without the culture edging into chaos.

6. Bonds appeal to investors because of their scope for capital appreciation.

7. Investors consider investing some money in bonds because they will be able to achieve a higher return than cash deposits.

8. In a nutshell, an investor should consider investing in bonds as an alternative for the purpose of diversification in investment.

9. In recent years, financial markets have become increasingly polarized between growth and security.

10. Credit rating agencies, such as Moody's and Standard & Poors, assign ratings both to entities issuing bonds and to specific corporate bond issues, and indicate possible risk in financial investment.

11. Silicon Valley is a magnet to which numerous talented engineers, scientists and entrepreneurs from overseas flock in search of fame and gain.

12. First and foremost, Silicon Valley has the largest concentration of brilliant computer professionals and the best supporting services in the world.

13. The never-say-die approach is the sine qua non for the ultimate triumph in entrepreneurship and technological breakthrough.

14. They willingly support promising start-ups with urgently needed initial capital to get them started.

15. Paper qualification, though useful, is not a be all and end all.

16. Because of its high-risk nature, for every success story there are hundreds who will fall by the wayside.

17. Today, we, pioneers and leaders of electronic commerce, are meeting here to call together for changes in the existing patent laws.

18. I propose a one-month period of public consultation before patents are issued.

参考译文
Reference Version

女士们,先生们,

下午好!今天我以安然公司的教训为例,谈一下企业文化的重要性。

在20世纪90年代的大部分时间里,旧经济公司的首席执行官们都在努力地将运作缓慢的公司向敏捷、更富有弹性的公司转型。但实际情况是,真正转型的却是极个别的现象。转变一家大型公司的核心理念、态度和基本关系极其困难。这就是20世纪90年代末大批学者和顾问涌入安然公司并推崇其为管理功效典范的原因。当时的安然似乎已经从一家平庸、节制的公用事业公司转型为一家快速运营、业绩出众的企业。

可惜这并非事实,安然栽了。当年那批学者中很多人现在忙于从安然的崩溃中分析企业文化和领导方面的教训。目前他们的结论是:安然的失败并不仅仅因为做了假账或者所谓的高层腐败,其失败还应归咎于它的企业文化,正是这种企业文化曾经使安然引人注目、备受青睐。过分强调收益增长和个人主动性,加之缺乏那种常规的公司制约平衡机制,使安然的企业文化从推崇进取性战略转变为日益依赖不道德的手段。最终,公司对没有经验的年轻管理人员过度宽容,又缺乏必要的控制手段使失败的可能性降至最小的程度。

2001年杰弗莱·斯基林就任安然首席执行官。他改变公司的方法完全出自新经济攻略手册。安然取消了一些管理层,从外界招募了数百名职员,鼓励他们给受传统束缚的企业注入新思想。公司废除了以资历为基础的薪水制度,取而代之的是更有激励性的分配制度,表现出众的员工可以获得丰厚的现金奖励和公司股票。公司的年轻人,其中不少是刚毕业的本科生或工商管理硕士专业的研究生,他们被授予了非常高的权力，无需上级领导的批准便可自行做出金额高达 500 万美元的决策。

像 IBM 这样的大公司，尽管也出现了不拘一格降人才的趋势，但是那些青年才俊身边不乏资深职员提供指导。但你在安然看到的却是一群不受大人监管的孩子在自说自话地任意行事。

新型的企业文化鼓励"张弛有度"的企业环境。这种张弛结合的理念是指把严格控管与最大限度的个人权限相结合，从而使企业家才能得到充分发挥，同时也避免企业文化陷入混乱。

然而在安然做假账的压力往往压倒了一切。安然的企业环境发展成为一种可以为所欲为的温床。公司内没有人提出切中要害的问题，企业完全处于一种放任自流的管理模式，公司就像一匹脱缰的野马。

我就讲到这里，下面请各位提问。

11—2 认识债券
Getting to Know Bonds

你们中间有多少人购买债券？越来越多的人对投资债券感兴趣。

债券吸引人的一大特点是让投资者有一笔固定的收入，到期时能收回借出的资金。

债券也有增值的机会。例如在利率下跌时，那些在利率高时发行的债券价格将会升高，让持有人有机会赚取利润。

此外，如果利率在过去一段时间里明显下跌，这会刺激经济增长，因为较低的贷款成本和储蓄利率将鼓励商家投资，带动家庭消费。在这样的低利率环境下，投资人仍可以考虑把一些资金投资在债券上，因为投资者将会取得高于现金存款的回报。

总的来说，投资者应该考虑把债券投资当作一个投资选择，以达到多元化投资和整体投资的目的。

债券定期支付利息，可能比较适合那些在某一时期内需要有定期收入的投资者，如退休人士。

股票和政府债券很合一些投资者的胃口。年轻投资者一般从股票的资本增值中获益，因为他们通常是作长线投资，不太在意眼前的收益。想规避风险的投资者则愿意购买目前收益相对低的政府债券。

但是很多人的投资选择介于股票和政府债券两端之间。近年来金融市场的投资增值与投资安全日趋两极分化。那些只愿承受中低风险的投资人都转向公司债券。公司债券是股票和政府债券的理想替代品,两头的好处都沾点边。投资公司债券的风险小于投资股票,而收益又高于政府债券。

公司债券的主要缺点是投资者只能通过信用等级间接分享公司的收益,而不能像股东那样从公司的扩张中获益。另一方面,这些债券投资者承担的绝对风险却又低于股东,因为息票支付是不能勾销的,而当公司无法偿付时,债券持有人在债权人中享有很高的优先权。

不过,某个公司的信誉等级是评估该公司债券的价值和风险的关键因素。信誉评级机构在评估公司债券的价值和风险过程中起着重要作用。穆迪和标准普尔是两家主要评估机构。它们给债券发售单位以及具体签发的公司债券评级。这些信息为投资者了解有关公司及其债券的信誉质量提供了风险指南。

资金的变现灵活性也是一个重要因素。投资者必须明白,即使是美国和英国这些成熟的资本市场,公司债券的二级市场也是相当有限的。换言之,公司债券与股票和政府债券不同,不太容易转售给其他投资者。

公司债券的风险虽然大于政府债券,但这种风险在很大程度上可借助信用分析,以及对债券发售者和债券条款采取其他一些制约手段加以控制。而作为回报,投资者则有机会获取不错的现金收益。

买股票还是买债券,请自己做主。

11—3　硅谷之贵
The Unique Silicon Valley

硅谷成功的原因何在？硅谷为什么如此独一无二呢？

硅谷犹如一块磁铁,把许许多多天资聪颖的工程师、科学家、企业家从世界各地吸引到这里,他们寻求功名,希望快速致富,积极投身于技术革命,而这场革命对人类带来的影响必将超过昔日的具有划时代意义的欧洲文艺复兴运动和工业革命。

因特网急速普及,以及因特网带来的势不可挡的技术创新,使我们真正地进入了信息时代,深刻地影响并改变着我们的生活、工作、商务活动、思维以及沟通的方式。

值得注意的是,包括工程师、科学家和企业家在内的硅谷地区技术人员近一半来自亚洲,表现尤为突出的是印度人、中国人和新加坡人,他们中有声名卓著的升阳微系统创始人之一文诺·考斯拉、雅虎帝国的创始人杨致远以及新加坡的沈望博。

有些国家已有自己的"硅谷",有些国家正在创建自己的"硅谷",但是美国正统硅谷的龙头地位未受到威胁。那么美国硅谷为何会如此与众不同呢?我认为有这么几个至关重要的因素。

首先,硅谷有着全球最密集的优秀电脑专业人才群和最佳支持性服务体系,有着毗邻斯坦福大学这类世界一流的研究机构,这些研究机构源源不断地培育着电脑业赖以发展的明日天才。没有这些优势,硅谷便将面目皆非。

其次,硅谷积极提倡,甚至极力颂扬冒险精神。所以,失败不可怕,出师不捷无人耻笑,失败反而使人再接再厉,加倍奋斗。这种永不言败的作风是企业成功和技术创新必不可缺的。

第三个决定性因素是风险投资公司的重要作用,风险投资者愿意支持那些前途看好的创业者,给予他们急需的启动资金,帮助他们起步。对于曾遭遇过失败的企业,有些风险投资者甚至只要确认企业的新观念能带来最终的成功,他们也会进行第二次投资。

创业公司为了将合适的人才收入自己的麾下,通常向企业员工们转让数量可观的股票。这一有力的激励措施旨在鼓励员工们为公司尽心尽职,以共同分享公司成功的成果。许多人认为参股是企业成功的基础。

网景、英特尔、思科、雅虎等出类拔萃的公司使许多包括秘书等后勤职工在内的许多员工一夜致富,许多员工年仅二三十岁便成了身价百万的网络富豪。

硅谷的专业人士工作之勤奋,举世罕见。一天 15 小时、一周 7 日的工作日程司空见惯,尤其是在创业初期。他们放弃社交生活,减少与家人生活的时间,去寻求事业彩虹尽头处的那一桶金。正是这种对卓越一心一意的追求,加上优良的团队精神,支持着他们的奋斗理念,不达目的决不罢休。

在硅谷,文凭虽然有用,却不是一切,一纸定不了终生,硅谷更看重求职者的真才实学和岗位资质。最有说服力的例子莫过于行业偶像,如苹果公司的创始人乔布斯与沃茨尼亚克、微软的创始人盖茨,他们都是一些在讲究学历的社会里可能无出头之日的大学辍学者。

美国无疑仍然存在着种族歧视,但在硅谷却难寻踪影。硅谷看人最重要的是看其视野和成长历程,而不是看其国籍、肤色或宗教信仰。这种观念,加上硅谷多种族的社会、不拘礼仪的生活方式、宜人的气候,使外国人近悦远来。

硅谷的非凡成功在全球掀起了创办网络公司的热潮,致使众多青年才俊放弃原本稳定的工作而投身于这场网络竞赛。但是事实上,网络创业本身是一种高风险的行为,一家公司的脱颖而出,可能意味着数百家公司的落败道旁。

然而,随着美国纳斯达克股市指数的狂泻,众多账面百万富翁所持的网络公司股票在突变中实际上已一文不值。经不起打击者大失所望,离职而去。

尽管如此,硅谷人大多把这次惨痛经历只看做行业的暂时挫折,他们仍然乐观地认为网络业的远景依然看好,信息时代最大潜力的发挥还有待时日。他们坚信,网络业只要保持锐利的科技进步势头,还会在本世纪内持续繁荣下去。

11—4 专利法规
On Patent Laws

今天,我们这些的电子商务的创始人和领导人在此集会,共同呼吁修改美国专利法。我们认为互联网的发展形成了一些新商业模式,专利法必须加以修改才能应付这种新形势。

我同在线书店亚马逊电子商务公司的首席执行官杰夫·贝索斯持有相同的观点。贝索斯先生在一封公开信中指出,现行的专利法若不加以修正以适应电子商务的新商务模式,最终将伤害所有商务活动。

我认为,制订美国专利法的根本出发点是为了保护那些投资开发新产品、新系统和新方法的人的商业权利。我在这里提议,专利权的保护期应该从原来的17年缩短为4年。同时我也建议,专利发布前应该有一个月的公示咨询期。这些改革的目的是为了确保获得专利权的商务模式和软件能更快地传达到公共范畴。

亚马逊公司曾遭到一些批评,有人指责亚马逊公司滥用现行法律,把一些十分一般的商务方法给予专利保护,而这些商务方法人人都应该有权使用。亚马逊公司有两个典型的专利保护例子,一个是所谓网上一次点击购物法,另一个是有关将客户介绍给亚马逊网址的其他网站付费的操作程序。

凭我在加州硅谷高科技公司的工作经验,当现行的商务行为的专利保护同因特网联系在一起时,就会出现最严重的问题。

当你把商务行为专利保护能力同使用因特网结合在一起时,你会发现一个十分有趣的巧合。因特网是一项新生事物,可以提供做每一件事的新方法。你可以在网上使用电子购物手推车,这是现实生活中手推车的一种模拟车,但是由于它出现在一个新环境中,出现在一个新媒体中,这个模拟方法就足以新到可以申请专利保护。

如果想让专利法的修改能真正起到作用,那就必须加快修订步伐,不然等到越来越多的对商务方法新专利颁布之后,为时就太晚了。电子商务产业的一些同行已开始游说立法者修改法律。但是我们还得耐心等待,现在提出的修改建议至少要等上两年才能被立法部门批准,成为正式法律。

句子精练
Sentences in Focus

1. 今天我从几个突出的案例给予我们的教训来谈一下企业文化的重要性。
2. 事实是,真正成功转型的公司是极个别的现象。
3. 转变一家大型公司的核心理念、态度和基本关系极其困难。
4. 过分强调收益增长和个人主动性,加之缺乏那种常规的公司制约平衡机制,使这个公司的企业文化从推崇进取性战略转变为日益依赖不道德的手段。
5. 新型的企业文化鼓励"张弛有度"的企业环境。这种张弛结合的理念是指把严格控管与最大限度的个人权利相结合,从而使企业家的才能得到充分发挥,同时也避免企业文化陷入混乱。

6. 债券吸引投资者是因为债券有增值的机会。

7. 投资人考虑把一些资金投资在债券上是因为可以取得高于现金存款的回报。

8. 总的来说,投资者应该考虑把债券投资当作一个投资选择,以达到多元化投资的目的。

9. 近年来金融市场的投资增值与投资安全日趋两极分化。

10. 信誉评级机构,如穆迪和标准普尔评估机构,给债券发售单位以及具体签发的公司债券评级,提供金融投资可能遇到的风险。

11. 硅谷犹如一块磁铁,把许许多多天资聪颖的工程师、科学家、企业家从世界各地吸引到这里寻求功名和财富。

12. 首先,硅谷有着全球最密集的优秀电脑专业人才群和最佳支持性服务体系。

13. 这种永不言败的作风是企业成功和技术创新必不可缺的。

14. 他们愿意支持那些前途看好的创业者,给予他们急需的启动资金,帮助他们起步。

15. 文凭虽然有用,却不是一切,一纸定不了终生。

16. 由于其高风险的特点,一家公司的成功,可能意味着数百家公司的落败。

17. 今天,我们这些的电子商务的创始人和领导人在此集会,共同呼吁修改现行的专利法。

18. 我提议,专利发布前应该有一个月的公示期。

第12单元 商务性口译(汉译英)

UNIT 12 Interpreting Business Speeches
Chinese-English Interpretation

12—1 金融扩展
The Growing Financial Industry

词汇预习
Vocabulary Work

引人瞩目	贴现市场
总设计师	保险市场
已故	金银买卖市场
决策层	辐射全国
抢滩上海	综合国力
外资财务公司	蓝图
代表处	全天候交易
证券市场	大展鸿图

课文口译
Text for Interpretation

Interpret the following passage from Chinese into English：
女士们、先生们：

我今天想谈一下上海金融业的现状与发展趋势。

众所周知,目前的亚洲是全球经济发展最为迅速的地区,中国是亚洲经济增长最快的国家,上海更是中国经济发展最引人瞩目的城市之一。在上个世纪三四十年代,上海曾是远东最大的国际金融中心。今天,鉴于上海特殊的历史地位与地理优势,亦基于中国经济强劲发展的实力,这座城市重建远东国际金融中心的势态已成定局。中国改革的总设计师、已故的邓小平先生早在 1992 年来沪时便明确提出,"中国在金融方面取得国际地位,首先要靠上海。"中国决策层已决心尽快将上海建成国际经济、金融、贸易中心城市。

经过 15 年的金融发展与改革,上海金融机构迅速扩展。目前上海已形成了以中央银行(即中国人民银行)为领导,以国有商业银行为主体,各种金融机构并存,发展比较健全的金融机构组织体系。近 10 年来,外资金融机构纷纷抢滩上海,其中包括外资银行、外资财务公司、外资保险公司和外资金融机构代表处。与此同时,上海金融市场迅速发展。迄今为止,上海已建成了具有一定规模与相当影响的比较完整的金融市场体系,其中包括证券市场、外汇市场、贴现市场、保险市场、金银买卖市场等。上海证券市场的发展最为瞩目,已成为辐射全国、影响深远的国内最大的资本市场。

随着我国改革开放的深入和综合国力的增强,上海金融业必将在更高层次上得到全面拓展。根据上海市政府制定的社会和经济发展蓝图,到 2010 年,上海将基本建成国际经济、金融、贸易中心之一,全方位介入国际金融活动,外汇市场、资本市场、黄金市场实现与世界各金融中心的全天候交易,人民币实行自由兑换。

女士们、先生们,新世纪的上海充满着希望,是各国富有远见的金融家和企业家大展鸿图的黄金宝地。让我们携手合作,共图发展大业。谢谢。

12-2 亚洲合作
Asian Cooperation

博鳌亚洲论坛   恪守入世承诺

文化博大精深   有步骤地扩大开放领域

东盟   取消非关税壁垒

提供重要渠道和机制   不断完善法治

独到见解   透明和可预见的市场环境

全方位合作   大力实施"走出去"战略

自我封闭   勤劳智慧

排他性集团   自强不息

新跨越

课文口译
Text for Interpretation

Interpret the following passage from Chinese into English:

我很高兴参加博鳌亚洲论坛首次年会,与大家共同探讨新世纪亚洲区域合作与发展的问题。

亚洲是地球上最大的洲,聚居着世界 60％的人口,资源十分丰富,历史源远流长,文化博大精深。近年来,在亚洲国家共同努力下,包容、平等和渐进的地区合作意识日益加强,开放、健康和互利的合作局面正在形成。亚太经合组织不断发展,东亚区域合作方兴未艾,"上海合作组织"顺利运转。我国与东盟国家一致同意今后 10 年内逐步建立中国—东盟自由贸易区,并正就启动谈判进行接触。这些将为亚洲国家和地区扩大交流、深化合作,提供重要渠道和机制。但是,与欧洲和北美区域合作相比,亚洲区域合作相对落后。一段时间以来,许多方面对亚洲区域合作的发展方向提出不少独到见解。这里,我谈几点看法:

第一,以经济合作为重点,逐步拓展全方位合作。发展经济是亚洲各国的首要任务。从实际需要和实践看,可以把贸易、交通、农业、信息、能源作为优先合作领域,并逐步向其他领域扩展。

第二,立足现有合作渠道,不断扩大合作范围。东亚、南亚、西亚和中亚地理上相对独立,经济发展各有特色。从便利性和有效性看,应首先加强次区域合作,在此基础上,积极探索泛亚合作的途径。

第三,进一步拓展双边合作,增强区域合作的基础。加强双边合作有利于推动区域合作的顺利发展。区域合作也有利于为双边开辟更广阔的空间。两者可以形成良性互动。

第四,实行开放式地区合作。合作不可能自我封闭,更不应形成排他性集团。亚洲国家应通过 APEC、亚欧会议和东亚—拉美合作论坛等渠道,进一步加强与各大洲国家的合作。

中国是亚洲的一员。20 多年来,中国坚定不移地推进改革开放,加速国民经济发展。中国改革开放和现代化的新跨越,不仅将给中国人民带来巨大福祉,也必将提供无限商机,为亚洲和世界经济合作开辟新的广阔空间。

加入世贸组织,是中国对外开放的新起点。我们将在更大范围和更深程度上参与国际经济合作与竞争。中国将进一步向亚洲和世界开放,向各国的企业家、投资者开放。我们恪守入世承诺,有步骤地扩大开放领域,降低关税水平,取消非关税壁垒。我们也将不断完善法治,创造更加公平、透明和可预见的市场环境。同时,我们还将大力实施"走出去"战略,鼓励中国各种所有制企业走向世界。

中国人民热爱和平,中国的发展需要和平。亚洲人民勤劳智慧,自强不息。中国人民愿与亚洲各国人民一道,携手共创美好未来。

12-3 外资企业
Foreign-Capital Enterprises

词汇预习
Vocabulary Work

法规	办理变更／注销登记手续
合法权益	设置会计账簿
利润	独立核算
国务院	报送会计报表
审查批准	财政税务机关
工商行政管理机关	免税
法人资格	缴纳所得税
吊销营业执照	清算

课文口译
Text for Interpretation

Interpret the following passage from Chinese into English：

我愿借此机会向各位介绍国家有关外资企业的法规。

为了扩大对外经济合作和技术交流，促进中国国民经济的发展，中华人民共和国允许外国的企业和其他经济组织或者个人在中国境内开办外资企业，保护外资企业的合法权益。

设立外资企业，必须有利于中国国民经济的发展。国家鼓励开办产品出口或者技术先进的外资企业。外国投资者在中国境内的投资获得的利润和其他合法权益，受到中国法律保护。

设立外资企业的申请，由国务院对外经济贸易主管部门或者国务院授权的其他机关审查批准。设立外资企业的申请批准后，外国投资者应当在接到批准书之日起30天内向工商行政管理机关申请登记，领取营业执照。外资企业符合中国法律条件规定的，依法取得中国法人资格。

外资企业应当在审查批准机关核准期限内在中国境内投资；逾期不投资者，工商行政管理机关有权吊销营业执照。

外资企业分立、合并或者其他重要事项变更，应当报审查机关批准，并向工商行政机关办理变更登记手续。

外资企业雇佣中国职员应当依法签订合同，并在合同中订明雇佣、解雇、报酬、福利、劳动保护、劳动保险等事项。外资企业的职工可依法建立工会组织，开展工会活动，维护职工的合法权益。外资企业应当为本企业工会提供必要的活动条件。

外资企业必须在中国境内设置会计账簿，进行独立核算，按照规定报送会计报表，并接受财政税务机关的监督。

外资企业依照国家有关税收的规定纳税并可以享受减税、免税的优惠待遇。外资企业将缴纳所得税后的利润在中国境内再投资的，可以依照国家规定申请退还再投资部分已缴纳的部分所得税税款。

外国投资者从外资企业获得的合法利润、其他合法收入和清算后的资金，可以汇往国外。外资企业的外籍职工的工资收入和其他正当收入，依法缴纳个人所得税后，可以汇往国外。

外资企业终止，应当及时公告，依照法定程序进行清算，并向工商行政管理机关办理注销登记手续，缴销营业执照。

谢谢各位听讲。

12－4　经济关系
Economic Links

```
词汇预习
Vocabulary Work
```

世界多极化	科学技术突飞猛进
经济全球化	前所未有

广阔前景	商机
日新月异的科技进步	全面建设小康社会
指导思想	与时俱进
贸易自由化	以更加积极的姿态
处于"弱者"地位	透明的贸易和投资政策
公正配置世界资源	全方位、多层次、宽领域的对外
加深"数字鸿沟"	开放

课文口译
Text for Interpretation

Interpret the following passage from Chinese into English：

各位贵宾，女士们、先生们：

　　我们进入新世纪，这不仅意味着年代上的更新，而且意味着国际社会开启了经济发展和社会进步的新时期。主要标志是：世界多极化、经济全球化的不断发展，尤其是科学技术的突飞猛进，为全球经济和社会发展提供了前所未有的物质技术条件，打开了广阔的前景。

　　日新月异的科技进步，正在深刻地影响着人们的经济、政治和文化生活。推动新经济的发展，不仅要求我们用先进科学技术更新经济，而且要求我们适应这个发展趋势来更新经济结构、经济体制、经济机制，更新国与国、企业与企业之间的经济关系，更新推进各国开展经济技术合作的指导思想。

　　在经济全球化不断发展的背景下，贸易自由化问题日益受到人们的关注。正确认识和把握经济全球化和贸易自由化问题，对促进全球经济健康发展具有十分重要的意义。经济全球化和贸易自由化的发展，总体上对全球经济发展有好处。但也必须看到，在当前全球经济发展很不平衡的情况下，这个问题处理不好，也会给发展中国家和中小企业带来不利影响。因此，世界贸易组织、亚太经合组织以及各国政府在推动经济全球化和贸易自由化的过程中，应充分考虑经济发展处于"弱者"地位的国家和人民的利益。

　　经济全球化和贸易自由化的进程，可以有两种发展趋势。一种是，推动它们朝着合理的方向发展,促进有效而公正地配置世界资源,促进各国生产力的发展,促进全球多边贸易体制和公正合理的国际经济新秩序的建立,从而造福各国人民。一种是,任凭它们按照不合理的规则运行,进一步扩大南北发展差距,加深"数字鸿沟",加剧贫富两极分化和环境恶化。毫无疑问,我们应该选择并推进前一种趋势,警惕并控制后一种趋势,弘扬合作发展精神,大力加强经济技术合作,赋予经济全球化和贸易自由化以互利合作的内涵,促进其健康发展。

加强企业间的合作是当今世界企业发展的重要方向。不少企业家认为,企业间开展平等竞争固然重要,但开展合作更为重要,合作的空间要大于竞争的空间。这个看法是很有见地的。在经济全球化和新经济不断发展的条件下,如果不能与其他企业建立良好的合作关系,任何企业都难以获得成功。

中国进一步发展经济、扩大开放,对各国企业就意味着更多的商机。改革开放以来,中国企业与国外、海外企业积极开展经济技术合作,取得了巨大成就。这些企业帮助了中国企业的成长,同时也在合作中获得了利益,取得了互利和共赢的结果。中国政府愿意继续提供便利和条件,推动中国企业与国外、海外企业进一步开展合作。

进入了全面建设小康社会的中国与时俱进,加快社会主义现代化建设。中国将以更加积极的姿态参与区域及全球范围的经济技术合作。中国将严格遵循国际通行的市场规则,实行公开、透明、平等的贸易和投资政策,进一步推动全方位、多层次、宽领域的对外开放。一个稳定、发展、进步的中国,将为促进世界和地区的和平与发展做出更大的贡献。

谢谢。

句子精练
Sentences in Focus

Interpret the following sentences from Chinese into English:
1. 我很高兴能应邀与各位一起研讨上海金融业的现状与发展趋势。
2. 鉴于上海特殊的历史地位与地理优势,亦基于中国经济强劲发展的实力,这座城市重建远东国际金融中心的势态已成定局。

3. 上海已形成以中央银行(即中国人民银行)为领导,以国有商业银行为主体,各种金融机构并存,发展比较健全的金融机构组织体系。

4. 上海已建成包括证券市场、外汇市场、贴现市场、保险市场、金银买卖市场在内的比较完整的金融市场体系。

5. 上海证券期货市场的发展最为瞩目,它已成为辐射全国、影响深远的国内最大的资本市场。

6. 在不久的将来,上海将全方位地介入国际金融活动,外汇市场、资本市场、黄金市场将实现与世界各金融中心的全天候交易,人民币将实行自由兑换。

7. 亚洲是地球上最大的洲,资源十分丰富,历史源远流长,文化博大精深。亚洲人民勤劳智慧,自强不息。

8. 包容、平等和渐进的地区合作意识近年来日益加强。

9. 从实际需要和实践看,可以把贸易、交通、农业、信息、能源作为优先合作领域,并逐步向其他领域扩展。

10. 区域合作和双边合作两者可以形成良性互动。

11. 我们恪守入世承诺,有步骤地扩大开放领域,降低关税水平,取消非关税壁垒。

12. 设立外资企业的申请,由国务院对外经济贸易主管部门或者国务院授权的其他机关审查批准。

13. 外资企业分立、合并或者其他重要事项变更,应当报审查机关批准,并向工商行政机关办理变更登记手续。

14. 外资企业终止,应当及时公告,依照法定程序进行清算,并向工商行政管理机关办理注销登记手续,缴销营业执照。

15. 推动新经济的发展,不仅要求我们用先进科学技术更新经济,而且要求我们适应这个发展趋势来更新经济结构、经济体制、经济机制,更新国与国、企业与企业之间的经济关系,更新推进各国开展经济技术合作的指导思想。

16. 在推动经济全球化和贸易自由化的过程中,世贸组织应充分考虑经济发展处于"弱者"地位国家和人民的利益。

17. 改革开放以来,中国企业与国外、海外企业积极开展经济技术合作,取得了巨大成就,取得了互利和共赢的结果。
18. 中国将以更加积极的姿态参与区域及全球范围的经济技术合作,进一步推动全方位、多层次、宽领域的对外开放。

参考译文
Reference Version

12—1 金融扩展
The Growing Financial Industry

Ladies and gentlemen,

Today I'd like to talk about the current situation and the trend of development of Shanghai's financial industry.

It is known to all that Asia is an area with the fastest economic growth in world economic development, and China boasts the fastest growing economy in Asia. Meanwhile, Shanghai is one of the most attractive cities in China's economic development. Back in the 30s and 40s of the last century, Shanghai was then the largest international financial center in the Far East. Today, thanks to Shanghai's distinct historical position and superior geographic location, and in view of China's actual economic strength as a result of its vigorous economic development, it is inevitable that this city will reestablish itself as an international financial center in the Far East. As early as in 1992, the late Mr. Deng Xiaoping, known as the chief architect of China's reform program, explicitly stated during his Shanghai tour that "China's success in obtaining an international status in finance will first of all depend on Shanghai". China's decision-makers are determined to turn as soon as possible the city of Shanghai into an international center of economy, finance and trade.

With 15 years of financial development and reform, the financial institutions in Shanghai have expanded rapidly. Shanghai has formed a comparatively complete financial system with the Central Bank (i. e. , People's Bank of China) as the leader and state commercial banks as the main body, and with various financial institutions developing together. In recent 10 years, foreign-funded financial institutions have swarmed in, each trying to secure a place in Shanghai. Among them are foreign-funded banks, foreign-funded financial companies, a foreign-funded insurance company and representative offices of foreign-funded financial institutions. Meanwhile, Shanghai's financial market has developed rapidly. By now, Shanghai has established a relatively complete financial market system with a fair size and a quite strong influence, a system which includes a securities market, a foreign exchange market, a discount market, an insurance market, and a bullion trading market, etc. . The development of the Shanghai securities market has attracted the widest attention. It has grown to be the largest domestic capital market, radiating its profound influence across the country.

With the deepening of China's reform and opening drive and the strengthening of its comprehensive national strength, Shanghai's financial industry will certainly embark on an all-round development at a higher level. According to the blueprint for social and economic development drawn by Shanghai Municipal Government, by the year 2010, Shanghai will have primarily grown to be one of the economic, financial and trade centers in the world, participating in an all-round manner in international financial activities. Our foreign exchange market, capital market and gold market will have 24-hour trading operations with all the financial centers in the world, and our RMB will enjoy free convertibility.

Ladies and gentlemen, Shanghai in the new century is a city with great expectations. It is a most valuable place where foreign financiers and entrepreneurs with a broad vision can very well realize their ambitions. Let us join hands and work together on our grand task of development. Thank you.

12—2 亚洲合作
Asian Cooperation

It gives me great pleasure to attend this First Annual Conference of Boao Forum for Asia and discuss with you issues concerning Asia's regional cooperation and development in the new century.

As the biggest continent on the earth, Asia takes up 60 percent of its population. It has abundant resources, a long history and profound cultures. In recent years, thanks to the joint efforts of Asian countries, there has been a growing awareness of regional cooperation featuring greater tolerance, equality and gradual progress, while a situation of open, healthy and mutually beneficial cooperation is taking shape. APEC is making steady progress. The East Asia regional cooperation is developing in full swing and the Shanghai Cooperation Organization is functioning smoothly. China and the ASEAN members agree to gradually build a China-ASEAN free trade area in the coming decade, and are making contacts for an early launch of negotiations. These developments will provide important channels and mechanisms for wider exchanges and deeper cooperation among Asian countries and regions. However, compared with Europe and North America, Asia's regional cooperation is lagging behind. Lately, there have been quite a few insightful views offered on the orientation of regional cooperation in Asia. Here, I would like to make some observations.

First, we should focus on economic cooperation and develop all-round cooperation in a step-by-step fashion. Economic development is the primary task of Asian countries. Given our real needs and experience, such areas as trade, communications, agriculture, information and energy can be made priorities of cooperation, which will be gradually expanded to include other areas.

Second, we should build on existing channels of cooperation to steadily broaden the scope of cooperation. As East Asia, South Asia and central Asia are relatively independent in terms of geographic location and different in ways of achieving economic development, it would be more advisable just for the sake of convenience and effectiveness to reinforce sub-regional cooperation as the first step and, on that basis, to actively explore ways of pan-Asia cooperation.

Third, we should further step up bilateral cooperation to consolidate the basis of regional cooperation. A closer progress at bilateral level will facilitate the smooth progress of regional cooperation, while regional cooperation will open even broader horizon for bilateral cooperation. The two can very well complement each other.

Fourth, we should ensure an open regional cooperation. Cooperation by definition must not be self-reclusive, still less lead to the formation of exclusive groups. Instead, Asian countries should further enhance their cooperation with countries of other continents through such channels as APEC, ASEM, East Asia-Latin America Forum.

China is an Asian country. Over the past twenty-odd years, thanks to its unswerving pursuit of the reform and opening up policy, China has accelerated the development of its national economy. The new leap forward in China's reform, opening up and modernization drive will not only bring enormous benefits to the Chinese people, but also provide unlimited business opportunities, ushering in broad prospects for economic cooperation in Asia and around the world.

China's accession to the World Trade Organization represents the new starting point for its opening to the outside world. Our participation in worldwide economic cooperation and competition will assume greater scope and depth. China will open its door still wider to the rest of Asia and the world, to entrepreneurs and investors of all countries. We will honor our WTO commitments, opening more areas in a step-by-step manner, lowering our tariffs and removing non-tariff barriers. We will continue to improve our rule of law, thus bringing about in China a market environment that is fairer, more transparent and more predictable. In the meantime, we will energetically carry out our "going global" strategy, encouraging more Chinese firms of multiple ownerships to operate globally.

The Chinese people love peace. China's development needs a peaceful environment. The people in Asia are diligent, talented and persistent in self-development. The Chinese people are ready to work hand in hand with the people in other Asian countries to build a better future.

12—3 外资企业
Foreign-Capital Enterprises

I'd like to take this opportunity to introduce China's laws and regulations concerning foreign-capital enterprises.

To expand economic cooperation and technological exchanges with foreign countries and promote the development of China's national economy, the People's Republic of China permits foreign enterprises, other foreign economic organizations and individuals to set up enterprises with foreign capital in China and protects the legitimate rights and interests of such enterprises.

Foreign-capital enterprises shall be established in such a manner as to help the development of China's national economy. The State shall encourage the establishment of export-oriented and technologically advanced foreign-capital enterprises. The investments of foreign investors in China, the profits they earn and their other lawful rights and interests are protected by Chinese laws.

The application to establish a foreign-capital enterprise shall be submitted for examination and approval to the department under the State Council which is in charge of foreign economic relations and trade, or to another agency authorized by the State Council. After an application for the establishment of a foreign-capital enterprise has been approved, the foreign investor shall, within 30 days from the date of receiving a certificate of approval, apply to the industry and commerce administrative authorities for registration and obtain a business license. A foreign-capital enterprise that meets the requirements for being a legal entity under Chinese law shall acquire the status of a Chinese legal entity, in accordance with the law.

A foreign-capital enterprise shall make investments in China within the period approved by the authorities in charge of examination and approval. If it fails to do so, the industry and commerce administrative authorities may cancel its business license.

In the event of separation, merger or other major changes, a foreign-capital enterprise shall report to and seek approval from the authorities in charge of examination and approval, and register the change with industry and commerce administrative authorities.

When employing Chinese workers and staff, a foreign-capital enterprise shall sign contracts with them according to the law, which shall clearly prescribe matters concerning employment, dismissal, remuneration, welfare benefits, labor protection and labor insurance. Workers and staff of foreign-capital enterprises may organize trade unions in accordance with the law to conduct trade union activities and protect their lawful rights and interests. Foreign-capital enterprises shall provide necessary conditions for the activities of the trade unions in their respective enterprises.

A foreign-capital enterprise must set up account books in China, conduct independent accounting, submit the accounting statements as required and accept supervision by the financial and tax authorities.

Foreign-capital enterprises shall pay taxes in accordance with relevant State provision, and may enjoy preferential treatment for tax reduction or exemption. An enterprise that reinvests its profits in China after paying income tax may, in accordance with relevant State provisions, apply for a refund of the portion of the income tax already paid on the reinvested amount.

The foreign investor may remit abroad profits that are lawfully earned from a foreign-capital enterprise, as well as other lawful earnings and any funds remaining after the enterprise is liquidated. Foreign employees in a foreign-capital enterprise may remit abroad their wages, salaries and other legitimate income after the payment of individual income tax in accordance with the law.

When terminating its operation, a foreign-capital enterprise shall promptly issue a public notice and proceed with liquidation in accordance with legal procedures. At the termination, the foreign-capital enterprise shall nullify its registration with the industry and commerce administrative authorities and hand in its business license for cancellation.

Thank you for your attention.

12—4 经济关系
Economic Links

Distinguished guests, ladies and gentlemen,

We have entered a new century. This is not merely a chronological change; it also marks a new era of economic development and social advancement for the international community. This new era distinguishes itself from others by a growing trend towards a multi-polar world and economic globalization, and, particularly, by the rapid progress in science and technology. All these have laid unprecedented material and technological conditions for continued economic and social progress worldwide and promise a broad prospect.

The scientific and technological progress with each passing day is bringing a profound impact on economic, political and cultural life of all human societies. To promote the development of the New Economy, we must not only update our economy with advanced science and technology, but also, in response to this new trend of development, revamp the economic structures, systems, and mechanisms accordingly, readjust the economic relationships between states and between enterprises and update our philosophies and concepts for economic and technological cooperation across national boundaries.

Against the backdrop of growing economic globalization, trade liberalization has attracted increasing attention. To put economic globalization and trade liberalization in their right perspective is of overarching importance to a healthy development of the global economy. They are generally conducive to world economic development. But one must be aware that given the unbalanced global economic development, any improper handling of this process will bring a negative impact on developing countries and small and medium-sized enterprises. In view of this, the WTO, APEC and national governments should give full regard to the interests of the economically disadvantaged countries and people while pushing forward economic globalization and trade liberalization.

There are two possible development scenarios for the process of economic globalization and trade liberalization. If the process moves along a rational track, it may not only allocate world resources more effectively and fairly and expand the productive forces of all countries, but also promote the establishment of a global multilateral trading system and of a new, just and rational international economic order to the benefit of people of all countries. But, if it should be allowed to proceed along an irrational way, it may widen the gap between the North and the South, worsen the "digital divide," sharpen the polarization between the rich and the poor and cause further environmental degradation. Without any doubt, we should opt for and facilitate the former scenario and guard against the latter. We must carry forward the spirit of development through cooperation and vigorously strengthen economic and technical cooperation. And we must make mutually beneficial cooperation a part and parcel of economic globalization and trade liberalization so as to ensure their sound development.

Closer cooperation between enterprises is a major trend in enterprise development today. Many entrepreneurs believe that although competition among enterprises is important, cooperation is even more so and that there is a bigger scope for cooperation than for competition. This is a sensible and well-grounded view. Given the development of economic globalization and the New Economy, enterprises can hardly succeed without good cooperative relations with other enterprises.

China will develop its economy further and open itself still wider to the outside world, which offers more business opportunities to overseas enterprises. Since China's reform and opening up, Chinese enterprises have vigorously undertaken economic and technical cooperation with overseas enterprises and scored tremendous achievements. While helping Chinese enterprises develop, overseas enterprises have also benefited from the cooperation, hence mutual benefit and all-win. The Chinese Government stands ready to continue to offer facilities and necessary conditions for closer cooperation between Chinese enterprises and their overseas counterparts.

China has entered a stage of building a well-to-do society throughout the country, advancing with the times and speeding up socialist modernization. China will take a more active part in regional and global economic and technical cooperation. China will strictly comply with the universally acknowledged market rules, implement open, transparent and equality-based policies of trade and investment and endeavor to promote a multi-directional and multi-level opening-up in a wide range of areas. A China that enjoys stability, growth and progress will make even greater contribution to peace and development in the region and the world at large.

Thank you.

句子精练
Sentences in Focus

---

1. I am very pleased to be invited and to discuss the current situation

and trend of development of Shanghai's financial industry.

2. Today, thanks to Shanghai's distinct historical position and superior geographic location, and in view of China's actual economic strength as a result of its vigorous economic development, it is inevitable that this city will reestablish itself as an international financial center in the Far East.

3. Shanghai has formed a comparatively complete financial system with the Central Bank (i. e. , People's Bank of China) as the leader and state commercial banks as the main body, and with various financial institutions co-existing and developing together.

4. Shanghai has established a relatively complete financial market system, a system includes a securities market, a foreign exchange market, a discount market, an insurance market, and a bullion trading market.

5. With the most remarkable development, the Shanghai securities and futures market has grown into the largest domestic capital market, radiating its profound influence across the country.

6. In the near future, Shanghai will participate in an all-round manner in international financial activities, its foreign exchange market, capital market and gold market will have 24-hour trading operations with all the financial centers in the world, and meanwhile, China's currency RMB will enjoy free convertibility.

7. As the biggest continent on the earth, Asia has abundant resources, a long history and profound cultures. The people in Asia are diligent, talented and persistent in self-development.

8. In recent years, there has been a growing awareness of regional cooperation featuring greater tolerance, equality and gradual progress.

9. Given our real needs and experience, such areas as trade, communications, agriculture, information and energy can be made priorities of cooperation, which will be gradually expanded to include other areas.

10. Regional cooperation and bilateral cooperation can very well complement each other.
11. We will honor our WTO commitments, opening more areas in a step-by-step manner, lowering our tariffs and removing non-tariff barriers.
12. The application to establish a foreign-capital enterprise shall be submitted for examination and approval to the department under the State council which is in charge of foreign economic relations and trade, or to another agency authorized by the State Council.
13. In the event of separation, merger or other major changes, a foreign-capital enterprise shall report to and seek approval from the authorities in charge of examination and approval, and register the change with industry and commerce administrative authorities.
14. When terminating its operation, a foreign-capital enterprise shall promptly issue a public notice and proceed with liquidation in accordance with legal procedures. At the termination, the foreign-capital enterprise shall nullify its registration with the industry and commerce administrative authorities and hand in its business license for cancellation.
15. To promote the development of the New Economy, we must not only update our economy with advanced science and technology, but also, in response to this new trend of development, revamp the economic structures, systems, and mechanisms accordingly, readjust the economic relationships between states and between enterprises and update our philosophies and concepts for economic and technological cooperation across national boundaries.
16. The WTO should give full regard to the interests of the economically disadvantaged countries and people while pushing forward economic globalization and trade liberalization.
17. Since China's reform and opening up, Chinese enterprises have vigorously undertaken economic and technical cooperation with

overseas enterprises and scored tremendous achievements, hence mutual benefit and all-win.

18. China will take a more active part in regional and global economic and technical cooperation, and endeavor to promote a multi-directional and multi-level opening-up in a wide range of areas.

第 13 单元　科普性口译(英译汉)

UNIT 13　Interpreting Popular Science Speeches
English-Chinese Interpretation

13—1　睡眠与梦
Sleep and Dream

> ### 词汇预习
> ### Vocabulary Work

irritable   slow-wave sleep
emotional   rhythm
psychological rest   dream cycle
alternate   exception
active sleep

> ### 课文口译
> ### Text for Interpretation

Interpret the following passage from English into Chinese:

It is clear that we all need to sleep. Most people rarely think about how or why they sleep, however. We know that if we sleep well, we feel rested. If we do not sleep enough, we often feel tired and irritable. It seems there are two purposes of sleep: physical rest and emotional, or psychological, rest. We need to rest our bodies and our minds. Both are important for us in order to be healthy.

Each night we alternate between two kinds of sleep: active sleep and passive sleep. Passive sleep gives our body the rest that is needed, and prepares us for active sleep, in which dreaming occurs. In passive sleep, the body is at rest, the heart beat slows down, and the body processes become very slow. We move very little, and the brain becomes very inactive. This stage of sleep is known as slow-wave sleep because the brain waves move in a very slow, regular rhythm.

If we continue to sleep, we will enter a more active stage, in which the body goes through several changes. In this new stage, the brain temperature rises, the amount of blood in the brain increases, the body becomes very still, and the brain goes from being very inactive to being active. As the brain becomes more active, the eyes begin to move rapidly. The eye movement signals that the person is dreaming.

Throughout the night, we alternate between passive and active sleep. The brain rests, then it becomes active, then dreaming occurs. This cycle is repeated several times throughout the night. During eight hours of sleep, we dream for a total of one and a half hours, on the average.

We all experience these dream cycles; no one is an exception. Many people say that they do not dream, or that they rarely dream. This is not what actually happens, because everyone dreams and in fact, everyone needs to dream in order to stay healthy. The truth is we need both kinds of sleep: we need passive sleep to rest our bodies, and active sleep in order to dream. Dreaming helps us to rest our minds.

13—2 音响今昔
The Sound Reproduction Industry

词汇预习
Vocabulary Work

---

bone whistle

phonograph

concentrate

orchestral

phonogram

affordable

mass-produced

turntable

portable record player

mono

real enthusiastic listener to music

realistic reproduction of music

high fidelity

transistor

hi-fi stereo system

compact cassette

magnetic tape

hardware

Walkman

compact disc

music information stored and reproduced digitally

digital format

digital audio tape

digital compact cassette

minidisc

mutually incompatible

obsolete

课文口译
Text for Interpretation

Interpret the following passage from English into Chinese:

From recorded time, man has been fascinated and delighted with music. Bone whistles, used as a type of flute, have been found dating back to 3000 BC. Paintings from the Stone Age show early musical instruments.

In modern times, man has further developed his interest in music and in recorded sound with the hardware of sound reproduction. American inventor Thomas Edison, who was considered the father of sound recording, developed the phonograph in 1877, the first device to record music in the world. While Edison concentrated at first mainly on the reproduction of the voice, it was not long before the musical uses of his invention were recognized and marketed. The modern recording industry was born to satisfy an enormous market for all types of music, folk, classical, orchestral and popular.

The phonogram, the first affordable and mass-produced device, played records on a turntable. The device was mechanical and was wound up by means of a handle on the side of the machine. Such machines were common as late as the 1950s.

The widespread use of electricity in the post-World War Two period led to the invention of the modern, portable record player. It was, however, "mono". The real enthusiastic listener to music wanted a realistic reproduction of music with "high fidelity" or "hi-fi".

The invention of transistors and the rise of the giant electronic companies in the developed world in the 1970s fed the growing demand for hi-fi stereo systems using compact cassettes containing magnetic tape.

The 1980s saw an even greater series of developments in sound reproduction hardware. The examples are the Sony Corporation's invention and development of the tiny portable tape players known as the "Walkman", and the compact disc, or CD, system based on the technology of computers with music information stored and reproduced digitally.

In the 1990s the developments of music hardware continue, with the main purpose of transferring and recording the astonishingly clear digital sound of CD, without the "hiss" noise often affecting magnetic tape. The digital formats vary and include digital audio tape (DAT), digital compact cassette (DCC) and the minidisc (MD). They are mutually incompatible, so the user must make a choice when they make a purchase.

Will this ever-improving technology produce another development beyond digital sound, making the CD as obsolete as the record? The answer is a definite "yes". When will this occur, then? No one can tell yet.

13—3 遗传信息
Genetic Information

词汇预习
Vocabulary Work

unique	mate
light hair	amazement
living creature	offspring
biologist	gene
pea plant	ethical

课文口译
Text for Interpretation

Interpret the following passage from English into Chinese:

There are over five billion people in the world. But every person is unique. Some people have black eyes; others have brown eyes, blue eyes, or gray eyes. Some have dark hair; others have light hair. Some are tall or thin; others are short or fat. Besides humans, there are millions of other living creatures. Some are so tiny that we simply can't see them with our own eyes. Whatever it is, every living creature is different from every other. Every living thing is a unique combination of characteristics.

Why is each living thing unique? Where do its characteristics come from? Do people receive characteristics from their mothers, or fathers, or both? Which characteristics do they receive? How? These are some of the questions that biologists try to answer. The work of a man by the name of Mendel a hundred years ago was especially important.

Mendel studied plants, especially pea plants. In some ways these plants were all the same. For example they all had flowers. But some had red flowers, and some had white flowers. Some pea plants were tall, and some were very short. Mendel was especially interested in these differences. He wondered why each plant was of a certain color, shape and size.

Mendel experimented with thousands of pea plants. First he mated a red flower plant with a white one. To Mendel's amazement, all the offspring plants had red flowers. Mendel was very curious to know what happened to the white color. Then he mated two offspring plants. Every time he did this, they produced three red flower plants and one white flower plant. Now Mendel knew that even red flower plants somehow passed on whiteness. Mendel decided that pea plants carried factors, and parents passed these factors onto their offspring. Today we call these factors **genes.**

Genes are tiny pieces of matter that carry information from parents to offspring. Based on Mendel's work, biologists began to ask such questions as "Can we apply our information about genes to people?" They discovered that in a person genes told whether he would have brown eyes or blue eyes, whether he would have dark hair or light hair, whether he would be tall or short, whether he would be thin or fat. Now we know that every person is unique. A major reason is that every person is a unique combination of genes.

What would happen if we combined animal genes with plant

genes? And animal genes with human genes? One species with another? Obviously, these are bold ideas that have upset many people for ethical reasons. Probably these questions will soon to be answered.

13—4　左脑之优
Left Hemispheric Dominance

词汇预习
Vocabulary Work

neuron	hemisphere
microcircuit	coordinate
perception	nerve pathway
cortex	perceptual skill
wrinkled	nonlinguistic sound
mantle	melody
tissue	muscular
layer	paralysis
neurological development	dominance
comparable	portion
cognitive	crucial
mammal	asymmetry
symmetrical	

课文口译
Text for Interpretation

Interpret the following passage from English into Chinese:

My topic today is the human brain and its relationship with language.

The human brain contains an average of ten billion neurons, or nerve cells, each of which is linked with one thousand to ten thousand other neurons. These nerve cells participate in countless electrical micro-circuits, which makes possible thought, perception, communication, and other types of mental activity.

The outside surface of the brain, which is known as the cortex, consists of a thin wrinkled mantle of gray tissue made up of millions of neurons. This layer of the brain represents man's relatively recent evolutionary step in neurological development and is not present to a comparable degree in any other species. Many of the cognitive abilities that distinguish humans from other mammals reside in the cortex. These cognitive abilities include sophisticated reasoning, linguistic skills and musical ability.

The brain is divided into two roughly symmetrical hemispheres, some-times called right and left brains. The activity of the two hemispheres is coordinated by a number of interconnecting nerve pathways.

The two sides of the brain, while fairly comparable in size and form, appear to specialize in handling various tasks. Current evidence suggests that the left and right hemispheres differ in some way in their function. For example, specialized linguistic and perceptual skills are each associated with a particular hemisphere of the brain. In most individuals, the left hemisphere has primary responsibility for language, while the right hemi-sphere controls visual and spatial skills as well as the perception of nonlin-guistic sounds and musical melodies.

Both hemispheres of the brain are involved in control over muscular activity as well as in sight and hearing. However, each hemisphere con-trols these activities for the opposite side of the body. Thus the right side of the brain is responsible for the movement of the left arm and leg, while the left hemisphere controls the movement of the right arm and leg. This is why someone who suffers damage to the right side of the brain will exhibit paralysis on the left side of the body.

You may ask which part of the brain is responsible for linguistic communication. Although there is no final answer to this question, studies have shown that the language center is located primarily in the left hemisphere of the brain in well over 90% of right-handers, who themselves make up about 90% of the population. Although the figure is somewhat lower for left-handers, about 60%, it is clear that the left side of the brain is somehow special as far as language is concerned.

Scientists believe that left-brain dominance in linguistic functions appears to exit prior to birth. It is now known that a portion of the left brain that is crucial to language is larger in fetuses than the corresponding portion of the right brain. This asymmetry is maintained throughout life.

So much for this session. May I stop to take your questions?

句子精练
Sentences in Focus

Interpret the following sentences from English into Chinese:

1. Sleep, in the form of active or passive sleep, serves the purpose of physical and emotional rest.
2. Passive sleep is also known as slow-wave sleep because the brain waves move in a very slow, regular rhythm, during which the body is at rest, the heart beat slows down, and the body processes become very slow.
3. From recorded time, man has been fascinated with music and the hardware of sound reproduction.
4. The modern recording industry was born to satisfy an enormous

market for all types of music: folk, classical, orchestral and popular.

5. The widespread use of electricity led to the invention of the portable record player, while the rise of the electronic industry fed the growing demand for hi-fi stereo systems.

6. The CD system is based on the technology of computers with music information stored and reproduced digitally.

7. It is certain that the ever-improving technology will give rise to another development beyond digital sound, making the CD obsolete from general use.

8. Every living thing is a unique combination of the tiny pieces of matter called genes that carry information from parents to offspring.

9. There are people who are obsessed with cloning experiments and wish to apply the theory of genetical replication in cloning human beings.

10. The idea of combining animal genes with plant genes, or animal genes with human genes, has upset many people for ethical reasons.

11. The human brain contains an average of ten billion neurons that participate in countless electrical microcircuits, the process of which makes possible thought, perception, communication, and other types of mental activity.

12. In the cortex of the brain reside human cognitive abilities such as sophisticated reasoning, linguistic skills and musical ability.

13. The cortex, which is not present to a comparable degree in any other species, represents man's relatively recent evolutionary step in neurological development.

14. The brain is divided into two roughly symmetrical hemispheres which appear to specialize in handling various tasks.

15. Current evidence suggests that in most individuals, the left hemisphere has primary responsibility for language, while the right

hemisphere controls visual and spatial skills as well as the perception of nonlinguistic sounds and musical melodies.

16. It is believed that left brain dominance for linguistic functions appears to exit prior to birth and this linguistic asymmetry is maintained throughout life.

参考译文
Reference Version

13—1　睡眠与梦
Sleep and Dream

显然我们都需要睡眠。大多数人很少考虑他们是如何睡眠的,他们为何要睡眠。我们知道如果我们睡得好,我们就会感到有了充分的休息。如果我们睡眠不充足,我们常会感到疲倦和烦躁。看来睡眠有两个目的:体力休息和精神休息(或叫做心理休息)。我们需要让自己的身体和大脑都得到休息。

每天晚上我们有两种交替出现的睡眠方式,即积极睡眠和消极睡眠。消极睡眠给我们的身体以所需要的休息,并让我们向积极睡眠过渡。积极睡眠时人会做梦。消极睡眠时我们的身体处于一种安宁的状态,我们心脏的跳动减缓,我们人体机能的运行变得非常缓慢。我们身体很少移动,大脑几乎处于静止状态。这一阶段的睡眠叫做慢波睡眠,因为这时的脑电波处于一种非常缓慢的、有节奏的波动状态。

如果我们继续睡眠,我们便会进入一个比较积极的睡眠阶段,人体会历经几种变化。在这个新的阶段,大脑温度会上升,大脑血液流量会增加,人体会变得几乎纹丝不动,大脑由静止不动状态转为积极活动状态。随着大脑活动变得较为积极,人的眼睛开始快速运动起来。人眼运动表明了我们正在做梦。

整个晚上我们始终处于消极睡眠阶段和积极睡眠阶段相互交替的过程。大脑保持静态,然后积极活动起来,然后我们开始做梦。整个夜晚这一过程会循环出现好几次。在八小时的睡眠过程中,我们做梦的总时间平均为一个半小时。

　　人人都会经历这些做梦过程，无一人例外。许多人说自己不做梦，或者说很少做梦。而实际情况并非如同他们所说的那样，因为每个人都做梦，事实上人人都需要通过做梦来保持身心健康。实际情况是，我们需要两种睡眠：我们需要消极睡眠以休息身体，我们还需要积极睡眠以进入梦乡。做梦有助于休息我们的大脑。

13—2　音响今昔
The Sound Reproduction Industry

　　有史记载以来，人类一直痴迷于音乐，为音乐所陶醉。用作笛子的骨哨早已出现在公元前三千年。从石器时代的画中我们可以见到早期乐器的模样。

　　现代人进一步发展了对音乐的兴趣，对用声音复制设备来录音的方式情有独钟。被誉为录音之父的美国发明家托马斯·爱迪生于1877年发明了留声机，这是世界上第一台录音设备。爱迪生最初的精力主要放在说话声的复制上，而时隔不久，他这项发明的音乐应用价值便为世人所认识，并被推向了市场。旨在满足人们对各种音乐的需求，如民间、古典、管弦、流行等音乐需求的现代录音产业便应运而生。

　　留声机是一种在转盘上播放唱片的机器，是有史以来第一批为人们所消费得起的、大批量生产的音响设备。留声机为机械结构，机子边上有一只用以上发条的摇柄。时至20世纪50年代这种留声机还很普遍。

　　二次大战后电的广泛使用使现代便携式电唱机面市。不过这种电唱机只能单声道放音，而真正的音乐发烧友想要一种能给人以一种身入其境感觉的有高保真度的音响设备。

　　晶体管的发明以及20世纪70年代发达国家中大型电子公司的崛起使人们对使用盒式磁带的高保真音响的需求升温。

　　到了20世纪80年代，声音复制设备的发展迈出了一系列更大的步伐，例如推出了由索尼公司首创开发的被称之为"随身听"的袖珍便携式磁带放音机，以及采用电脑技术以数码储存与再现音乐信息的激光唱片（CD）音响。

进入 20 世纪 90 年代后的音响行业还在继续发展,重点放在转录 CD 那种无比清晰的数码声音的技术上,这种技术不会产生使用磁带时通常会出现的那种"咝咝"噪声。使用数码声音技术可以有各种不同的编排格式,其中包括数码音带(DAT)、数码微型盒式带(DCC)和数码微型光盘(MD)等格式。由于这些编排格式互不兼容,所以客户在购买音响时需作选择。

音响技术改进的永无止境是否会开发出一种超越数码阶段的音响,使 CD 片像从前的唱片那样退出历史舞台吗? 回答是肯定的。那么这种替代何时发生? 目前尚无人可知。

13—3 遗传信息
Genetic Information

世界上有 50 多亿人。每个人都与众不同。有些人的眼睛为黑色,有些人的眼睛为褐色、蓝色或灰色。有些人头发乌黑,有些人头发浅淡。有些人瘦长,有些人矮胖。除了人类之外,还有数以百万计的其他生物。有些生物微乎其微,是我们无法用肉眼所能见到的。无论何种生物,个个都与众不同。每个生物都是特性的一种独特组合的产物。

为什么每个生物都会与众不同呢? 生物的特性又是从何而来? 人们的特性是遗传自母亲,还是遗传自父亲,或者是遗传自父母双亲? 人们从父母亲身上所得到的又是哪些特性呢? 他们又是如何得到这些特性的呢? 生物学家试图找到这些问题的答案。一百年前一个名叫孟德尔的人所做的研究工作具有特别重要的意义。

孟德尔的研究对象为植物,他尤其注重对豌豆植株的研究。从某些方面来看,豌豆植株都完全一样,例如它们都开花。但是有些豌豆植株开红花,有些却开白花。有些豌豆植株长得很高,有些却很矮。孟德尔对这些差异特别感兴趣。他很纳闷,为什么一棵植株会有某种颜色、形状和大小呢?

孟德尔对数以千计的豌豆植株进行了实验。他先将一棵开红花的植株与一棵开白花的植株杂交。孟德尔惊愕地发现杂交后的植株其后代都开红花。他很想知道白颜色的结果,于是他又将两棵后代植株进行了杂交。实验的结果是出现了三棵红花植株和一棵白花植株,每次实验的结果都一样。孟德尔明白了,即使红花植物也会因某种原因而遗传白颜色。他断定,豌豆植株带有遗传因子,父辈植株将这些遗传因子传给了子辈植株。今天我们称这种遗传因子为**基因**。

基因是一种将遗传信息从父辈传给子辈的微小物质。依据孟德尔的实验结果,生物学家开始提出了诸如"我们能否将我们有关基因的理论运用到人的身上"等问题。他们发现一个人的基因可以告诉我们他是否会有褐色眼睛还是蓝色眼睛,是否会有乌黑的头发还是浅色的头发,是否会是个瘦子还是胖墩。现在我们知道每个人都与众不同,其中一个主要原因在于每个人都是基因独特组合的产物。

倘若我们把动物的基因与植物的基因组合起来,那将会出现何种结果呢?如果我们把动物的基因与人的基因组合起来,或把一种物种的基因与另一种物种的基因组合起来,那又将出现什么样的结果呢?显然,这些大胆的想法由于伦理方面的原因使很多人颇感不安。也许这些问题很快就会有答案。

13—4 左脑之优
Left Hemispheric Dominance

我今天要讲的题目是人的大脑及其与语言的关系。

人的大脑平均有 100 亿个神经元,或者叫做神经细胞。每个神经元与 1 千至 1 万个其他神经元相连。神经元从事着不可悉数的微电路脉冲活动,由此而产生了思维、感觉、交流以及其他一些脑力活动。

大脑的外表层叫做脑皮层,脑皮层很薄,有皱褶,是一层由数以百万计的神经元组成的灰色组织。大脑的这层表皮代表着人类在其神经发展过程中的一次相对较晚的进化,任何其他物种的脑皮层都无法与人脑皮层相提并论。将人与其他哺乳动物区别开来的许多认知能力都寓于脑皮层中,如复杂的推理能力、语言技能以及音乐技能。

整个大脑划分为两个大致对称的半球,有时叫做右半脑和左半脑。这两半球的活动由一些互为连接的神经束协调。

大脑的两半球虽然就其大小和形状而言比较相像,却又各司其职。据目前所知,左右半球的功能各有所不同。例如:语言和感知的专项技能分属不同的半球。大多数人的左半球主要负责语言操作,而右半球则掌管着与视觉与空间有关的技能，负责对非语言声音以及音乐旋律的感知。

　　大脑的两半球都掌管着肌肉活动并对视觉与听觉负责，不过每半球只控制身体另一侧的活动。因此右半球只能对左半身的活动负责，左半球只能对右半身的活动负责。这就是为什么右半球受伤者的左半身会瘫痪的原因。

　　也许你们会问究竟哪一部分的大脑负责语言交际。这个问题虽未有最终结论，但是研究表明，占人口总数 90％ 的惯用右手者中 90％ 以上的人其语言中枢主要位于左半球。虽然语言中枢位于左半球的人数在惯用左手者中相对较低，约占 60％，但是大脑的左半部分因某种原因有着专辖语言的功能。

　　科学家认为，左半脑的语言功能优势似乎在婴儿出生前便已存在。据目前所知，与语言有着至关重要关系的左半脑的某一部分在胎儿期就比右半脑中的相对称的那部分大一些。这种大小不对称现象伴随着人生的始终。

　　这一部分讲完了，下面请各位提问。

句子精练
Sentences in Focus

---

1. 睡眠有积极和消极两种形式，其目的是使人在体力上和精神上都得到休息。
2. 消极睡眠又叫做慢波睡眠，因为消极睡眠时脑电波处于一种非常缓慢的、有节奏的波动状态，人体处于一种安宁的状态，心脏的跳动减缓，人体机能的运行变得非常缓慢。
3. 有史记载以来，人类一直痴迷于音乐，痴迷于复制音乐的音响设备。
4. 现代录音行业的诞生旨在满足市场对各种音乐如民间乐、古典乐、管弦乐、流行乐等音乐的巨大需求。
5. 电的广泛使用使便携式电唱机面市，而电子行业的出现则刺激了人们对高保真音响系统不断增长的需求。
6. CD 音响系统是一种采用以数码储存音乐与再现音乐的电脑技术

的音响设备。

7. 可以断定,不断改进的技术必将产生一种超越数码阶段的音响系统,致使 CD 光碟退出大众使用的舞台。

8. 每个生物都由一些叫做基因的物质独特组合而成的,基因则是一种将遗传信息由父辈传给子辈的微小物质。

9. 某些热衷于克隆试验的人们想把遗传复制的理论运用到复制人类上去。

10. 一想到将动物的基因与植物的基因组合起来,或者将动物的基因与人的基因组合起来,许多人出于伦理方面的原因而颇感不安。

11. 人的大脑平均有 100 亿个神经元,每个神经元都从事着不可悉数的微电路脉冲活动,由此而产生了思维、感觉、交流以及其他一些脑力活动。

12. 人类的认知能力,如复杂的推理、语言、音乐等能力,无不寓居于人类大脑的脑皮层上。

13. 任何其他物种都不具有人类的脑皮层,脑皮层的出现代表着人类在其神经发展过程中相对较晚阶段所经历的一次进化。

14. 大脑划分为两个大致对称的各司其职的半球。

15. 据目前所知,大多数人的左半球主要负责语言行为,而右半球则掌管着与视觉与空间有关的技能,以及对非语言类声音和音乐旋律的感知。

16. 据认为,左半脑的语言功能优势似乎在婴儿出生前便已存在,而且这种大脑的语言不对称现象伴随着人生的始终。

第14单元 科普性口译(汉译英)

UNIT 14　Interpreting Popular Science Speeches Chinese-English Interpretation

14—1　汉语概要
The ABC of Chinese

词汇预习
Vocabulary Work

特征　　　　　　　　　词形变化表

截然不同　　　　　　　史前的混沌时期

书写体系　　　　　　　同宗同源

错综复杂　　　　　　　华夏祖先

动词变化形式　　　　　神喻圣言

名词变格　　　　　　　单音节

课文口译
Text for Interpretation

Interpret the following passage from Chinese into English：

　　欢迎各位参加汉语学习班。作为学习班的第一课,我想介绍一下汉语有别于欧洲语言的一些普通特征。

　　对于那些只熟悉普通欧洲语言的人来说,汉语是一种截然不同的语言。但是,如果我们仔细观察一下汉语的结构,我们便可发现汉语的结构并非特别复杂。事实上汉语在许多方面较之西方语言更为简单。既然汉语与欧洲语言之间存有一些根本性的不同点,那么对汉语结构及其历史发展过程有所了解将有助于各位学习汉语。

在西方人看来,汉语的书写体系是一种全新的体系;他们所看到的不是排列整齐、笔划简单的字母,而是数以千计、形态各异的文字,许多文字看上去错综复杂,笔划纵横交错得令人难以置信。对许多西方人来说,汉语听上去颇有旋律感,或许有点像在歌唱。你若透过汉语的表象看其内部结构,也许会有更多的惊讶。汉语基本上没有什么动词变化形式,也没有名词变格。汉语的语法全然没有那些令西方学童生畏的、语法手册中必有的词形变化表。例如,英语动词 to buy 有各种变化形式,如 buy、bought 和 buying,而汉语只有一种形式"买"。又如英语名词 book 有单复数之分,而汉语只有"书"一种形式。语言的上下文常常可以清楚地表明动词的时态和语态,以及名词的数。因而,汉语无需依靠这种特别的语法重复结构。也许正因为汉语这种结构上的简洁性才使著名的美国人类学暨语言学家爱德华·萨丕尔将汉语描绘为一种有着"合理的逻辑性"的语言。

汉语常被认为是一种非常古老的语言。从某种意义上看,这种说法不免失之偏颇。人类的所有语言都可追溯到朦胧的史前时期,但目前我们还无法确定这些语言是否都同宗同源。五千年前华夏祖先说汉语的方法同英语人士的祖先说英语的方法大致相似。而从另外一种意义上说,汉语确实也是一种很古老的语言。今天所存的最早的汉字已有近四千年的历史。这些文字均为甲骨雕文。大部分的铭文为神喻圣言,内容大都与政治和宗教事件有关,有些则与天气或战争有关。汉语有丰富的古代文字作品,源远流长,远非任何其他一种语言的文字可与之媲美。一些最古老的汉字属象形文字。虽然大部分汉字无法从其图案的形态来解意,一般说来,汉语书写文字的形与意比英语书写文字的形与意有着更为直接的联系。而且大部分汉字都为单音节。汉字的悠久历史及其艺术价值使其比任何其他一种书写体系的文字有更多的大小变化和形状变化。

汉语的基本句子结构为"主—谓—宾",与英语相同。例如"我会说英语"这句话同 I can speak English 的词序完全一样。但是汉语可以省略那些可有可无的、不会引起误解的主语或宾语。

近年来世界各地学汉语者与日俱增。对于这门拥有世界上使用人数最多、文学历史最悠久的语言来说，这股学习热潮早该出现了。随着各位学习汉语兴趣的上升，我们可以深入探讨汉语的历史与结构，探讨汉语对中华民族的文化和思维所起的影响作用。这样的研究一定能使我们对人类语言本质有一个更好的、全面的了解。我以后会安排时间与你们一起探讨这方面的问题。

今天就讲到这里。

14—2　热量传递
Energy Transfer

词汇预习
Vocabulary Work

反射	导体
吸收	绝缘体
转移	静止不动
辐射	水流
分子	对流
传导	固／液／气体

课文口译
Text for Interpretation

Interpret the following passage from Chinese into English：

我们知道热量来自太阳，但不是每个人都很明白热是如何从太阳传来的。当太阳光照射到某样东西时，太阳光可以使所照射到的东西变热，而太阳光自身却不热。虽然太阳光穿越空间照射到地球上，但事实上太阳与地球之间的空间非常之寒冷。

太阳光照到地球时，空气、土地以及一切被照射到的物体都会升温。有些光线被反射回去,有些光线则被所照之物吸收了。闪亮的表面比暗淡的表面可以反射更多的光,这是因为后者吸收的光比前者更多。我们认为太阳辐射热量,并称这种热量转移方式为**辐射**。辐射仅仅是热量从一处传向另一处的三种方式之一。

如果你将一把银制汤匙和一把木制汤匙同时浸入沸水中,银制汤匙的把柄很快会变热,而木制汤匙的把柄不会升温。这种现象的原因在于,银制汤匙一端的热量由一个银分子迅速传递给另一个银分子。而对木料来说,情况却不一样。

热量由一个分子传递给另一个分子的现象叫做**传导**。当热量以这种方式转移时,我们认为热量被传导了。能够迅速传导热量的材料叫做热传良导体。所有金属都属热传优良导体,而木料、橡胶、空气等物的分子因不易迅速传递热量,所以被认为是热传不良导体。

热传劣导体又常常被叫做绝缘体,由于绝缘体的分子不易迅速传递热量,所以可以防止散热。静止不动的空气属于一种最糟糕的导体,因而也是最优良的绝缘体。任何含大量空气的材料都属优良绝缘体。

你如果给水加温,便可看到水在运动。运动的水叫做水流。水在流动时带走了热量。我们将这种热传现象叫做**对流**。由于固体不会运动,所以热量无法在固体中进行对流转移。对流只存在于液体和气体之中。

我把以上所述小结一下:热量有三种转移方式,它们分别为辐射、传导和对流。通常,热量在空间或气体中辐射,在固体中传导,在液体和气体中对流。

14—3　蚊虫之祸
The Power of the Petty Mosquito

词汇预习
Vocabulary Work

（亚）热带　　　　　　　　　　病菌

吸血为生　　　　　　　　命归黄泉

宿敌　　　　　　　　　　产卵

致命的　　　　　　　　　稀释

吉尼斯世界纪录大全　　　周而复始的恶圈

疟疾　　　　　　　　　　免疫力

石器时代　　　　　　　　杀虫剂

直／间接杀手　　　　　　无生育能力

肆虐

> **课文口译**
> **Text for Interpretation**

Interpret the following passage from Chinese into English:

　　如果你生活在热带或亚热带地区,例如中国的海南岛或香港,你便无法免遭蚊虫叮咬之苦。这些小害虫似乎无处不有,它们携带传染病菌,以吸血为生,彻夜骚扰不止。

　　事实上蚊子是世界上最危险的虫子,也是人类最古老的宿敌和最致命的杀手。据《吉尼斯世界纪录大全》记载,人类除了死于战争和事故外,携带疟疾以及其他病菌的蚊子被认为是自石器时代以来致人类半数于死地的直接或间接杀手。即使在今天,肆虐世界各地的蚊子每年将2百万人送入黄泉,另外估计约有6亿人受到蚊子所携带病菌的威胁。

　　携带传染病菌的蚊子都是雌蚊子,而雌蚊子在产卵之前通常都要吸血。雌蚊子先在受害者身上射入一种可以稀释血液的物质,然后通过头上那根如针般的细管将稀释后的血液吸上来。起稀释作用的物质携带着病菌由蚊子传播给另一个人,于是形成了一个传播疾病与导致死亡的周而复始的恶圈。

　　蚊子产生免疫力的速度似乎与我们发明杀虫剂的速度一样快,也与我们开发药物、控制蚊子传播疾病的速度一样快。很多事例表明,蚊子产生抗体所需要的时间远比人类发明药物所需要的时间少得多。

　　那么我们可以采取什么样的措施来使人类免受蚊虫宿敌的致命伤

害呢？有人建议把无生育能力的蚊子放入蚊群,这样可以控制蚊子增长的数量。然而这样做是否可以将蚊子及其所携带的病菌一扫而光却非常值得怀疑。至少目前还做不到。现在的问题是如何控制蚊虫的危害,而不是如何彻底打败我们的宿敌。除了医生和科学家的努力之外,这场控制虫害的战争必须在全世界范围内展开,必须是一场全球性的战争。

14—4 用筷技艺
The Magic Chopsticks

词汇预习
Vocabulary Work

筷子	变色反应
荤／蔬菜	艺术性
竹子	海参
漆器	用餐规矩
玉石	平行
铝	咄咄逼人
象牙	乳猪

课文口译
Text for Interpretation

Interpret the following passage from Chinese into English：

　　筷子是中餐桌上最有特色的用餐工具。

　　几千年来我们中国人一直视筷子为一种可以将饭从碗中逐口送入口中的最简单同时也是最有效的工具。早在周朝时期(公元前 11 世纪—公元前 3 世纪)筷子便被人们用来夹取荤、蔬菜,而米饭则用手来取而食之。

这一时期的筷子叫做"箸",与"住"字谐音。可这个"住"字在船上被列为禁忌语,因为船是不可以在航行途中打住不前的,人们因而改"箸"字为"筷"字,与"快"字谐音。此后人们在"筷"字后又添加了后缀词"子"。中国许多厨房用品的名称都带有后缀词"子",如"杯子"、"盆子"、"锅子"、"桌子"等等。

掌握好筷子这件与生存有关的工具需要手指的熟练协调,而用好筷子则可以给孩子一次机会,向父母亲表明自己已无需再依赖汤匙进食,可以同常人一样为自己取食。

全国各地的筷子大小基本一样,而用材的种类则各有不同,选材包括竹子、木材、漆器、玉石、象牙、塑料、铝、银、金等。特长的竹筷通常为厨房用筷。过去人们用嵌有银器的木筷来测试是否有人在餐中下毒,因为银器碰到一些有毒物品会起变色反应。

我们中国人使用筷子的方法很有艺术性,各人有各人的方法,就好像签名一样,不尽一致。中国人一般都能随心所欲地用筷子夹起一粒米、一粒豌豆、一只滑溜溜的蘑菇或海参。对于那些用餐时只会使用刀叉的西方人来说,掌握用筷的方法和技巧开始时难度也许很大,也很有趣,需要很大的耐心,需要用心练习。如果他们希望享用一顿真正的中餐的话,那么花时间耐心学习用筷技艺不仅很有必要,而且也很有收益。

就餐时若自始至终握筷不放,这会被视为一种不礼貌的举动,与中国的用餐规矩不符。中国传统的用餐规矩要求就餐者将夹取到的食物送入口中后即把筷子平行放在饭碗或餐盘的一边。餐间交谈时用筷子指指点点也是一种不礼貌的行为。

在中国,餐桌上放一把刀是极其少见的现象。在许多人看来,刀会使人联想到虎视眈眈、咄咄逼人的武器,因而不可在友好温暖的餐桌上占有一席之地。根据中国的传统习俗,所有切割操作以及其他劳作都应该在厨房内进行。这样所有出现在餐桌上的食物都可一口送入口中,但是全鱼、全鸡、整头乳猪除外。这些菜经过一番烹调,可以用筷子夹开取用,因而也无需借助刀子切割。

句子精练
Sentences in Focus

Interpret the following sentences from Chinese into English：

1. 对于那些只熟悉普通欧洲语言的人来说，汉语是一种截然不同的语言。在他们看来，汉字的笔划令人难以置信的错综复杂。

2. 如果我们仔细观察一下汉语的结构，我们便可发现汉语在许多方面较之西方语言更为简单，例如，汉语基本上没有什么动词变化形式，也没有名词变格现象。

3. 由于上下文常常可以清楚地表明汉语动词的时态和语态，以及名词的数，因而汉语无需依靠这种特别的语法重复结构。

4. 尽管目前我们还无法确定人类的语言是否同宗同源，但是它们都可追溯到朦胧的史前时期。

5. 汉语有丰富的源远流长的古代文字作品，其悠久的历史远非任何其他一种语言的书面作品可与之相比。

6. 今天所存的最早的汉字均为甲骨雕文，其中大部分为神喻圣言，内容大都与政治和宗教事件有关，或者与天气或战争有关。

7. 让我们深入探讨一下汉语的历史与结构，探讨一下汉语对中华民族的文化和思维所起的影响作用。

8. 虽然太阳光自身不热，但是它照射到某一物体时，却可以使所照之物变热升温。

9. 热量由一个分子传递给另一个分子的现象叫做传导。

10. 运动的水可以带走热量，我们将这种热传现象叫做对流。

11. 通常，热量在空间或气体中辐射，在固体中传导，在液体和气体中对流。

12. 蚊子是世界上最危险的害虫，也是人类最古老的宿敌和最致命的杀手。

13. 肆虐世界各地的蚊子携带着疟疾以及其他病菌，每年将 200 万人送入黄泉。

14. 研究表明蚊子产生免疫力的速度远远快于人类发明杀虫剂的速度。

15. 我们必须在全球范围内展开这场控制虫害的战争。

16. 制作筷子这一最简单、最有效的进食工具所使用的材料可以多种多样，如竹子、木材、漆器、玉石、象牙、塑料、铝、银、金等。

17. 我们中国人使用筷子很有艺术性，各人有各人的方法，就好似签名一样百花齐放。

18. 对于那些用餐时只会使用刀叉的西方人来说，若想享用一顿真正意义上的中餐，那么花时间耐心学习用筷技艺是有好处的。

参考译文
Reference Version

14—1　汉语概要
The ABC of Chinese

Welcome to the Program of Chinese as a Foreign Language. For the first session of this program, I wish to highlight some general aspects of Chinese which distinguish this language from European languages.

To people who are familiar only with the common European languages the Chinese language is strikingly different. Yet, when we examine the structure of the Chinese language, we find that it is not conspicuously complex. Indeed, in many ways it is simpler than the Western languages. But since Chinese does differ from European languages in some fundamental respects, some knowledge of its structure and historical development will help you to learn the language.

To the Western eye the writing system of Chinese is altogether novel: instead of neat rows of simple alphabetic letters there are thousands of unique characters, many of which seem incredibly intricate. To the ear of many Westerners the language sounds rather melodious, perhaps a little like singing. When you peer below the surface, there may be more surprises for you. The language has virtually no conjugation for its verbs and no declension for its nouns. The inevitable paradigms that Western schoolchildren have come to dread in their grammar books are totally absent in a grammar of Chinese. For example, for the various forms of the English verb "to buy", such as "buy", "bought" and "buying", Chinese has the single form *mai*. For the singular and plural forms of the English noun "book", the Chinese is *shu*. Most of the time it is quite clear from the context what tense or mood is intended for a verb and what number is intended for a noun. Hence the Chinese language does not bother much with this particular type of redundancy in its grammar. Perhaps it is this structural simplicity of the language that moves the well-known American anthropologist and linguist Edward Sapir to characterize it as "soberly logical".

Chinese is often termed a very old language. In a sense such a statement is misleading. All human languages go back to the dim uncertainty of prehistory, and at present we have no way of knowing for sure whether or not they can all be traced back to the same root. Five thousand years ago the ancestors of the Chinese people spoke an early form of the Chinese language in much the same way that the ancestors of the English-speaking peoples were using an early form of the English language. In one sense, however, Chinese is indeed a very old language. The earliest written forms of Chinese in existence today date back nearly 4,000 years. These writings are incisions on bone and tortoise shell. Most of the inscriptions are oracular, dealing mostly with political or religious events, or with weather or warfare. Chinese has an abundance of ancient writings that reach back continuously in time further than the writings of any other language in the world. Some of the earliest written Chinese characters were quite pictographic. Although most of the words in the language cannot be suggested by a simple picture, generally, a written Chinese character has a more direct connection with its meaning than a written word in English does. And most Chinese characters are exactly one syllable long. The long history and artistic values of Chinese characters have given them a much greater range of variability in their size and shape than the characters of any other writing system.

The basic sentence structure in Chinese follows the order of subject-verb-object, as in English. For example, the sentence "*wo hui shuo yingyu*" is word for word "I can speak English". There is, however, a tendency in Chinese to omit either the subject or the object when it is considered unnecessary and causing no misunderstanding.

In recent years, interest in the Chinese language is increasing at an accelerating tempo throughout the world. Considering that the Chinese language has the largest number of speakers in the world and the greatest time depth in its literature, this interest is long overdue. With the increase in your interest we may look forward to deeper probing into the history and the structure of the language, and into the influence the language has had on cultural and intellectual development of the Chinese people. These studies will surely lead to a better general understanding of the nature of human language. I will schedule time for our discussions on these issues at a later time.

That's all for today.

14－2 热量传递
Energy Transfer

We know heat comes from the sun, but not everyone knows exactly how it comes. When the rays of the sun touch something in their way, they make it warm, although the rays themselves are not hot. As a matter of fact, the space between the sun and the earth remains quite cold, although the rays are traveling through it.

When the sun rays reach the earth, they warm the air, the ground, and everything else they touch. Some rays are reflected and some are absorbed by the things on which they fall. A shiny surface throws back more heat than a dull surface, which absorbs more heat than a shiny surface. We believe that the sun radiates heat, and we call this method of heating as heat transfer by **radiation**. Radiation is only one of the three methods by which heat is passed from one place to another.

If you put a silver spoon and wooden spoon into boiling water at exactly the same time, the handle of the silver spoon quickly gets hot, while the handle of the wooden one remains cool. The reason for this is that the heat at one end of the silver spoon is passed on quickly from one molecule of silver to the next. However, this is not true for wood.

The transfer of heat from one molecule to the next is known as **conduction**. When heat is transferred like this, we say that it is conducted. Materials in which this happens easily and quickly are said to be good conductors of heat, and all metals are good heat conductors. In materials such as wood, rubber and air, heat does not pass easily and quickly from one molecule to the next, in which case we consider these materials as bad conductors of heat.

Bad conductors of heat are often known as insulators that stop heat from getting away because their molecules do not transfer heat easily and quickly from one to the next. Still air is one of the worst conductors and therefore, it is one of the best insulator. Any material which contains plenty of air is a good insulator.

If you heat water, you can see the movement of water. The movement of water is known as current. As the water moves, it carries the heat with it, and we say that the heat travels by **convection**. Heat does not travel by convection in a solid, because the solid does not move. We find convection currents only in liquids and gases.

To put what I have just said into a few words: There are three methods of the heat transfer and they are respectively radiation, conduction, and convection. Generally, heat travels by radiation in space or in gases, by conduction in solids, and mainly by convection in liquids and gases.

14—3 蚊虫之祸
The Power of the Petty Mosquito

If you live in a tropical climate or sub-tropical climate like China's Hainan Island or Hong Kong, it is impossible for you to avoid the attacks of mosquitoes. It seems that these little pests are everywhere. Feeding on blood and carrying infection, these little insects make nuisance of themselves throughout the night.

In fact, the mosquito is the most dangerous insect in the world, and can be shown to be man's oldest and deadliest insect enemy. According to the *Guinness Book of Records*, the type of mosquito which carries malaria and other diseases is believed to be responsible, directly or indirectly, for half of all human deaths since the Stone Age, if you exclude deaths from wars and accidents. Even today, mosquitoes kill up to two million people a year worldwide, and an estimated 600 million more are said to be at risk or threatened by the diseases they carry.

Infection is carried only by the female mosquito, which usually has to feed on blood before laying eggs. The insect injects the victim with a substance which thins the blood, before it is sucked up through a needle-like tube on its head. The thinning agent contains the disease, which will then be passed on to the next person by this mosquito. And so proceeds the vicious cycle of disease and death.

As quickly as we develop insecticides to kill them, mosquitoes seem to be able to develop resistance to our inventions. The same is true of efforts to develop drugs to control the diseases spread by mosquitoes. In many cases, it takes a much shorter time for mosquitoes to develop resistance to man's invention of a new drug than it takes man to develop the drug.

So what can be done to protect mankind from his deadly old

insect enemy? There have been suggestions that releasing sterile insects which cannot breed into the population might control the growth of mosquitoes in numbers. However, it is very doubtful that the mosquito and the diseases it carries will ever be completely wiped out. At least not for the present. The situation is now one of damage control rather than complete defeat of the old enemy. In addition to the efforts of the doctors and scientists, the war to control the damage this pest insect can do has to be carried out around the world. This has to be a global war.

14—4 用筷技艺
The Magic Chopsticks

Chopsticks, or *kuaizi*, are the most distinctive eating tool at the Chinese dining table.

For thousands of years we Chinese have always regarded chopsticks the simplest possible and the most efficient tool for transporting bite-sized morsels of food from a bowl to the mouth. As early as in the Zhou Dynasty (11th — 3rd century B. C.), chopsticks were used for picking up meat and vegetable, while hands were used for rice.

The Chinese term for chopsticks during this period was *zhu*, a character whose sound was homonymous with another word meaning "to stop". Since this character was taboo on ships, which were not supposed to stop en route, it was changed to *kuai*, a word homonymous with another word meaning "quick". Then, another character *zi* was added as a sort of suffix, as occurs with the names of many common objects, such as *beizi* (cup), *panzi* (plate), *guozi* (pot), *zhuozi* (table), etc.

The mastery of this survival tool requires a skillful coordination of fingers, which gives a child an opportunity to prove to his or her parents that he or she is no longer dependent on the spoon, and can reach out for his or her own food like everyone else.

Chopsticks, which are roughly uniform in size throughout China, can be made of a variety of materials, including bamboo, wood, lacquer, jade, ivory, plastic, aluminum, silver and gold. Special long bamboo chopsticks are generally used in the kitchen. In the past, wooden chopsticks inlaid with silver thread were used to test whether poison was put in a meal, since silver reacts to a number of poisonous substances by changing its color.

The way we Chinese handle our chopsticks is quite artistic and varied from person to person like one's signature. An average Chinese can very easily pick up a single tiny grain of rice, or a tiny piece of peas, or a slippery button mushroom or sea cucumber. For those Westerners who use only forks and knives for their meals, the mastery of the method and skills for using chopsticks may be quite challenging, and amusing, at the beginning. A lot of patience and concentrated practice is required. This is not only very necessary and but also very rewarding if they wish to enjoy a real Chinese dinner.

As far as Chinese table manners are concerned, it is considered impolite to hold chopsticks throughout meal. The Chinese traditional table manners require the diner to lay down the chopsticks on the table parallel to one's rice bowl or plate when one has sent the picked food into his or her mouth. It is also considered impolite to point with chopsticks during a conversation over the meal.

In China, it is quite rare for a knife to appear on the table. For many people, a knife is associative with a menacing weapon that should not find itself landing on a friendly, warm dinner table. It is also a Chinese custom for all chopping and other "manual labor" to be performed behind the kitchen door. Thus, all food which appears on the table is bite-sized or smaller, with the exception of entire fish, chickens, or suckling pigs, which are cooked in such a way that they can be served and eaten with chopsticks, and therefore there's no need for a knife to appear on the table.

1. To people who are familiar only with the common European languages the Chinese language is strikingly different. For them, Chinese characters are formed with many strokes that appear incredibly intricate.

2. If we examine the structure of the Chinese language more closely, we find it simpler in many ways than Western languages. For example, the Chinese language has virtually no conjugation for its verbs and no declension for its nouns.

3. Because most of the time it is quite clear from the context what tense or mood is intended for a verb and what number is intended for a noun, the Chinese language does not bother much with this particular type of redundancy in its grammar.

4. Although at present we have no way of knowing for sure whether or not human languages can be traced back to the same root, they go back to the dim uncertainty of prehistory.

5. Chinese has an abundance of ancient writings that reach back continuously in time further than the writings of any other language in the world.

6. The earliest written forms of Chinese in existence today are incisions on bone and tortoise shell. Most of these inscriptions are oracular, dealing mostly with political or religious events, or with weather or warfare.

7. Let us probe into the history and the structure of the Chinese language, and into the influence this language has had on cultural and intellectual development of the Chinese people.

8. Although the rays of the sun themselves are not hot, they warm up the objects they touch in their way.

9. The transfer of heat from one molecule to the next is known as

conduction.

10. The phenomenon that the heat travels as the result of the water moving and carrying the heat with it is known as convection.

11. Generally, heat travels by radiation in space or in gases, by conduction in solids, and by convection in liquids and gases.

12. The mosquito is the most dangerous insect pest in the world, and man's oldest and deadliest killer.

13. Carrying malaria and other diseases and flying rampant all over the world, mosquitoes are believed to be responsible for the death of up to two million people every year.

14. Studies show that it takes a much shorter time for mosquitoes to develop resistance to man's invention of a new drug than it takes man to develop the drug.

15. We must fight a global war to control this mosquito rampage.

16. Chopsticks, the simplest and most effective eating tool, can be made of a variety of materials, such as bamboo, wood, lacquer, jade, ivory, plastic, aluminum, silver and gold.

17. The way we Chinese use chopsticks is quite artistic and varies from person to person, similar to the way people write their signatures.

18. For Westerners who use only forks and knives for the meals, spending some time and learning to use chopsticks with patience can be very rewarding if they wish to enjoy a real Chinese dinner.

第三部分　口译测试

PART THREE
Interpretation Test in Brief

口译测试概要与实践
Interpretation Test: Essentials and Practice

英语中级口译测试的要求、题型及形式

"上海市英语中级口译资格证书考试"的口译部分有其特定的测试内容、形式和操作程序。本单元根据《上海市英语中级口译资格证书考试大纲》的测试框架及原则,将口译测试的要求、题型及形式作简要介绍,然后提供模拟试卷六套,以供教师检测学生的口译能力和应考水平。

测试要求

"上海市英语中级口译资格证书考试"要求凡获得"上海市英语中级口译资格证书"者均具有良好的口语能力和基本口译技能,可从事一般的生活翻译、陪同翻译、国际研讨会翻译以及外事接待、外贸业务洽谈等工作。

英语中级口译考试旨在测试考生的"英译汉"和"汉译英"的口译能力以及对口译基本技巧的掌握程度。考生在口译时应能准确传达原话意思,语音语调正确,表达流畅通顺,句法规范,语气恰当,用词妥切。

试题题型

口译测试采用微型演讲文翻译的形式。翻译总量为四篇短文,其中两篇为"英译汉",两篇为"汉译英"。短文题材与本教程的课文题材大体吻合,体裁一般为介绍、宣传、发言、演讲、祝词、报告等。每篇短文的篇幅大致为 120～140 个词。每个考生的口译测试时间约 10 分钟。

测试形式

　　口译测试采用个别面试的形式。考生逐句听事先录制好的原文，然后逐句将原文的内容准确而又流利地从来源语翻译成目标语。测试顺序通常以"英译汉"部分为先，然后再做"汉译英"部分。每部分均含两篇短文，每篇短文一般含四个句子，每个句子的长度一般不超过 35 个单词。口译均以句子为单位进行。考生可得到一张口译记录纸，用以在听录音时作一些必要的笔记。考生听完一句话后约有 20～30 秒左右的间隙供口译。口译时间的长短由口译录音信号控制，即考生必须在"始译信号"和"止译信号"之间完成有关句子的口译。

　　以下为六套口译模拟试卷，其题材、形式与要求同"上海市英语中级口译资格证书"的口译部分相吻合。

英语中级口译模拟测试

Model Tests for the Intermediate Interpretation Test

Model Test One

PART A (E—C)

Directions: In this part of the test, you will hear two passages in English. Each passage consists of four sentences. After you have heard each sentence, interpret it into Chinese. You will start at the signal ... and then stop at the signal ... . You may take notes while listening. Now let us begin Part A with the first passage.

Passage 1

Since we arrived, the gracious hospitality with which we have been received has been truly heartwarming. //

A Chinese proverb best describes my feeling: When the visitor arrives, it is as if returning home. //

One of the purposes of my visit was to make new friends, but I'm very pleased to find that instead of making friends, I am among friends. //

And I'm also very pleased with our cooperation in the joint venture which has been very successful: We both gained and profited, and we both survived the fierce competition in the world market.

Passage 2

Ladies and gentlemen, I suppose you've all read the report about the restructuring of the group's organization, which has given rise to the problem of relocating the new group. //

One possibility is to move all the head offices to Shanghai, and that is basically what the report recommends. //

Alternatively, we could continue to run the two companies quite separately in their present locations with the smaller company in Shanghai. //

I'm not sure how efficient the second option would be, but I'd like to hear your ideas on the subject.

PART B (C—E)

Directions: In this part of the test, you will hear two passages in Chinese. Each passage consists of four sentences. After you have heard each sentence, interpret it into English. You will start at the signal ... and then stop at the signal ... . You may take notes while listening. Now let us begin Part B with the first passage.

Passage 1

中国有一句话是这么说的，"上有天堂，下有苏杭。" //

这句话毫无夸张之意，苏杭这两座邻近上海的历史名城以其秀丽的景色每年吸引了数以百万计的海内外游客。//

例如，中国南方园林建筑艺术之典范、迷人的苏州造景园林在有限的空间里造就了无数自然景观。//

园林的池塘、河水、石头、花朵、树木给游客带来了如诗般的意境，是赴苏州观光客的必游之地。

Passage 2

女士们,先生们,进入 21 世纪的上海正在迅速发展为世界经济、金融和贸易中心之一。//

上海金融业的发展尤为引人注目,现已逐渐形成了一个具有相当规模与影响的金融市场体系。//

浦东新区近年来的崛起使这块黄金宝地成了海外投资的热点,投资总额已达 830 亿美元。//

上海这颗璀璨的东方明珠以其特有的魅力召唤富有远见卓识的金融家和企业家来此大展鸿图。

Model Test Two

PART A (E—C)

Directions: In this part of the test, you will hear two passages in English. Each passage consists of four sentences. After you have heard each sentence, interpret it into Chinese. You will start at the signal ... and then stop at the signal ... . You may take notes while listening. Now let us begin Part A with the first passage.

Passage 1

Permit me to say again this evening: Let us act according to the principle of mutual respect and mutual benefit, to the principle of both dignity and fairness. //

It is certainly in the fundamental interest of our people to trade and be friends with the Chinese people. //

We are very impressed by your modernization program, an ambitious undertaking which makes our future cooperative relationship very promising. //

China today, as I understand, is taking a practical and effective approach and we wish you success and offer you our cooperation in this great endeavor.

Passage 2

We know that the human brain is divided into two roughly symmetrical hemispheres, which are comparable in size and form, but not in function. //

The left hemisphere is primarily responsible for linguistic communication, i. e., the language center is located in the left side of the brain in most people. //

The right hemisphere, on the other hand, controls one's visual and spatial activities, including also musical perception. //

The most important differences between humans and other animals are the creative aspect of human language and man's sophisticated cognitive abilities.

PART B (C—E)

Directions: In this part of the test, you will hear two passages in Chinese. Each passage consists of four sentences. After you have heard each sentence, interpret it into English. You will start at the signal ... and then stop at the signal ... . You may take notes while listening. Now let us begin Part B with the first passage.

Passage 1

欢迎科林斯先生和太太来上海。我叫孟诗琪,是上海联华制衣(集团)公司海外营销部的经理。//

我很高兴能代表公司总经理陈先生在此接待您和夫人。//

我受陈先生的委托,代表公司在今后的几天里同您进行业务洽谈。//

我将同科林斯先生商谈有关建立公司海外销售网的事宜。请您多多指教。

Passage 2

"远亲不如近邻"是中国人民推崇的、经得起时间考验的信条。//

这一广为人们所接受的信条很有意义地表明了相互照顾在中国社区生活中所起的重要作用。//

中国现有 350 万左右的义务工作者为年老体弱者、残疾人以及需

要帮助的人士提供服务。//

　　这些来自社会各界的社区服务自愿助工出于"人人为我，我为人人"的信念为社区服务。

Model Test Three

PART A (E—C)

Directions: In this part of the test, you will hear two passages in English. Each passage consists of four sentences. After you have heard each sentence, interpret it into Chinese. You will start at the signal ... and then stop at the signal ... . You may take notes while listening. Now let us begin Part A with the first passage.

Passage 1

I am delighted to extend this personal welcome to Chinese visitors to the Sydney Agricultural Technology Exhibition. //

Here we present to our Chinese friends a comprehensive display of Australian agricultural achievements and advanced technology in farming that we have to offer. //

I greatly value the friendship and confidence that we enjoy as your trading partner. //

I am certain that this Exhibition will strengthen our economic cooperation and contribute directly to our further trade expansion.

Passage 2

As an American manager of a Sino-American joint venture for two years, I have to say that there are differences in business management between Chinese and Americans that we American businessmen in China should try to understand and respect. //

We are more direct and straightforward than most Chinese

colleagues due to our different cultural traditions. Often times they consider our way of business practice rather aggressive and we consider their process of decision-making time-consuming. //

I can't say our way of doing business is absolutely superior. After all, there are merits and demerits inherent in both types of management. //

It must be pointed out that in recent years, more and more American business executives have recognized the merits of the more humane Oriental way of Chinese management. It seems to offer something that we are lacking in.

PART B (C—E)

Directions: In this part of the test, you will hear two passages in Chinese. Each passage consists of four sentences. After you have heard each sentence, interpret it into English. You will start at the signal ... and then stop at the signal ... . You may take notes while listening. Now let us begin Part B with the first passage.

Passage 1

今晚,我们很高兴在北京大学接待格林博士和夫人。我代表学校的全体师生员工向格林博士和夫人及其他新西兰贵宾表示热烈的欢迎。//

中新两国教育界人士的互访,增进了相互间的了解和学术交流。//

我相信格林博士这次对我校的访问,必将为进一步加强两校的友好合作关系做出重要的贡献。//

明天,贵宾们将要赴南京和上海访问,我预祝大家一路旅途愉快。

Passage 2

我很高兴应邀参加本届中外文化交流节,向诸位介绍中国书法这

一人类文化财富和中国宝贵的旅游资源。//

　　中国有这么一句话，叫做"山不在高，有仙则名；水不在深，有龙则灵。"//

　　各位在中国旅游胜地所看到的包括铭文石碑在内的中国书法笔墨，就好比高山上的仙，大川中的龙。许多汉字属象形文字，我们可以从字形猜测词义。//

　　无论是刀刻书法还是笔墨书法都可以通过字形的夸张产生引人入胜的艺术效果。书法是一门研究艺术，观赏旅游景点的古代书法遗迹自然是一种艺术享受。

Model Test Four

PART A (E—C)

Directions: In this part of the test, you will hear two passages in English. Each passage consists of four sentences. After you have heard each sentence, interpret it into Chinese. You will start at the signal ... and then stop at the signal ... . You may take notes while listening. Now let us begin Part A with the first passage.

Passage 1

I'm very glad to have the opportunity to work in your company, and I'm particularly pleased to be able to work with a group of brilliant people in China's automobile industry. //

I had been looking forward to this job for many years and you have made my dream come true. //

I'm deeply grateful to you and appreciate all you have done for me. I really love my new residence by the beach that you have chosen for me. //

If you don't mind, I wish to tour around your company properties and meet my Chinese colleagues and lab assistants tomorrow.

Passage 2

Welcome to the official launch of IBM of Shanghai. I regard it as a great honor and a sign of good business that you show so much interest in IBM products and be with us on this important occasion in the IBM history. //

As the world leader in personal computers, IBM would like to share with Chinese customers our success. //

Among other things, IBM products enjoy an excellent price versus performance ratio and high quality, which I believe, are very important to our Chinese customers. //

We are looking forward to a long-term relationship with our clients and strategic partners which will help further strengthen our position we enjoy as the leader in the world's computer market.

PART B (C—E)

Directions: In this part of the test, you will hear two passages in Chinese. Each passage consists of four sentences. After you have heard each sentence, interpret it into English. You will start at the signal ... and then stop at the signal ... . You may take notes while listening. Now let us begin Part B with the first passage.

Passage 1

中外合资是一种互补互惠的合作关系。外国在华投资可以最大限度地发挥各自的优势。//

我国幅员辽阔、资源丰富、劳动力低廉、消费市场潜力大。此外我们还有稳定的政治社会环境和优惠的投资政策。//

发达国家有雄厚的资金、先进的技术和管理知识。投资兴办合资企业时，外方可以提供资金、机械、技术和管理方法。//

中方可以提供土地、劳工和部分资金。应该说，这种投资方法对合作双方来说，具有丰厚的经济回报率。

Passage 2

在这个举国同庆的美丽夜晚，我谨代表公司的全体同仁，感谢各位来宾从百忙之中拨冗光临我们的春节联欢晚会。//

春节是我国一年中的良辰佳时，我希望各位中外同事共度一个轻

松、欢快的夜晚。//

我愿外国来宾能尽情品尝中国的传统佳肴和美酒。我希望这次晚会能使我们有机会彼此沟通、增进友谊。//

最后我再次感谢各位嘉宾的光临，并祝各位新年身体健康、事业有成。

Model Test Five

PART A (E—C)

Directions: In this part of the test, you will hear two passages in English. Each passage consists of four sentences. After you have heard each sentence, interpret it into Chinese. You will start at the signal ... and then stop at the signal ... . You may take notes while listening. Now let us begin Part A with the first passage.

Passage 1

On behalf of all the members of my delegation, I would like to thank your company for the gracious invitation and hospitality. //

During our stay, we met a lot of friends and visited many factories. The new progress you have made impressed us deeply. //

We have a long friendly relationship with China. We have made great progress in many areas, especially in high-tech areas. //

Our cooperation is sincere and effective. We are no longer remote and strange to each other, but cordial friends and important trading partners.

Passage 2

This is a happy and memorable occasion for me personally as well as for all the members of my delegation. //

I wish to thank you for the generous hospitality and the warmth with which we have received. //

In accepting your gracious invitation to visit Shanghai, it has provided me with an excellent opportunity to learn about the investment environment here. //

It is my sincere wish that we would reach an agreement on the establishment of a joint venture in this most promising city.

PART B (C—E)

Directions: In this part of the test, you will hear two passages in Chinese. Each passage consists of four sentences. After you have heard each sentence, interpret it into English. You will start at the signal ... and then stop at the signal ... . You may take notes while listening. Now let us begin Part B with the first passage.

Passage 1

今天我们聚会在一起,在平等互利的基础上,就广泛领域里建立合作伙伴关系交换我们彼此的看法。//

这是一次具有历史意义的开拓性的会议,它反映了我们希望进行交流与合作、增进相互理解和信任的共同愿望。//

我深信这次会议将对我们的双边和多边关系产生积极的影响。我愿借此机会,向会议的东道主表示衷心的感谢。//

让我们携手合作,为会议在相互尊重、平等互利的气氛中圆满结束而共同努力。

Passage 2

浦江商务旅游公司是经国家旅游局批准的我国首批商务旅游公司之一。//

公司集科、工、贸、旅游、娱乐于一体,以外国在华的商社和三资企业为主要服务对象。//

公司的宗旨是拓展国内外商务旅游市场,以旅游促进商务,为改善上海及其周边地区的投资环境提供全方位的服务。//

公司竭诚与客户建立互惠互利的合作关系,坦诚相待,共同发展商务旅游事业。

Model Test Six

PART A (E—C)

Directions: In this part of the test, you will hear two passages in English. Each passage consists of four sentences. After you have heard each sentence, interpret it into Chinese. You will start at the signal ... and then stop at the signal ... . You may take notes while listening. Now let us begin Part A with the first passage.

Passage 1

I wish to take this opportunity to thank you on behalf of all my colleagues for your warm reception and incomparable hospitality. //

The past five days in China have been truly pleasant and enjoyable, and most memorable. //

Here, I particularly want to pay tribute to our Chinese partners whose effort has made possible the successful conclusion of the cooperative agreements. //

May I ask all of you present here to join me in raising your glasses, to the lasting friendship and cooperation between our two companies.

Passage 2

Ladies and gentlemen, I'd like to report on my recent investigation of the current situation of China's automobile market. //

Considering the fact that there is only one car for every 250 Chinese at present, the potential auto market is extremely attractive. //

China has cut its average tariff rate several times and promised to continue to cut its automobile import tariff. China has virtually opened its auto market to the outside world. //

China is seeking partners for its automobile industry, and we should walk up and take the opportunity.

PART B (C—E)

Directions: In this part of the test, you will hear two passages in Chinese. Each passage consists of four sentences. After you have heard each sentence, interpret it into English. You will start at the signal ... and then stop at the signal ... . You may take notes while listening. Now let us begin Part B with the first passage.

Passage 1

中国国际旅行社为各位安排了富有中国民族文化特色的有趣的旅游路线。//

各位将要游览举世闻名的景点和名胜,参观雄伟的古建筑群,观赏珍贵的文物。//

你们还将有机会欣赏中国的戏剧和杂技表演,品尝纯正的中国烹调和地方风味小吃。//

我国人民传统的热情和好客将使各位的这次访问愉快而又难忘。

Passage 2

欢迎各位参加对外汉语学习班。我们很高兴地看到,近年来世界各地学汉语者与日俱增。//

对于这门拥有世界上使用人数最多、文学历史最悠久的语言来说,这股学习热潮早该出现了。//

从某种意义上说,汉语是一种很古老的语言,其最早的汉字已有近

四千年的历史了。//

随着各位学习兴趣的提高，我将适时介绍汉语对中华民族的文化和思维所产生的影响。

参考译文
Reference Version

Model Test One

PART A (E—C)

Passage 1

自我们抵达这里时起，便一直受到暖人心房的盛情款待。//

中国有一句俗话最能表达我的感受，那就是"宾至如归"。//

我此次访问的目的之一是结交新朋友。然而我很高兴地发现，我不用结交朋友，我已处在朋友中间。//

我们合资企业成效斐然，我对我们之间的合作深为满意：我们双方都有收获，我们都经受住了国际市场剧烈竞争的考验。

Passage 2

女士们，先生们，我想各位已经看到了有关我集团组织重新调整的那份报告，由此而产生的问题是如何为新组建的集团选择所在地。//

一种设想是将所有的总部机构都迁移到上海，这也是这份报告所提出基本意见。//

另一种设想是继续在两处经营我们两家公司，公司的现址不变，小公司设在上海。//

虽然我对第二种选择的经营效率有所怀疑，但是我想听听各位的高见。

PART B (C−E)

Passage 1

A Chinese saying goes like this: "Just as there is a paradise in Heaven, there are Suzhou and Hangzhou on earth." //

This saying is no exaggeration about the scenic beauty of the two historic cities near Shanghai which attract millions of tourists from home and abroad every year. //

For example, the charming landscaped gardens of Suzhou, typical of China's southern garden architecture, contain numerous created landscape scenes within limited space. //

The ponds, water, stones, flowers and trees of these gardens create a poetic mood for tourists and therefore, a visit to these gardens is a must for every tourist visiting Suzhou.

Passage 2

Ladies and gentlemen, Shanghai, upon entering the 21st century, is developing rapidly into one of the world's economic, financial and trade centers. //

The development of Shanghai's financial industry is particularly spectacular, with a fairly large and influential system of a financial market coming into shape. //

The rise of Pudong New Area in recent years has turned this most valuable place into a hot destination of overseas investment, with a total investment volume reaching US $ 83 billion. //

Shanghai, the brilliant Oriental Pearl with its unique charm, invites financiers and entrepreneurs with broad visions to this city, where they will readily materialize their ambitions.

Model Test Two

PART A (E—C)

Passage 1

请允许我今晚重申，让我们以相互尊重、互惠互利的原则，以尊严与公正共存的原则为行动指南。//

同中国人民进行贸易往来，同中国人民交朋友，必定符合我国人民的根本利益。//

贵国的现代化建设给我们留下了深刻的印象，这一雄心勃勃的伟业，使我们未来的合作关系前程似锦。//

据我所知，今日中国采取了一种务实的、行之有效的方法。我们祝愿你们取得成功，并愿意在这项伟大的事业中与你们合作。

Passage 2

我们知道人脑分为大致相称的两个半球，它们的大小与形状比较相近，而功能则不同。//

人脑的左半球主要负责语言交际活动，也就是说，大多数人的语言中枢位于左半球。//

而人脑的右半球负责与视觉和空间有关的活动，同时也负责对音乐的感知。//

人类与其他动物之间最大的不同在于人类语言的创造性以及人类复杂的认知能力。

PART B (C—E)

Passage 1

Welcome to Shanghai, Mr. and Mrs. Collins. I'm Meng Shiqi, manager of the Overseas Marketing Department of the Shanghai Lianhua Garment Manufacturing (Group) Corporation. //

It's my pleasure to meet you and your wife here on behalf of Mr.

Chen, general manager of the company. //

Mr. Chen would like me to represent the company at our business talks in the next few days. //

I will talk with you about the establishment of the company's overseas sales network. Your advice will be very much appreciated.

Passage 2

"Distant relatives are not as helpful as close neighbors" is a cherished and time-honored belief in China. //

This widely recognized belief indicates quite meaningfully the important role of mutual care in China's communities. //

In China there are about three and half million volunteers who provide service for the aged, sick, handicapped and people who need help. //

These community service volunteers, who come from all walks of life, act upon their belief of "All for one and one for all".

Model Test Three

PART A (E—C)

Passage 1

我怀着愉快的心情,以我个人的名义,向光临悉尼农业技术展览会的中国来宾,表示热烈的欢迎。//

我们在这里向中国朋友全面展示我国的农业成就,并介绍我们所能提供的先进的农业技术。//

我非常珍视澳中两国在贸易合作中发展起来的友谊和建立起来的信心。//

我确信,这次展览会将进一步加强我们的经济合作,并直接对扩大我们之间的贸易往来作出贡献。

Passage 2

作为一名在一家中美合资企业工作了两年的美国经理,我认为中国人和美国人在经营管理中存在着差异,这些差异是我们这些在华工作的美国商务人士应该去理解和尊重的。//

由于我们有着与中国人不同的文化传统,所以我们比大部分中国人来得直率。中国人经常认为我们的经营方式咄咄逼人,而我们却认为他们的决策过程过于冗长。//

我不能说我们的经营之道一定优于中国的同事,毕竟各有各的优点和弊端。//

必须指出的是,近年来越来越多的美国经理人员开始认识到中国人的那种更具人情味的、东方式的管理方法的长处,这正是我们所欠缺的。

PART B (C—E)

Passage 1

It gives us great pleasure to play host to Dr. and Mrs. Green in Beijing University. On behalf of the faculty, students and staff of the university, I wish to extend our warm welcome to Dr. and Mrs. Green and other distinguished New Zealand guests. //

The exchange of visits between Chinese and New Zealand educators has facilitated our mutual understanding and academic exchanges. //

I am convinced that Dr. Green's current visit to our university will surely make an important contribution to further strengthening the friendly relations and cooperation between our two universities. //

Our distinguished guests will leave for Nanjing and Shanghai tomorrow. I wish you all a pleasant journey.

Passage 2

I am very pleased to be invited to attend this gathering to celebrate the current Sino-Foreign Cultural Exchange Festival, and to talk about Chinese calligraphy, mankind's cultural heritage and China's highly valued tourist resources. //

The Chinese saying goes that "Any mountain can be famous with the presence of an immortal, and any river can be holy with the presence of a dragon." //

The Chinese calligraphic works that you have seen in China's tourist resorts are like an immortal in a high mountain and a dragon in a great river. Many Chinese characters are pictographs and often the meaning of a particular character is apparent in the pictorial form of the character. //

Whether done with a knife or brush, Calligraphy can be rendered in ways that exaggerate the form, and consequently yields the inviting effects of artistic beauty. Calligraphy is a subject of artistic study, and the appreciation of ancient calligraphic relics seen in places of tourist attraction is certainly an artistic entertainment.

Model Test Four

PART A (E—C)

Passage 1

我很高兴有此机会来贵公司工作。令我特别高兴的是我能与中国汽车工业的杰出人士合作共事。//

我多年来一直盼望着能有这份工作,现在您使我的梦想得以实现。//

我很感激您为我所做的一切。我很喜欢您给我安排的这处与大海为临的新居。//

要是可能的话,明天我想去公司看一看,与我的中国同事和实验室的助手们见见面。

欢迎诸位光临 IBM 上海公司的开张典礼。各位如此钟情 IBM 的产品,愿意与我们一起度过 IBM 历史上的这一重要日子,我感到万分荣幸,这对我们的业务来说是一个好兆头。//

作为世界上个人电脑行业的龙头老大,IBM 公司希望同中国客户分享我们的成功。//

IBM 成功的因素很多,其中之一就是其优异的性能价格比以及产品的优质,而我认为这些品质对中国客户来说是非常重要的。//

我们期待着同我们的客户和战略伙伴建立一种长期的关系,这将有助于进一步强化我们在世界电脑市场上所享有的领先地位。

PART B (C—E)

Passage 1

A Sino-foreign joint business is one of complementary and mutual beneficial partnership. Foreign investment in China can maximize the strengths of both parties concerned. //

Our country has massive land, abundant resources, cheap labor and a potential consumer market, in addition to the stable political and social environment and favorable investment policies. //

Developed countries have sufficient funds, advanced technology and managerial expertise. When establishing a joint venture, a foreign partner may bring into the cooperative business capital funds, machinery, advanced technology and management. //

The Chinese partner, on the other hand, may supply land, labor and a portion of the funds. Therefore, this type of investment is supposed to yield fat economic returns for both parties in the partnership.

Passage 2

On the occasion of this beautiful evening of national celebration, and on behalf of all my colleagues of the company, I wish to thank all the guests here for taking the time off their busy schedule to come to this party and celebrate our Spring Festival. //

The Chinese Spring Festival is a very wonderful and joyous occasion in our tradition, and I wish all the Chinese and foreign colleagues a most relaxing and delightful evening. //

I hope our overseas visitors will have a good time enjoying to their hearts' content the finest traditional Chinese food and wine. I hope this party will give us an excellent opportunity to get to know each other and to increase our friendship. //

In closing, I'd like to thank you again for your presence and wish everyone good health and a successful career in the new year.

Model Test Five

PART A (E—C)

Passage 1

我谨代表我们代表团的全体成员,十分感谢贵公司的盛情邀请和款待。//

在访问期间,我们会见了很多老朋友,参观了许多工厂。你们取得的新成就给我们留下了很深刻的印象。//

我们同中国有着长久的友好关系。我们在许多领域,尤其是在高科技领域里的合作,取得了很大的进展。//

我们的合作是真诚的、富有成效的。我们彼此之间不再感到遥远和陌生了,我们已成了和睦的友邦和重要的贸易伙伴。

Passage 2

对我本人以及代表团的全体成员来说,这是个愉快而又难忘的时刻。//

我对我们所受到的热情欢迎和盛情款待谨向你们表示感谢。//

我接受您的盛情邀请来访上海,这使我有极好的机会来了解这里的投资环境。//

我真诚地希望我们能达成一项协议,在这座最有发展前途的城市建立一家合资企业。

PART B (C—E)

Passage 1

Today, we meet here to exchange views on cooperation in a wide range of areas on the basis of equality and mutual benefit. //

This meeting is one of pioneering endeavor and historic significance, one that reflects our common desire for exchange and cooperation, and for mutual understanding and trust. //

I am deeply convinced that this meeting will exert a positive impact on our bilateral and multilateral relations. I wish to take this opportunity to express my heartfelt thanks to the host of this meeting. //

Let us work together for a successful conclusion of this meeting in the spirit of mutual respect, equality and mutual benefit.

Passage 2

Pu Jiang Business Travel Company is one of the first business travel agencies approved by the Chinese National Tourism Administration. //

Integrating scientific research, manufacturing industry, trade, tourism and entertainment, the company provides service to foreign business establishments and foreign-funded enterprises in China. //

We operate under the principle of expanding our business travel markets at home and abroad, promoting business activities with the tourist development and offering an all-round service to improve the investment environment in Shanghai and its surrounding areas. //

The company does its best to establish cooperative relations with all its interested clients on the basis of mutual benefit and promote business tourism in an honest partnership.

Model Test Six

PART A (E—C)

Passage 1

我愿借此机会,谨代表我所有的同事,对你们热情的接待以及无与伦比的款待表示感谢。//

在中国度过的这五天,确确实实令人愉快,令人难以忘怀。//

我在这里要特别赞颂我们的中国合作者,他们的努力使我们成功地达成了合作协议。//

我敬请各位与我一起举杯,为我们两家公司的永久友谊和合作而干杯。

Passage 2

女士们,先生们,我向诸位汇报一下我对中国汽车市场现状所作的调查。//

目前中国的轿车拥有量为每250人仅一辆车。因此,这个潜在的市场具有极大的诱惑力。//

中国已数次下降关税,并承诺将继续降低汽车进口关税,中国汽车市场的大门已经敞开。//

中国正在寻求汽车工业的合资伙伴。我们的机会就在眼前。

PART B (C—E)

Passage 1

China International Travel Service is offering you an interesting tour program which is characteristic of Chinese national culture. //

You will visit world-famous scenic spots, historical sites and magnificent ancient architectural complexes, and appreciate precious cultural relics. //

You will also have the opportunity to enjoy Chinese operas and acrobatic shows, as well as authentic Chinese cuisine and local delicacies. //

The traditional warmth and hospitality with which the Chinese people entertain our guests will make your visit a pleasant and memorable experience.

Passage 2

Welcome to the Program of Chinese as a Foreign Language. We are glad to see that the worldwide interest in Chinese is increasing at an accelerating tempo. //

Considering that Chinese has the largest number of speakers in the world and the greatest time depth in its literature, this interest is long overdue. //

In a sense, Chinese is a very old language, with its earliest writings dating back nearly four thousand years. //

As your interest grows, I will discuss in due time the influence of the Chinese language on the cultural and intellectual development of the Chinese nation.